AMPHION

THINKING LITERATURE
A series edited by Nan Z. Da and Anahid Nersessian

Amphion

LYRE, POETRY, AND
POLITICS IN MODERNITY

Leah Middlebrook

The University of Chicago Press
Chicago and London

The University of Chicago Press, Chicago 60637
The University of Chicago Press, Ltd., London
© 2024 by The University of Chicago
All rights reserved. No part of this book may be used or reproduced
in any manner whatsoever without written permission, except
in the case of brief quotations in critical articles and reviews. For
more information, contact the University of Chicago Press, 1427
East 60th Street, Chicago, IL 60637.
Published 2024
Printed in the United States of America

33 32 31 30 29 28 27 26 25 24   1 2 3 4 5

ISBN-13: 978-0-226-83551-8 (cloth)
ISBN-13: 978-0-226-83552-5 (paper)
ISBN-13: 978-0-226-83553-2 (e-book)
DOI: https://doi.org/10.7208/chicago/9780226835532.001.0001

Library of Congress Cataloging-in-Publication Data

Names: Middlebrook, Leah, 1966– author.
Title: Amphion : lyre, poetry, and politics in modernity / Leah
     Middlebrook.
Other titles: Lyre, poetry, and politics in modernity | Thinking
     literature.
Description: Chicago ; London : The University of Chicago Press,
     2024. | Series: Thinking literature | Includes bibliographical
     references and index.
Identifiers: LCCN 2024016863 | ISBN 9780226835518 (cloth) |
     ISBN 9780226835525 (paperback) | ISBN 9780226835532 (ebook)
Subjects: LCSH: Amphion (Greek mythological character)—In
     literature. | European poetry—Renaissance, 1450-1600—
     History and criticism. | European poetry—17th century—History
     and criticism. | European poetry—History and criticism. |
     Spanish poetry—Classical period, 1500-1700—History
     and criticism. | Lyric poetry—Political aspects. | European
     literature—Classical influences.
Classification: LCC PN1181 .M53 2024 | DDC 809.1—dc23/
     eng/20240416
LC record available at https://lccn.loc.gov/2024016863

♾ This paper meets the requirements of ANSI/NISO Z39.48-1992
(Permanence of Paper).

FOR JONATHAN MIDDLEBROOK

FOR JONATHAN MIDDLEBROOKS

Contents

LIST OF FIGURES ix

A NOTE ON ORTHOGRAPHY AND
TRANSLATIONS xi

PREFACE: THE MYTH xiii

INTRODUCTION · Clarinda's Stones 1

CHAPTER 1 · The Lyre and the World 25

CHAPTER 2 · Mercurial *Translatio*: Amphionic
Lyric Poetics from Du Bellay to Trevor Joyce 63

CHAPTER 3 · How to Do Things with *Copia* 93

CHAPTER 4 · Amphion in the Americas 119

CODA · Amphion Dancing 163

ACKNOWLEDGMENTS 165

NOTES 167

BIBLIOGRAPHY 199

INDEX 211

Figures

1   Lepautre, *Amphion* (1676) 4
2   Alciato, *Foedera Italorum* (early sixteenth century) 9
3   Valesio, *Amphion Building the Walls of Thebes* (early seventeenth century) 14
4   *Certamen Poético* (1636) 112
5   Zurita, "MAPA. Cuartel 13" (2016) 156
6   Laurens, *Amphion* (1953) 163

A Note on Orthography and Translations

Orthography in this book generally follows the language of my sources, except in cases where it unduly complicates reading (for example, *u* for *v*). I slightly modify wording in instances where the original presents a distracting archaism (for example, "sithens" for "since"). Translations are my own, unless noted otherwise.

Preface
The Myth

This is a book about a myth. King Amphion played his lyre so sweetly that he charmed stones into building walls for his city, Thebes. Amphion's myth descends to us from Euripides and Plato, and thence through Ovid and Horace to their Renaissance humanist emulators. Amphion and his lyre draw together some of the most significant riddles in Western modernity. The story is about politics, about power, and about cultural production—both as the term is used today (the creation of poems, stories, treatises, essays, plays, music, and works of visual art) and as it connotes the generation of culture itself. Having said that, among the phenomena that Amphion's lyre sets in motion is destruction, which precedes the building up of new structures. The myth accounts for the implosion and toppling of cities and states when social harmony falters and discord flares into violence.

One way to think about myth is to take it as a reservoir of stories we can't stop telling. Myths pose riddles and offer signposts that appear to point us toward answers. In fact, however, myths are famously evasive and turn back on themselves when we try to pin them down. The purpose of myth is not to solve the great conundrums. Rather, it might be said that myths function to keep us company. One motivation for this book is my conviction that in the manner Orpheus helped people to think through some of the core dilemmas attending nineteenth- and twentieth-century modernity in the West, Amphion may be a good thought partner for the twenty-first. This is the myth:

Amphion and Zethus were the twin sons of Zeus and Antiope. Their birth issued from a rape. Zeus attacked the maiden princess, who, fearing punishment by her family, fled her home. Lycus, her uncle, tracked her down and brought her back with him to Thebes, where his wife Dirce subjected her to cruel mistreatment. Antiope gave birth to twin sons. The babies were abandoned to exposure on Mount Cithaeron. However, they xiv **Preface**

were discovered by shepherds, who raised them as their own. Zethus became a hunter and herdsman, and was famed for his physical strength. Amphion became a musician whose skills attracted the favor of Hermes.[1] The god rewarded Amphion with a lyre, an instrument of Hermes's own invention.

Once grown, the two brothers discovered their mother by chance. They rescued her from Lycus's palace, in the process conquering their great-uncle's kingdom and refounding Thebes. The story recounts that despite Zethus's strength, it was Amphion who managed to build the magnificent walls for which the city became famed. The demigod played his lyre with such skill that great boulders rolled in from the plain, stacking themselves into place of their own accord.

Later, Amphion, now king of Thebes, married Niobe. The couple had seven daughters and seven sons. Amphion reigned over a prosperous and powerful city, and his family and his people were deemed happy and successful. But on a festival day honoring Latona, Niobe refused to honor the Titan, expressing disdain for a womb that had borne only two children, when the great Niobe herself had borne so many more. Niobe's arrogance angered Latona, who instructed her offspring, the gods Apollo and Diana, to avenge her name. The divine siblings struck down Niobe and Amphion's children, one by one. Amphion committed suicide upon hearing the news. Niobe turned to stone.

Introduction

Clarinda's Stones

I am thinking of something that is in the common pool of humanity, into which individuals and groups of people may contribute, and from which we may all draw if we have somewhere to put what we find.

D. W. WINNICOTT, "The Location of Cultural Experience"

The prompt for writing this book arrived in heaps and stacks. For a number of years, I worked on a project that involved spending time in the rare books and manuscripts room of the National Library of Spain. In addition to the volumes and microfiches I was there to examine, I sometimes ordered a random box or volume to see what I might be overlooking. Often what appeared on my desk was a bewildering assortment of materials: single pages or bound collections of poems, some in print, some in manuscript. Loose verses, boxed up with the proceedings of a meeting of an academy or a private society, a group of local wits in Valencia or Zaragoza whose existence is commemorated only in these stacks of logs, folders, and printed leaflets, in which snippets of academy business and often-pseudonymous lists of those who attended are interspersed with long poems full of inside jokes and what appear to be puns and double entendres on names—of fellow participants? Of the members of a rival society? I couldn't tell. I couldn't discern the significance of this poetry. It clearly meant something to someone or a group of people in the past. But its meaning was lost to me, beyond a general sense that something of value must inhere in this material. Otherwise, why preserve it?

This experience led me to reflect on how small a sample of poetry survives for us via the accidents of time and reputation, and via the critical tradition that dominates our approaches to Renaissance poetry. Oriented by Petrarchism, *imitatio*, influence studies, and self-fashioning, this criticism illuminates a great deal about many things. In particular, it helps us think about the subject-self, about our inner landscapes of feeling and desire. But it tells us little about other things. For example, it is nearly mute regarding the masses of nonsubjective poetry that make up a substantial portion of the sixteenth- and seventeenth-century lyric archives: occasional poetry, ballads, parodies, ditties, satires, extended cantos that cel-

2 Introduction

ebrate a country's Parnassian poets. *That* observation, in turn, brought to mind D. W. Winnicott's musings about how we discern and attach meaning, how cultural objects move in and out of legibility and usefulness, depending on our ability to place them, to "put what we find" in a context that makes it intelligible.

It also reminded me of lines from the *Discurso en loor de la poesía* (Discourse in praise of poetry) by the anonymous Peruvian poet "Clarinda" (1602):

> Luis Pérez Ángel, norma de discretos . . .
> Fabrican tus romances, y sonetos
> (como los de Anfión un tiempo a Tebas)
> muros a Arica, a fuerza de conceptos.

> (Luis Pérez Ángel, the model of sound judgment . . . / your *romances* and sonnets build / (as Amphion did once, for Thebes) / walls for Arica, by then power of your conceits.)[1]

Clarinda's lines raise questions. For example: Who was Luis Pérez Ángel? Who was Amphion? What were those powerful conceits? In addition: What is the basis for Clarinda's comparison? How is Luis Pérez Ángel, in turn-of-the-century vice-regal Peru, like Amphion in archaic Greece? How do poems build walls?

Scholarship helps with some of these questions. Luis Pérez Ángel and his poetry have disappeared from the record, but we know about his circle, the "Academia Antártica," a literary society composed of men and women of Peru's elite *criollo* caste.[2] And I began to answer "Who was Amphion?" in the preface, where I provide a summary of his myth. Another way to answer the question of who Amphion was, however, is to say that he is the frame, the place to "put" (in Winnicott's terms) poetry of the kind I puzzled over in the library. This is not only because the name Amphion is ubiquitous in both poetry and writing about poetry from antiquity through the early modern period (which it is, alongside Orpheus). More important, Amphion figures a specific kind of poiesis, a generativity that encompasses both poems and the civic form that is the polity: community with a fixed architecture (a structure of government, civic buildings), governed either by a single ruler (a despot, benevolent or otherwise) or an oligarchy, and encircled by walls. In antiquity and through the early modern period, these walls were often physical structures.[3] However, as countless legends about great cities make clear, physical walls need cultural bulwarks, and these bulwarks are what Amphion builds. He composes poems that define what work, play, and worship are. With his lyre, Amphion inspires people to collaborative effort. They create accumulations of things, from cities, their contents, and their products to more poetry: sonnets, ballads, hymns, madrigals, and epigrams whose cadences stir individuals to move in concert and adopt shared practices and beliefs. Consider the happy birthday song, the alphabet song, or a national anthem—all kinds of lyric poems that exercise sufficient social force to be mainstays across languages and cultures.[4] Amphion's songs also furnish the basis for defining actions, beliefs, and characteristics that set someone or some group *outside* the circle of belonging. Thus Amphion's lyre represents the human capacity to accomplish the magnificent, even miraculous collective feats that are represented in Renaissance discourse by the image of the city; however, Amphion's lyre razes civilizations as well. This is what Spain did, of course, before Clarinda, Pérez Ángel, and their fellows set about building Arica over the ruins of the Incan empire.[5]

This book examines Amphion's significance to sixteenth- and seventeenth-century Europe and, via Europe, to the present day. Amphion was a vital point of reference in writing about lyric poetry during the period in which ruling coteries in England, France, and Spain were remaking their countries into centralized states modeled on their ideas about ancient Rome. Barbara Fuchs describes Renaissance "cultures of imperium," in which rulers elaborated discourses, policies, and administrative and political systems and practices that centralized power domestically. These reforms were often made in conjunction with projects of conquest and colonialism abroad.[6] Lyric poetry flourished in this context, across all strata of society, from the courts, to the streets, to gathering rooms where humanists devised theories and created knowledges to facilitate the transformation of their societies and to grapple with the disruptions, upheavals, and opportunities introduced into European life after 1492. As a consequence of the intersection between this avid poetry-making and the Renaissance humanist appetite for theory, the sixteenth century also marks the point of emergence of an incipient "idea of lyric," to use María José Vega and Cesc Esteve's term.[7] The lyric genre as we know it today did not exist in the sixteenth century.[8] However, writers began to talk about lyrics—designated variously by terms such as *poemi piccoli*, rimes, *rimas*, small poetry, *pöesies*—as a distinct category within the more capacious art that Aristotle describes in his *Poetics*, where "poetry" designates imaginative writing, generally (in contrast to history, which is factual). Renaissance humanists adapted this emergent category from Horace, whose *Ars Poetica* describes *musa lyrae sollers* (songs of the lyric muse), an art he presents as important to the smooth functioning of civilized society (and, in fact, of empires, as the sphere of reference in the *Ars Poetica* is Augustan Rome). Horace describes *musa lyrae sollers* in terms of two mythical figures: "Orpheus, the priest and interpreter of the gods," and "Amphion . . . the builder of the Theban wall," who "was said to give the stones motion with the sound of his lyre, and to lead them where he would by engaging persuasion."[9] I argue in this book that those three phenomena—imperium, the polity, and lyric—are interrelated. Moreover, their clearest point of intersection is Amphion's lyre.

Amphion's Lyre

Images of Amphion abound in the sixteenth and seventeenth centuries. The engraving by the seventeenth-century artist Jean Lepautre (fig. 1) is a representative example. It depicts a man seated outdoors, playing a stringed instrument. In this image, Amphion plays a lute; other images may show him with a violin, a viola, or a zither. Bricks or stones dance through the air and stack themselves into orderly walls, animated by his music.

These images speak to poetic *efficacia*, the fact that poetry builds things in the world. In the eyes of sixteenth- and seventeenth-century artists and their patrons, the products of lyric poiesis encompassed both songs

1. Jean Lepautre, *Amphion* (1676). Photograph: National Gallery of Art, Washington, DC (accession no. 1988.49.3).

(*carmina*) and cities, feats of collaboration and construction that mirrored the perfection of Heaven in their harmonious and orderly design.[10] This design was a function of Orphic law, which traveled directly from Heaven through the *vates*, to be communicated to people,[11] and as a function of what might be called, following Pierre Bourdieu, "habitus," the "system of internalized structures, schemes of perception, conception, and action," by which a community or social group structures itself as a totality.[12] These systems are instilled through Amphion's skilled work with a stringed instrument, and the strings are important. In contrast, for example, to woodwinds such as flutes or panpipes, the lyre foregrounds the materiality as well as the transient nature of Amphionic poiesis. When a musician plucks at a harp, its strings vibrate and stir the air. This resonance catches listeners up in collective rhythms, while melodies and tones rouse feelings and attitudes. A skilled player can guide these responses, for example, to create a community that will serve as a building block to a larger political unit (such as a city or a state), or to establish cultural practices, or steer public opinion to consensus. When the vibrations cease, in a slow fade or through a sudden rupture, Amphion's structures weaken and disperse. However, verses and song forms crystallize Amphion's measures and the shared responses they inspire. Allen Grossman captures this idea when he writes that "line forms and verse forms in general are fundamentally discussable as mediations of relationships, as rules and orders of polities."[13] This idea is also captured in older senses of the word "canto," which in Latin and some romance languages means, variously, song and the cornerstone of a building.

The meaning of Amphion's lyre was intuitive enough in the sixteenth century that many writers didn't see the necessity of explaining it. However, George Puttenham's discussion in *The Art of English Poesy* (1589) draws forward the material dimensions of lyric *efficacia*. Like many of his contemporaries across Europe, Puttenham opens his discussion by identifying poets as "makers" and poetry as something made:

> [O]ur English name conforms with the Greek word: for of poiein, to make, they call a maker Poeta. Such as (by way of resemblance and reverently) we may say of God: who without any travail to his divine imagination, made all the world of nought, nor also by any pattern or mold as the Platonics with their Ideas do fantastically suppose. Even so the Poet makes and contrives out of his own brain both the verse and the matter of his poem . . .[14]

Puttenham offers a variety of sources for the poet's ability to make things: Platonic furor, an innate "excellence of nature and complexion," great subtlety of spirit and wit, "much experience and observation of the

6 Introduction

world"—or, he allows, "all or most part" of these factors.[15] It is making born of experience that matters here. Puttenham identifies this kind of poetry with human creators, as opposed to God (who creates solely by imagination), or the theories of forms espoused by "fantastical" Platonists.

This worldedness of Puttenham's argument, the fact that he anchors it so firmly in both lived human experience and a specific place—Elizabeth's England—distinguishes *The Art of English Poesy* from many similar *ars* and poetic defenses from the sixteenth century.[16] Puttenham makes specific claims for a human creative capacity that is lodged in the brain (and not the soul, for example) and informed by local experience. These claims form the basis of his larger case for a kind of poetry that is culturally specific and politically useful. That is, the universal value of poetry lies in its capacity to communicate knowledge of nature and the fundamental laws of civilization to humankind. Puttenham acknowledges this dimension of poetry's value, observing, in a manner consistent with most writing on poetry from the period, that poets "were the first that intended to the observation of nature and her works, and specially of the Celestial courses, by reason of the continual motion of the heavens . . . they were the first that instituted sacrifices of placation . . . and invented and established all the rest of the observances and ceremonies of religion." Puttenham also describes poets as "the first lawmakers to the people, and the first politicians, devising all expedient means for the establishment of the Common wealth." These kinds of knowledge are generally valuable in and of themselves, and the poets Puttenham describes achieve success when they bring truths to life for their communities by using language that appeals to them in body and mind: poetry, "speech by meter . . . a kind of utterance, more cleanly couched and more delicate to the ear than prose is."[17]

While poetry stirs people universally, the particulars that make a song or verse compelling to a given community are specific to a time, a language, and a culture. Puttenham argues that English experience is different from Greek and Latin experience, for example.[18] Therefore, the challenge that confronts an English poet is to discover the "curious points" of English language that shape the "rime and tunable concords" that will accomplish this work:

> . . . there was no art in the world til by experience found out: so if Poesie be now an Art, and of all antiquity hath been among the Greeks and Latins, and yet were none, until by studious persons fashioned and reduced into a method of rules and precepts, then no doubt may there by the like with us. And if th'art of Poesie be but a skill appertaining to utterance, why may not the same be with us as well as with them, our language being no less copious, pithy and significative than theirs were? If again, Art be but a cer-

tain order of rules prescribed by reason, and gathered by experience, why should not Poesie be a vulgar Art with us as well as with the Greeks and Latins, our language admitting no fewer rules and nice diversities than theirs . . . our speech has in many things differing from theirs: and yet in the general points of that Art, allowed to go in common with them: so as if one point perchance which is their feet whereupon their measures stand, and indeed is all the beauty of their Poesie, and which feet we have not, nor as yet never went about to frame (the nature of our language and words not permitting it) we have instead thereof twenty other curious points in that skill more than they ever had, by reason of our rime and tuneable concords or symphony, which they never observed. Poesie therefore may be an Art in our vulgar, and that very methodical and commendable.[19]

The modern poet's task, in Puttenham's view, is to "contrive" a poetic music that draws the specific features of English into poems whose "symphony" (harmony) will inspire people to collective motion, "this way and that, withersoever the heart by impression of the ear shall be most affectionately bent and directed."[20] That is how Amphion, a poet and a composer, "built up cities and reared walls with the stones that came in heaps to the sound of his harp, figuring thereby the mollifying of hard and stony hearts by his sweet and eloquent persuasion."[21]

Puttenham indicates that Queen Elizabeth can do the same. His principal case in *The Art of English Poesy* is that poetic music, the art of Amphion, is a productive instrument of state—or rather, it is an instrument that produces states. Puttenham's meaning is especially clear given how he presents Elizabeth in his opening passages, where he draws two roles together. She is both an administrator ("whose contemplations are every hour more seriously employed upon the public administration and services") and a poet ("already, of any that I know in our time, the most excellent"). She is an Amphion. As a musician plays the lyre by skillfully plucking individual strings to sound chords, a good administrator manipulates just the right person, using precisely the right pressure, in combination with this or that other person, according to a given circumstance. Like Amphion, Elizabeth I was a maker of polities and poems.

Puttenham was not alone in identifying a resonant common ground between the lyre and politics. In the *Emblemata liber*, Alciato uses a lyre in his emblem of the *foedera*, the diplomatic pact (fig. 2). The device portrays a zither accompanied by a motto that compares the politician who negotiates a peace treaty to a musician with a balky instrument: "It is difficult, except for a man of skill, to tune so many strings, and if one string is out of tune or broken, which so easily happens, all the music of the instrument is lost and its lovely song disjointed."[22] The motto points to the fragility of

8 Introduction

political agreements. The ephemerality of civilizations is a theme Puttenham weaves through *The Art of English Poesy* as well.

Reading for Amphion

Both *The Art of English Poesy* and the *foedera* emblem point to a sphere of lyric activity that is often overlooked in Renaissance poetry: the poetic art whose sphere of operation is the social collective. Most poetic defenses, ars poetica, and treatises that humanists composed in the sixteenth and seventeenth centuries present lyric poetry as an art that is presided over by two figures, Orpheus (the vatic singer and the lawgiver) and Amphion (the politician and the city builder). Their pairing follows Horace, but there is an underlying logic to it as well, as the conjoined figure "Orpheus and Amphion" links two distinct lyric phenomena. Orpheus represents the capacities and limitations of the human individual.[23] Orphic poetry is anchored in the solitary human voice, which is both powerful and threatened by a death that inevitably silences it. In contrast, the art of Amphion is not rooted in the one, but in the many. The name "Amphion" indicates dualities ("Amph" means "two"), and Amphion is one half of a pair (twins Amphion and Zethus). The multiplicities that attend both the king and his art proliferate from there, a point I will develop throughout this book. Furthermore, Amphion's power is the power of the lyre, an instrument of *translatio* (movement across space and time) and transmediation. It transforms air to song, song to "stones" (in the sense of cultural bulwarks), and people to stones (as the building blocks of polities).[24] The scene of Amphion's lyric poiesis is therefore the polity, in its mobile, burgeoning, earthbound reality, and the purview of his lyre is the polity. The poetic tradition of Amphion grapples with the relentless, often violent, play of order and disorder in human social life.[25] Thus, while the Orphic task is to conserve the human image—in Susan Stewart's words, to create lasting images that render persons "visible, tangible, and audible" through time[26]—Amphion's lyre creates something different and is harder to pin down. Primarily, it inspires people to join into productive, collective action, even as one of the "products" of this action is destruction. Poems take shape as part of this activity and can serve as documents of it.

Because Amphionic poiesis is a phenomenon of animation and motion, it is useful to approach it with some questions that extend beyond what literary training directs us to look for. In general, reading lyric poetry entails directing close attention to a stable object, "the poem," assumed to be a discrete work of art. As scholars and critics, we analyze and evaluate the interplay of form and content by which poets render the worlds of emotion, experience, and insight we hold within ourselves in language. This

Exiliens infans sinuosi e faucibus anguis,
  Est gentilitijs nobile stemma tuis.
Talia Pellæum gessisse nomismata regem,
  Vidimus, hisq; suum concelebrare genus.
Dũ se Ammone satũ matrẽ anguis imagine lusaue,
  Diuini & sobolem seminis esse docet.
Ore exit, tradunt sic quosdam enitier angues,
  An quia sic Pallas de capite orta Iouis.

FOEDERA ITALORVM.

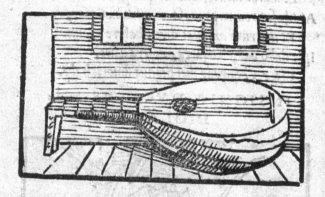

Hanc cytharã à lembo, quæ forma halieutica fertur,
  Vendicat, & propriam musa latina sibi.
Accipe Dux, placeat nostrũ hoc tibi tẽpore munus
  Quo noua cum socijs fœdera inire paras.
Difficile est nisi docto homini tot tendere chordas,
  Vnaq; si fuerit non bene tenta fides.
                                           Ruptaue

2. Andrea Alciato, *Foedera Italorum* (early sixteenth century). Photograph with permission of University of Glasgow Archives & Special Collections (Sp Coll S.M. 20, folio A2v).

interiority is a singular feature of us as a species. This practice of "lyric reading" can be not only pleasurable, but profoundly illuminating. Yet it is of limited usefulness when a poem, a collection of poems, or a vast archive of lyrics does not exhibit the aesthetic qualities that literary training teaches us to value. Furthermore, as Puttenham has begun to show us, prosodies and vocabularies encode a wealth of information about the groups who devised, embraced, and elaborated on them. The significance of these lyric devices—what the "curious points" of language can tell us about people, about communities, about polities—can be lost over time. The poetry feels stale or tedious.[27] This is what happened with the sheaves of lyrics I found myself puzzling over in the library.

Piecing together the lost or dormant meaning conveyed by Amphionic poetry can be a powerful and moving experience. As a point of departure, it is helpful to recognize the expansive field of lyric culture that Europeans recognized in the sixteenth and seventeenth centuries. Second, it is useful to entertain the possibility that the object of some kinds of poetry-making is not literary. Oren Izenberg observes that "poetry is not always and everywhere understood as a literary project aiming to produce a special kind of verbal artifact. . . . Nor is it always understood as an aesthetic project seeking to provoke or promote a special kind of experience . . . in its readers."[28] He recommends looking beyond poems themselves to "poetry" understood "as an occasion for reestablishing or revealing the most basic unit of social life." This "unit," for both Izenberg and this book, is the person, an essential component of communities. Another essential element of "social life" is, of course, *another* person or a group of people. Sociality is not a phenomenon of isolated or exclusively inward-looking individuals. Thus, in place of the literary critic's judgments ("Is this a lyric poem?" and "Is it a *good* lyric poem?"), a reader of Amphion might approach with curiosity, asking, "Here is a curious fragment. What is it doing?" "What is it building?" "Why is it here?" "What larger formations might it form part of?" If the poem is mute or resistant, it is useful to investigate when, where, and how it resonated and what it built in some other place or time.

Finally, and crucially, Amphion invites us to seek out the contexts in which a poem, verse, fragment, collection, or archive might be set back in motion to build and dismantle anew. This last area of inquiry blurs boundaries between lyric poetry and varieties of creative verbal and linguistic activity such as translation, glossing, and parody, as we will see at a number of junctures in this book.

Reading for Amphion uncovers meanings that are constantly forming, deforming, dismantling, sorting, shifting, and restaging themselves in multiple asynchronous ways. Thus, in accompaniment to a familiar path that extends from the Renaissance poetry of self-fashioning, *imitatio*, and

Petrarchan desire, through the Romantics, to the varieties of twentieth- and twenty-first-century lyrics that issue "out of a solitude, to a solitude," directing "mimesis toward the performance of the mind in solitary speech,"[29] Amphion opens new through lines across a wide swath of forms that variously issue from, contribute to, erode, and sometimes destroy altogether social conditions and political formations. The route can lead us from sixteenth-century poetry to varieties of modern and postmodern poetries and criticism that are similarly concerned with sociality, collectives, and polities. I draw connections between these two kinds of poetry, the early modern and the modern/postmodern, throughout this book.

Amphionic Formations

In reading the iconography of Lepautre's engraving of Amphion, above (fig. 1), I described the stones as flying up. But they are not necessarily ascending. It is possible that they are flying *down*. Amphion is a figure for what Alice Oswald has called the "bright, unbearable fact" of communities: that as a species, we are stirred both to form them and to tear them apart.[30] Amphion's music makes and unmakes, and what is constant is not the made thing but the inspiration to motion.

Amphion thus prompts us to consider how we think and talk about the social and political structures he helps create in the sixteenth and seventeenth centuries. The concept of "imperial formations" developed by Ann Laura Stoler, Carole McGranahan, and Peter C. Perdue furnishes a useful framework. While the term "imperial formations" itself is common, they write, "the analytic of our choice is not. We think here of Louis Althusser and Etienne Balibar's use of 'social formation' to signal the 'concrete complex whole comprising economic practice, political practice, and ideological practice at a certain place and stage of development.'" To this constellation, they add Raymond Williams's sense of "formation" as a social form suggesting "effective movements and tendencies" that have "variable and often oblique relations to formal institutions.'" Imperial formations is useful as a critical lens, they explain, because it underscores "not the inevitable rise and fall of empires, but the active and contingent process of their making and unmaking. . . . Empires may be 'things,' but imperial formations are not. . . . Imperial formations are . . . states of becoming, macropolies in states of solution and constant formation."[31] The distinctions they draw harmonize provocatively with claims I make about Amphion's lyric in this book. By opening space to think through and conceptualize a phenomenon that many of us feel intuitively to be true—that however modest, frivolous, or impromptu activities such as singing a work song, participating in a poetry contest, or preparing a gloss of a culturally

12 Introduction

significant poem or fragment of text might appear, these are fundamentally important to the functioning of society—"formation" accommodates the diverse ways in which verbal and linguistic activity contributes to the making and undoing of polities and states. This diversity is both featured and concealed in poems such as W. B. Yeats's "Lapis Lazuli":

> On their own feet they came, or on shipboard,
> Camel-back, horse-back, ass-back, mule-back,
> Old civilizations put to the sword.
> Then they and their wisdom went to rack:
> No handiwork of Callimachus
>
> . . . .
>
> . . . stood but a day;
> All things fall and are built again
> And those that build them again are gay.[32]

These lines describe civilization as a singular totality that rises and falls in a rhythm.[33] The work of Callimachus, a master artist, rises and falls with it. Within that greater frame, however, unnamed, uncounted numbers of participants are at work. "Those" people—perhaps they are named Mary or Jacques or Inés or Anonymous, or perhaps there is a group of them working in concert—proceed along, unremarked and gaily building. They are active agents of the micro and contingent acts of making and unmaking that resonate with or diverge from the larger process. We will examine a good deal of poetry created by these kinds of persons. "Formations" facilitates considering the multiple relationships people develop to the ongoing presence of social, physical, and psychological conditions imposed by power. Amphion and formation, taken together, open new ways of describing how poetry-making mediates those relationships.

As a critical framework, "imperial formations" also supports a comparatist approach that brings sixteenth- and seventeenth-century lyrics and poetry and criticism from more recent periods to bear on each other. "Empire," as a singular term, often connotes a specific bounded temporality that accords with narratives of unidirectional historical movement. According to this linear history, structures created at one point are subsequently displaced by new and different regimes. Formation "encourages us to attend to the consistency of the practices, the habits of thought, and the physical and mental terrain upon which political domination is carried out, in colonial periods and subsequently."[34] The "subsequently" that Stoler, McGranahan, and Perdue refer to is what I mean when I use the term "modernity" in this book. In keeping with formulations such Walter

Mignolo's at the start of *The Darker Side of Western Modernity*, this book takes the modern to be inextricably linked to Renaissance imperial expansion and to coloniality, one of Renaissance imperium's most enduring formations.[35] In the sixteenth and seventeenth centuries, "Amphion" names a poetic discourse that contributes to Renaissance imperial formations. Readings in this book draw together poetry composed in those contexts and poetry that reflects on the legacies and "debris" of imperial formations as people navigate them in postcolonial and postmodern culture.[36] The "consistency" of practices, thought, and terrain that subtend modernity (early, high, late, and post-) furnishes context for the witty manner that Trevor Joyce makes use of Renaissance poetry as he fashions a postcolonial Irish poetics in the lyric sequence *Rome's Wreck* (chapter 2). It also speaks to the harsh and compelling lyric music that Raúl Zurita uses to render the Chilean experience of the Pinochet regime in poetic form (chapter 4). Constantly in motion and constantly creating, Amphion points us to life, growth, and energy at play, even in the shadow of what Stoler calls "ruination."[37] Additional evidence of this process in this book includes writing by Morisco poets, exiled from their homes in Spain (chapter 1); a trilingual project of poetic composition, citation, and translation prepared by self-identified Mapuche poets active in the southern cone of the Americas (chapter 4); and emergent scholarship and criticism that uncovers the simultaneous presence of multiple worlds that flourish and decay, variously aware and unaware of each other, on the same geographic sites.

Mercury

That Amphion is a figure for mobility, plurality, and change is signaled by the god who serves as his divine patron. His lyre was a gift from Mercury (in Greek, Hermes). A drawing by Giovanni Luigi Valesio (fig. 3) depicts the pair. Mercury here is a faintly traced figure, crowned with laurels, standing behind Amphion's right shoulder. He appears to be encouraging Amphion, perhaps guiding his song.

While Apollo is the god more famously associated with poetry, Mercury invented the lyre. He subsequently gave it to Apollo, in apology for a transgression. He awarded one to Amphion in recognition of the youth's skills as a musician. The god of eloquence, Mercury delights in beguiling speech. His utterances, while technically true, double back and reverse themselves, just as Amphion's walls rise and crumble. Mercury presides over travel, commerce, and contracts. It is thus fitting that he sponsors Amphion, the maker of poems and songs that ease the business of daily life and the smooth operation of polities and states.[38] Renaissance hu-

3. Giovanni Luigi Valesio, *Amphion Building the Walls of Thebes* (early seventeenth century). Joseph F. McCrindle Collection. Bequest of Joseph F. McCrindle, 2008 (accession no. 2009.31.3). Photograph: The Metropolitan Museum of Art, New York.

manists followed Horace in associating Mercury with the dual spheres of creative activity, the lyric poiesis of poems and states.[39] However, Mercury also represented a disturbing conundrum that confronted sixteenth- and seventeenth-century moralists: poetic discourse harbors marvelous, truth-disclosing powers, and yet it is made up of lies.

Early Amphion

The foregoing pages paint, in broad strokes, the conceptual and poetic terrain of this book. What follows is a short review of the key sources for Amphion as sixteenth- and seventeenth-century writers understood him, with brief discussions of the themes these sources furnish to lyric tradition. A sense of these sources will be helpful as we begin to explore the world of Amphionic lyric.

AMPHION AND ZETHUS

An important source for the story of Amphion is Euripides's play *Antiope*. The full text is now lost, but the existing fragments present a debate between Amphion and his twin brother, Zethus. Zethus chastises his brother for wasting his time on music while he, Zethus, exerts himself in physical labor. At the end of the play, Zethus convinces Amphion to take violent action to avenge their family's abuse of Antiope. Hermes (Mercury) descends to interrupt the scene. He affirms the superiority of harmony over conflict and music over force. Handing Amphion a lyre, he delivers a prophecy that the poet's songs will create walls for Thebes.

In the *Gorgias*, Plato draws on *Antiope* to structure a debate about political philosophy. Zethus and Amphion represent two kinds of politician: the man who, in the manner of Zethus, argues forcefully and crushes his challengers, and the leader who emulates Amphion and fosters harmonious agreement. Like *Antiope*, *Gorgias* presents a core question that it leaves unresolved. What is the most successful way to govern a city, by physical force or through eloquence? Plato introduces a poetic solution, as Socrates recounts a myth about the fate of the soul after death.[40]

Sixteenth- and seventeenth-century writers did not have access to the *Gorgias*, but they knew that Amphion had a twin named Zethus, and a number of poems discussed in this book invoke Amphion in the context of violence, harmony, and the threats posed to society by civil war. Ben Jonson and Joachim du Bellay each devise Amphionic music as a means to sublimate violence and reconcile, at least in poetry, brewing conflicts. Yet if we limit our reading of Amphion and Zethus to the conundrums of governance (music versus force, eloquence versus violence, questions that perplex rulers), we may be overlooking what the brothers have to show us by taking Mercury too much at his word. When the god prophesizes that Amphion will build Thebes's walls with his music, what he is talking about is a narrative that takes shape over time to recount how great cities came to be. Poetry has the power to fix the names of queens, kings, and heroes in cultural memory, while the people who actually performed the labor of

16 Introduction

building cities disappear from the record, as in the case of Yeats's "those who build them."

If this were all there is to say about Amphion, he would not be a twin. The myth would be a story about the rise and fall of kings. Over the course of preparing this book, I have come to a different understanding of Amphion and Zethus, and this understanding helps us read and interpret Amphion's lyric. The pair figures the fundamental ambivalence of polities, in which rulers and laborers each play essential roles. Rulers establish laws and priorities and guide group efforts to accomplish goals. Laborers furnish effort and make things. Their labor includes the physical work that lifting boulders to raise walls represents. However, it also consists of cheerful participation in collective endeavors that generate culture. I have referred to some kinds of activity already: glossing, translating, participating in poetry contests and festivals, and writing poems and verses in culturally specific forms shaped by the "curious points" of a community's or a society's language. It is possible to read Amphion as a sign of co-presence, an Amphion-Zethus pair that represents the simultaneous operation of two distinct worlds—two perspectives, two frames of experiences, two visions of what collective living is about and for—within the same greater body. The relationship between the two is sometimes conflictual, even murderous. But it is also sometimes blithely indifferent or mutually beneficial. Chapter 3 furnishes a view into the dual worlds of Amphions and Zethuses as those worlds are realized in early modern poetry contests.

Amphion also receives mention in *The Odyssey*, in Pausanias, in Statius, and in Seneca.[41] But for the sixteenth- and seventeenth-century writers who established the Amphionic tradition in Western lyric, the most significant references to the king appear in Ovid, Horace, and Dante. Ovid and Dante draw on Amphion in the contexts of the polis and the city, so I will discuss them together. Horace creates the Amphion-Orpheus pair that forms the basis for early modern lyric poetics, and we will look at him last.

THEBES: THE CARNIVOROUS POLIS

Ovid mentions Amphion twice in the *Metamorphoses*: in book 6, Amphion appears briefly in the story of Niobe, as he suffers the slaughter of the couple's children. In book 15, Ovid folds Thebes into the seer Pythagoras's harangue on the law of change that governs the cosmos:

. . . We see times change and civilizations
rise and fall. Yes, Troy was great in her riches and people;
for ten long years she was able to spend the blood of so many
sons in her cause; but now she is humbled and all she can show

for her glorious wealth is ancestral barrows and ancient ruins.
Sparta was highly renowned and so was powerful Mycénae;
so flourished the cities of Cecrops at Athens and Theban Amphion.[42]

It makes sense that the myths of Amphion and Thebes are useful to Ovid. Amphion's association with Thebes's rise and fall conforms to the *Metamorphoses*' central project: the recitation of "changes of shape, new forms . . . [in] . . . a thread from the world's beginning / down to my own lifetime, in one continuous song."[43] Pythagoras's prophecy provides a sort of mise en abyme of a greater poem, and Ovid draws in "Amphionis arces" (literally, Amphion's citadel, which David Raeburn translates as "Theban Amphion") as an example. For Renaissance humanist writers, this passage offers an important justification for imperium as a form of power that constitutes an advance over archaic imperial cities. Pythagoras sets Thebes in a metonymic chain with great archaic cities such as Troy, *poleis* that prey on their inhabitants. Priam, Hector, Andromache, and tens of thousands of nameless men, women, and children, from heroes to weavers to farmers, are no more than sacs for the blood that fuels the city's domination of surrounding regions. Apologists for empire link their states to formations of the past, but draw a distinction between the appetitive, carnivorous polis and the just and orderly operations of modern imperium. In Europe, this imperium is imposed by the Christian God and structured in accordance with His grace.

AMPHION IN DANTE

In the *Inferno*, Dante describes Hell with successive images of a walled city. In canto 18, Malebolge, the eighth circle of Hell, is a well "tutto di pietra di color ferrigno / come la cerchia che d'intorno del volge" (made of / stone the color of iron, like the circle that encloses it),[44] whose concentric, walled trenches lead farther and deeper into the underworld. Amphion and Thebes shape the symbolism of walled Hell. Dante invokes the myth directly in canto 25, where he compares his virtuoso, extended description of the punishments carried out by serpents and snakes to Ovid's description of Cadmus, the first founder of Thebes, in the *Metamorphoses*. In canto 32 of the *Inferno*, Dante develops the conceit he establishes with the walls of Malebolge and links Amphion to the walls of the most extreme region of Hell, Cocytus, the great, frozen lake populated by traitors and the instigators of civil wars:

S'io avessi le rime aspre e chiocce
come si converrebbe al tristo buco

18   Introduction

sovra 'l qual pontina tutte l'altre rocce,
io premerei di mio concetto il suo
più pienamente; ma perch' io non l'abbo,
non senza tema a dicer mi conduco:
ché non è impresa da pigliare a gabbo
descriver fondo a tutto l'universo,
né da lingua che chiami mamma o babbo.
ma quelle donne aitutino il mio verso
ch'aiutaro Anfione a chider Tebe,
sì che dal fatto il dir non sia diverso.

(If I had harsh and clacking rhymes such as befit / the dreadful hole toward which all other rocks point / their weight, / I would press out the juice from my concept more / fully; but because I lack them, not without fear do I bring / myself to speak; / for it is not a task to take in jest, that of describing / the bottom of the universe, nor one for a tongue that / calls mommy or daddy. / But let those ladies aid my verse who helped / Amphion enclose Thebes, so that word may not be different from the fact.)[45]

Dante foregrounds the ambivalence of Amphion's music, which wields the power to sway minds and convene collectives, but does not ensure (as a more angelic song might) that the assembled crowd sings and labors in the cause of the common good. Indeed, the inhabitants of Cocytus share close space with neighbors they have come to loathe. Trapped, immobilized in ice, they seethe and rail against each other. Their condition, neighbor turned against neighbor, renders them vulnerable to the casual predations of outsiders—indeed, inspires this kind of violence. Dante captures the mercurial power of Amphion's lyre, which fans political implosion within the walls it created. As he passes through the place, Dante finds himself moved, to his bewilderment, to kick at a prisoner's head:

E mentre ch'andavamo inver'lo mezzo
al quale ogne gravezza si rauna,
e io tremava ne l'etterno rezzo,
se voler fu o destino o fortuna,
non so, ma, passeggiando tra le teste,
forte percossi 'l piè nel viso ad una.
Piangendo mi sgridò: "Perché mi peste?"

(And while we were walking to the center toward / which all weight collects, and I was trembling in the eternal chill, / if it was by wish or destiny or fortune, I do not / know, but, pacing among the heads, I struck my foot / hard in the face of one. / Weeping, it scolded me: "Why do you pound me?")[46]

Incivility is a powerful and contagious disease. This is something Dante knew from his own lived experience as well as from his classical sources. He modeled his "bottom of the universe" on his contemporary Florence, which was racked by civil war throughout much of Dante's lifetime. The myths of Thebes and Amphion supply narratives and imagery with which to parse and analyze the breakdown of community within a city's walls. The *Inferno* reserves the eighth circle of Hell for fraudsters and the ninth circle for traitors. Both kinds of sinners break down the bonds of collaboration and community with their destructive eloquence.

To illustrate his point, Dante describes Cocytus in lines that are ugly and dissonant. Translator Robert Durling captures their awkwardness in English by studding the passage with hard consonants and buffeting sense through changes in tone and register; for example, in the contrast between the elegant, aspirational opening of the first line, "S'io avessi le rime" (If I had the rhymes . . .), and the childish "mamma o babbo" (mommy or daddy) in line 9. This lack of harmony is a deft aesthetic rendition of the perversion of community. Dante also creates jarring imagery, such as the metaphor of "juicing" (premerei) used to describe the divine activity of form giving by devising conceits ("concetto," in lines 1–5). The brilliant trick here, of course, is that these clamorously perverse poetics create the appropriate aesthetic form for political disaster: stanzas of terza rima that give order to the chaotic contents of Hell—pains, sorrows, grievances, cries of anguish and recrimination—and buttress, by means of their mass and also their formal ugliness, a rotten city. In this way, "the words are not different from the fact" (dal fatto il dir non sia diverso).

Dante's Amphion furnishes formal and thematic resources to sixteenth- and seventeenth-century writers. Many employ terza rima in the great canon-building poems they prepare for France, England, Spain, and the Spanish-American vice realms. The Dantean canto furnishes a material form by which long lists of names and accomplishments may be transformed into cultural bulwarks, harmonized and secured by means of Dante's rhyme. Furthermore, since terza rima always points to Dante, poets who use the form align themselves with Dante's authority.

Horace, Amphion, Orpheus, and the *Musa Lyrae Sollers*

With the *Ars Poetica*, Horace moves Amphion out of his archaic contexts and refurbishes him for usefulness in cosmopolitan, imperial Rome. For both reasons—his poetics of imperium and his influence on Renaissance

20 Introduction

poetry and theory—Horace is, in this book, the author and the architect of modern lyric.

The *Ars Poetica*, also called the "Letter to the Pisos" (*Epistola ad Pisones*), serves as a touchstone in histories of poetics. Memorable phrases such as "ut pictura poiesis" (let poetry be like painting) or "aut prodesse aut delectare" (generally translated as "teach and delight"[47]) are widely accepted as universal, if somewhat antiquated, advice. What is often forgotten is that Horace directed his remarks to a particular audience. The "Pisos" to whom the letter is addressed were the sons of Lucius Calpurnius Piso (c. 48 BCE–c. 32 CE), a senator during the time of the emperor Augustus (63 BCE–14 CE). We can assume that the letter served the dual purpose of pleasing the senator and his family while also speaking more broadly to the scions of Rome's patrician houses. When we overlook this context, we miss a key element of the value of the *Ars Poetica* to Renaissance and early modern writers. The *Ars Poetica* held special appeal during the period in which the rulers and Renaissance humanists in Spain, France, and England were engaged in both projects of political and administrative reform based on Roman imperium. Renaissance humanists recognized aspects of their world in the portraits of Rome and Romans that Horace offered across his odes and epistles, among them the *Ars Poetica*. Horace framed his writing in the social and political conditions of empire, a context that he recognized extended opportunities as well as dangers and imposed constraints.

As Horace lays them out, these constraints are vocational, professional, and political. Romans did not enjoy the same access to the gods granted to the ancient Greeks: "To the Greeks, the Muse gave native talent, to the Greeks speech in well-rounded utterance; they craved nothing except to praise the gods."[48] Furthermore, Rome's youth were trained to be merchants and accountants, not poets: "Romans, by contrast, learn in school by means of lengthy calculations how to divide the *as*[49] into a hundred parts . . . once this canker, this thirst for petty cash, has blighted their souls, do we expect that poems can be fashioned worthy of being smeared with cedar-oil and kept in a polished cypress chest?"[50] Finally, although Horace does not say so directly, aspiring poets needed to consider the potential social and political costs of excelling in their art, given that poetic feats drew scrutiny on the part of the emperor and his family, and could lead to disaster. Horace himself navigated a number of dangerous exchanges with Augustus. Propertius faced similar pressure. Later, Augustus exiled Ovid to a remote city on the coast of the Black Sea because of what the poet characterized as "a song and a mistake" ("carmen et error").[51] For a host of reasons, then, Horace counseled his readers to rein in their ambition: "[C]hoose a theme that is equal to your powers" and

Clarinda's Stones 21

"reflect a long while on what your shoulders refuse, and have the strength to carry."[52]

It is in this context that Horace introduces Orpheus and Amphion as the two ancient figures who confer authority and prestige on what Horace presents as an art that is minor, but of significant social value. In a passage we will come back to at a number of junctures in this book, Horace writes that

> Orpheus, the priest and interpreter of the gods, deterred the savage race of men from slaughters and inhuman diet; hence he is said to tame tigers and furious lions: Amphion too, the builder of the Theban wall, was said to give the stones motion with the sound of his lyre, and to lead them where he would by engaging persuasion. This was the ancient wisdom, to distinguish the public good from private benefit; the sacred from the profane; to prohibit promiscuity; to give laws to married people; to plan out cities; to engrave laws on tablets of wood. Thus divine poets and their songs came to be honored. After these, excellent Homer and Tyrtaeus animated the manly mind to martial achievements with their verses. Oracles were delivered in poetry, and the economy of life pointed out, and the favor of sovereign princes was solicited by Pierian strains, games were instituted, and a cheerful period put to the tedious labors of the day; I remind you of this lest by chance you should be ashamed of the lyric muse [musa lyrae sollers] and Apollo, the god of song.[53]

We have already examined the myth of Amphion, but to understand this passage fully, it is useful to review Orpheus. The acclaimed singer of Thrace, Orpheus is a favorite of Apollo and admired by the rest of the gods for songs that charm all creation. They tame the beasts, inspire trees to create shady forests on bare hillsides, and even sway the gods of the underworld. When Orpheus's wife, Eurydice, dies from a snakebite, he persuades Pluto (Hades) and Proserpine (Persephone), king and queen of the underworld, to release her. He does so by arguing that his overwhelming love for his wife is an emotion common to gods and humans alike, and that he is in this respect equal to the gods. He should therefore receive the privilege of making the forbidden journey back from Hades to the daylight world, bringing Eurydice with him:

> . . . I came
> For my wife's sake, whose growing years were taken
> By a snake's venom. I wanted to be able
> To bear this; I have tried to. Love has conquered.

22 Introduction

> This god is famous in the world above,
> But here I do not know. I think he may be,
> Or is it all a lie, that ancient story
> Of an old ravishment, and how he brought
> The two of you together? By these places
> All full of fear, by this immense confusion,
> By this vast kingdom's silences, I beg you,
> Weave over Eurydice's life, run through too soon.[54]

The gods consent, with one condition: that Orpheus not turn back to look at Eurydice before the two have emerged from death's caverns. Tragically, humanly, Orpheus does turn to look, just as he crosses into the sunlight, while Eurydice is still in the cave. This turn marks the unbreachable difference between men and gods. The gods deny Orpheus's second suit to bring Eurydice back. He returns to earth heartbroken but still singing. Even after his body is torn apart by the frenzied Maenads, his head continues to sing as it travels over the sea to wash up on the island of Lesbos.

Orpheus and Amphion do not intersect in ancient myth. They come from different cities, Orpheus from Thrace, Amphion from Thebes. Furthermore, Orpheus plays a lyre furnished by Apollo, not Mercury. When Horace pairs them and associates them with *musa lyrae sollers*, he establishes new parameters for a practical, viable art that is accommodated to the constraints and the culture of his time and place—imperial, cosmopolitan Rome.[55] Orpheus and Amphion provide dignified, archaic origins for a poetry whose creative powers and *efficacia* are circumscribed by the real-world circumstances of poetry-making under an autocratic ruler, in a society organized in terms of military conquest and imperial commerce. Although Orphic poetry arises from the most sacred human experiences (desire, loss, the recurring, unfulfillable wish for permanence), and though Amphion represents the human capacity to create and destroy cities, *musa lyrae sollers* is a modern, circumscribed variant of these arts. These poems turn the awesome, archaic powers to the service of the daily rhythms of society. *Musa lyrae sollers* remind people of the rules and the fated outcomes communicated by oracles; they help them keep abreast of routine tasks; they cultivate favor with patrons and serve as accompaniment to various kinds of entertainment.

Horace's *Ars Poetica* wielded tremendous influence on sixteenth- and seventeenth-century lyric culture.[56] The political conditions that shaped its composition constituted one important factor in its success. Just as significant, however, was the political structure of the society that *musa lyrae sollers* builds up and supports. The lyric space Orpheus and Amphion delimit is composed of (1) a *vates* (Orpheus), (2) a political leader (Amphion), and (3) a populace that follows Orpheus's and Amphion's dictates. The people are crucial to the vision. Orpheus's laws and Amphion's songs have no meaning if no one responds to them. Moreover, a civilization doesn't exist if people don't live, work, play, and rest there. Rome was run by patricians, and Horace was an uncritical member of that group. His vision of society is neither egalitarian nor democratic. However, the domain of *musa lyrae sollers* is one in which everyone participates, whether or not they are named, in a variety of ways: the select few (the Orpheuses and Amphions) and the everyday people who are for the most part occupied by their business, but who appreciate poetry, perhaps because they like to compose little songs and epigrams, perhaps because they like to sing, or dance, or work in time to them, or perhaps because they are in love.

What happens next is the terrain of this book. In the hands of Renaissance humanists, Horace's lines on Orpheus, Amphion, and *musa lyrae sollers* establish the parameters of a lyric culture built up on the ground and, increasingly, elaborated in theory. The early chapter of lyric tradition that ensues unfolds through the seventeenth century and well into the eighteenth. Furthermore, as readings in the following chapters demonstrate, although Amphion is excluded from lyric as that category is reshaped by modern criticism, his lyre persists as a vital, generative instrument. I build a case for Amphion and his relevance to both poetry and modernity in this book through four interlocking discussions. Chapter 1 considers the Amphionic powers of culturally specific verse forms. I present readings of a representative selection of poems drawn from the period in which the influence of Horace, Amphion, and Orpheus was at its height. With a focus on Joachim du Bellay's *Antiquitez de Rome* (The ruins of Rome, published in 1558) and its afterlives, chapter 2 examines an Amphionic *translatio* that proceeds along the long life of Renaissance imperial formations, from Valois France to twenty-first-century Ireland. Chapter 3 centers on the Amphionic generative power of great quantities of lyrics, prepared in community. Miguel de Cervantes held both this labor and its products sacred. Moreover, in late texts such as the *Viaje del Parnaso* (Journey to Parnassus, 1614) and *Don Quijote, Part II* (1615), he links ignorance of the true meaning and value of the lyre to the ethical and moral catastrophe that was Spain's expulsion of the Moriscos.

In chapter 4, I discuss Amphion's salience in the Spanish colonial project in the Americas. The discussions in chapters 1 through 3 address first and foremost the question of what Amphion meant to sixteenth- and seventeenth-century European writers. However, Amphion's embeddedness in Renaissance imperial formations makes his art a rich site through which to consider the interplay of poetry, sociality, community, and politics in a Western modernity that is shaped, fundamentally, by coloniality.

24 Introduction

In the Americas, moreover, a key intertext for Amphion is the *Divina Commedia*, which furnishes a poetic music that accompanies creation and ruination, both in the early modern period and in the twentieth century, as witnessed by the Dantean poetry of Raúl Zurita. The chapter concludes with a short look at poetry by a number of self-identified Mapuche writers who have prepared work for circulation among readerships outside their communities.[57] These lyrics offer a glimpse of what an American world might look like when perceived otherwise from the Eurocentric perspective.

This book makes a double argument. My first point is that Amphion is a key figure in the Renaissance humanist concept of lyric poetry. He accounts for a wide variety of lyric production that falls outside the purview of the Renaissance self, but which Horace and Renaissance humanists understood to be a vital source of culture. Yet Horace centers Amphion because of what this myth tells us about polities, and from the Renaissance on, the polity persists as the dominant social formation in Western modernity. As a consequence, the myth of Amphion helps underwrite this modernity.

Once we know Amphion's myth, we find it staged and refracted all around us. This book creates a place to "put what we find" when we encounter Amphion and the songs of his lyre.

The Lyre and the World

[CHAPTER ONE]

One of the most influential passages that classical tradition handed down to Renaissance poetry was penned by Horace, who writes in his *Ars Poetica*:

> Orpheus, the priest and interpreter of the gods, deterred the savage race of men from slaughters and inhuman diet; hence he is said to tame tigers and furious lions: Amphion too, the builder of the Theban wall, was said to give the stones motion with the sound of his lyre, and to lead them where he would by engaging persuasion.[1]

As a point of departure for thinking through Amphion's significance to lyric tradition, it is useful to pause on a simple historical fact: "lyric," as a category of poetry, was initially conceived as a social phenomenon. "*Musa lyrae sollers*," as Horace devised it, designates the wide range of non-epic song forms, hymns, work songs, lighthearted ditties that perform what Virginia Jackson terms the "stipulative functions" that lyrics carry out in society.[2] Lyric poetry is understood in terms of these functions, even as "the lyric" began to take on meanings that no longer account for occasional poetry and related genres in the nineteenth and twentieth centuries. *Musa lyrae sollers* and that category's descendants were composed and sung by people as they went about their daily lives, animating the chores, labors, obeisances, and rituals that structured community life; for example, as "Pierian strains" flattered kings and tunes leavened the tedium of daily labor and set routines (*longorum operum*).[3] Notably, this totality is hierarchical in Horace. It is organized to foster both internal peace and material and economic productivity.

These features of lyric's social nature informed Renaissance humanists' attraction to Horace's lines. The *Ars Poetica* helped them develop

26 Chapter One

arguments that lyric poetry be taken seriously as an instrument for the smooth functioning of civic life in emergent imperial states, as monarchs and their councillors remade their societies on the model of Rome (or what they imagined to be Rome). Luis Zapata's prologue to his translation of the *Ars Poetica* (1592) presents this line of thought. Zapata argues that Horace's treatise is useful

> ... para Poetas, para Oradores, para predicadores, para historiadores, para escribir, y hablar, para tratar a la gente, conocer las diferencias de las personas, de los estados, de las naciones, de las edades, en fin para en todas las cosas, maestra de la vida humana . . .

> (. . . for Poets, for Orators, for those who deliver sermons; on writing and speaking, on how to treat people, to learn of differences among people, among states, among nations, among ages, finally, it is our teacher in all things related to human life . . .)[4]

For these reasons, according to Zapata, a Castilian-language translation of the *Ars Poetica* is of value to the Spanish patria (*gran servicio a la patria*). As a secondary point, he argues that Spanish society was, at the time of writing, burgeoning with poets: "tanta multidud de Poetas . . . que escaramuzan desmandados, sin doctrina y sin letras" (such a multitude of Poets, who skirmish in unruly fashion, with neither doctrine nor letters). It is to the benefit of the state to "recogerlos a que estén debajo de bandera como aventureros sueltos, y reduzirlos a arte" (collect those who fly the flag of the solitary adventurer and subject them to training).[5]

Many translations and imitations of the *Ars Poetica* from the sixteenth century, the earliest stage of the treatise's career as a cornerstone of Western poetics, emphasize the relationship between lyric and law. Jacques Pelletier du Mans's translation of Horace, *L'Art Poétique* (1555), furnishes an especially well-developed example, as the writer expands on Horace's language to underscore the idea of a poetry that instills social codes and constrains individual impulses "without use of force" (sans user de force):

> La poésie a congrée les hommes, qui étaient sauvages, brutans et épaves; et d'une horreur de vie, les a retirés à la civilité, police et société. Et est ce qui a été dit d'Anfion e d'Orfée: que par le son de leur Lire, ils tirent es arbres et les pierres après soi. La poésie a été cause des édifications des villes, e constitutions des lois; a montré la distinction du bien public d'avec le prive; du sacre d'avec le profane; des concubinages vagabonds et incertains, les a retirés aux mariages; a fait que chacun s'est tenu au sien, et a contenu la main e la convoitise de celui d'autrui, sans user de force comme

les bêtes sauvages, sus les biens, les enfants, et la vie de chacun. Ce qui est manifesté par cela, que les lois furent premièrement insculpées en vers; les prophéties des Sibylles sentenciées en vers.

(Poetry has convened men, who once were savages, beastly and lost; and from a life of horror, it drew them into civility, policy and society. And that has been said of Amphion and Orpheus: that by the sound of their lyre, they drew the trees and the stones after them. Poetry has been the cause of the building of cities, and the constitution of laws; it has shown the distinction between the public and the private good; between the sacred and the profane; it has drawn vagabond, uncertain concubinage into marriage; it has made it so that each person keeps to his own, and has contained the hand and the covetousness of one and another, without the use of force like the savage beasts, over the goods, the children, and the life of each. This is all shown by this fact: that laws were first carved in verses, the prophecies of the Sybils delivered in verse.)[6]

Eloquence and political prudence can accomplish what violence cannot.

While these passages represent civil society, civilization, as something imposed from above, the power of *musa lyrae sollers* in fact rises up within groups of people. It is a function of collective energies that stir and inspire communities. The secret of Amphion's walls is cheerful collaboration.[7] This is true even if those walls harden into repressive regimes of power and forms capable of inflicting harm, as they exclude people or crush them beneath the structure, or as they close people in and cause them to turn on each other. Horace refers to the "modis ludus" (cheerful manner) in which lyrics accomplish their objectives. In Renaissance images, a musician gaily plays a stringed instrument, and bricks and stones dance into place.[8] The iconography represents energetic civic participation roused by a skilled player of the lyre. In the *Defense of Poesy* (published 1595), Philip Sidney refers to this power as "charm." Wary of the opprobrium of Christian religious authorities, he nonetheless finds no better way to describe the power of lyric music than to endorse the opinion of the Greeks and Romans: "Although it were a very vain and godless superstition," he writes, "as also it was to think that spirits were commanded by such verses—whereupon this word charms, derived of *carmina*, comes—so yet serves it to show the great reverence those wits were held in" by the ancients. Sidney does not altogether refute their view. He continues: ". . . not without ground, since both the oracles of Delphos and Sibylla's prophecies were wholly delivered in verses; for that same exquisite observing of number and measure in words, and that high-flying liberty of conceit, proper to the poet, did seem to have some divine force in it."[9]

28   Chapter One

Charm remains a compelling way to think about poetic music. Paraphrasing Roman Jakobson, Tiffany Beechy observes in a discussion of charms and riddles in Middle English poetry that "[w]hen a voice takes on a certain tone or when repetitions of words or sounds arrest the ear, we seem to shift into a poetic mode of reception, in which logic may be associative rather than linear and affect is allowed a seat at the table of what counts as meaningful." Beechy attributes this shift to the "keenly material qualities of poetic language."[10] Sixteenth-century writers similarly recognized that the lyre represents poetry's material properties, the "curious points," in George Puttenham's words, of a particular language—the prosodies, vocabularies, and turns of phrase that cause poetry to "lodge in the ear," to shape attitudes, beliefs, and behaviors. The metaphor of Amphion's stones, which build walls for Thebes, captures the way in which verses inscribe habitus, seemingly miraculously, so that to compose language in a pre-given, socially recognized verse or poem form constitutes a meaningful contribution to collective social life.

While not all writers drew distinctions between Orpheus and Amphion (we will encounter writers in these chapters who confuse them, or who invoke them interchangeably), the constellation of lyric attributes—sociality, materiality, and charm, with its connotations of the divine—were frequently associated with Amphion. Orphic power is a transcendent force. Whether the Orpheus a writer draws on is Horace's lawgiver, Ovid's and Virgil's tragic lover, or a combination of the two, Orpheus creates poetry that suspends the laws of nature: "So long as men can breathe or eyes can see, / So long lives this and this gives life to thee."[11] Moreover, while Orpheus plays Apollo's lyre, he tends to be associated with voicing. Amphion's sphere of reference is consistently material. His myth points to a poetry of stones and walls, his lilting melodies and beats strike ears and animate bodies, and his music raises and vanquishes polities in keeping with a fated rhythm. This cycle explains Amphion's close association with the lyre (unlike Orpheus, Amphion is never represented as a singer).[12] The lyre's strings vibrate and stir the air to create their music. This music moves people for a period of time. Inspired, they make things such as poems and laws. They build up cities, empires, and the institutions that support those creations: impressive buildings, monuments, canons of poetry, art, and music, et cetera. Then the chords fade, and the structure fissures and crumbles. Gaps appear, and the walls come down. New melodies, tones, and phrases catch on. A society may crumble, implode, or disband; it may disperse and reconstitute itself in new formations, animated by these new poems. Amphion's lyre figures both the materiality and the ephemerality of social cohesion, an interpretation that is supported by that lyre's mythical donor—not golden, truth-telling, Parnassus-dwelling Apollo, but

Mercury, the god of techne and the day-to-day functions that make up social and commercial life: communication, the making of contracts, travel. Mercury is also the Olympian most closely associated with change.

The material and political dimensions of Amphion's art help explain why much sixteenth- and seventeenth-century poetry seems decidedly *un*lyrical to us today. Occasional poetry, homiletic verse, parody, translation—a wide swath of verbal activity that early moderns associated with the lyre—fall outside the bounds of the poetry that tends to attract critical and literary interest. However, Amphion's poetry is generated as societies, polities, and worlds are made, undone, dispersed, and remade. If the lyrics composed in the course of these processes seem uninspired or uninspiring to a reader now, we might bear in mind that some lyrics are not composed to last. If a given example of this poetry retains its vibrance and its capacities to mean, that is a happy accident. In general, however, Amphionic poetry conforms to Horace's dictum that "charm and excellence of construction . . . is to say here and now what is to be said here and now."[13] Having said that, as the material remains of a once-vibrant, now-dormant social moment or civic or ceremonial occasion, an Amphionic poem carries within itself—like the veining of a rock—traces of prior situations and prior worlds. As an initial example, consider the particularly challenging case of the kind of lyric that is the poetic gloss, via the example of poetry composed by the sixteenth-century lawyer Alonso de Cervantes.[14]

At the opening of the sixteenth century, Alonso sits at a writing desk. He is lonely and homesick. Banished from Spain because of a political dispute, he resides in Portugal, a place that feels foreign and strange.[15] No one is interested in making use of his skills. He is a *licenciado*, a lawyer, yet he cannot find gainful employment. He has been adrift for four years now, he reports, anonymous, unmoored, buffeted by misfortune:

> . . . afrentado y molestado de varias y extremas necesidades sin hallar (conociendo de mi alguna habilidad que pudiera ser satisfactoria para merecer algún premio beneficio y merced que se me pudiera hacer) quien la mano me diese ni ayudase para llegar a algún puerto de donde alguna manera de descanso alcanzase: por tanto: pues en las cosas de mi facultad y sagradísimas leyes: en que de los tiernos años aca siempre fue ocupado: no hallé camino que me guiase ni menos estado: ni tierra donde plantase . . .[16]

> (. . . offended and troubled by a variety of urgent needs while failing to find (knowing of myself that I have some abilities that might be sufficiently satisfactory to warrant some gift, benefit, or consideration) anyone who might extend a hand or help me to gain some port where I might take some rest, so that, since by my mental abilities those most sacred laws which

30   Chapter One

have occupied me from the most tender age I could not find the path to guide me forward, much less an estate, or a plot of ground upon which to establish myself . . .)

In this state, and concerned about falling into what he fears will be a corrupting indolence, Alonso turns to a poem that signifies home: the *Coplas por la muerte de su padre* by the fifteenth-century Castilian aristocrat Jorge Manrique (1440–1479). Nearly everyone in Spain knows of the *Coplas*. In its printed form, it is among the best-selling printed books of the sixteenth century, and verses and fragments of it circulate widely in oral tradition.[17] The *Coplas* is an elegy for a Castilian aristocrat (Don Rodrigo Manrique de Lara, the poet's father), but for many sixteenth-century Spaniards, Manrique's expert verses re-create a lost world, an idealized Spain populated by noble Christian warriors. This world is regenerated by Manrique's deft skill with pie quebrado (broken foot), a Castilian form composed of octosyllables whose flow is punctuated by the regular, rhythmic insertion of a tetrasyllable at every third line (the "broken foot"). Manrique deploys the pattern to powerful effect as he frames a statement of stoic Christian forbearance. The following stanza is one of the most famous fragments of lyric in Spanish tradition:

Nuestras vidas son los ríos
que van a dar en la mar,
que es el morir:
allí van los señoríos,
derechos a se acabar
y consumir;
allí los ríos caudales,
allí los otros medianos
y más chicos;
y llegados, son iguales
los que viven por sus manos
y los ricos.

(Our lives are rivers / that flow into the sea / that is death: / to there seigneury flows / directly, to be consumed; / to there the great rivers, / and the more modest ones, / and the smallest ones; / upon arrival, all are equal / those who live by their hands / and those with wealth.)[18]

As he reads through this poem he knows well, Alonso is stirred to write. Meditating on the meaning of each *copla* (each unit of *pie quebrado* verse), he writes dozens of stanzas of his own: glosses (explications) that reproduce the stanza's form, four *coplas* of *pie quebrado* to a stanza, rhymed ABC ABC DEF DEF. Alonso stacks three *coplas* of his own on a fourth one he draws from Manrique. As an example, the first parts of his gloss of stanza 3 run as follows (the verses Alonso takes from Manrique are in bold):

Es muy poca la prudencia
del que piensa en el estado
desta vida
que aproveche diligencia
para nadie ser librado
de caída
ni estos tuyos ni estos míos
aprovechen a excusar
este decir
nuestras vidas son los ríos
que van a dar en la mar
que es el morir.

Este mar que a todos baña
por juicio y por sentencia
divinal
con su ira y con su saña
lo que es flaco a gran potencia
haze igual
si livianos poderíos
assi lleva sin mudar
su proseguir
alla van los señoríos
derechos a se acabar
y consumir.[19]

(What little prudence / has he, the man who thinks of his state / in this world / may he avail himself of diligence / for no one is spared / from falling / neither your state nor mine / has the luxury of eluding / this saying / Our lives are rivers / that flow into the sea / that is death. // This sea that bathes all / by the judgment and sentence / of the divine / with its anger and its fury / makes the weak equal / to the great and powerful / whose force is just as lightly / carried away, with no change / to its course. / To there all seigneury flows / directly, to be consumed.)

How counterintuitive to call this work lyric. Alonso interrupts the solemn procession of Manrique's fluid assonances, the smooth flow of short,

Chapter One

low "ah" sounds (nuestras vidas . . . van a dar . . . mar . . . alla . . . acabar) with the stops of alliterated p's, d's, and hard c's (poca . . . prudencia . . . del . . . desta . . . diligencia . . . caída, and so forth). Moreover, the essence of glossing is explanation,[20] and Alonso's prating commentary would seem to be at odds with what is, for many of us, the *Coplas'* most lyrical quality, which is its allusiveness. Yet in the sixteenth century, "poet" meant "maker." Nearly every treatise or defense of poetry from the period introduces this definition as its point of departure.[21] Thus, if we want to discover where and how Alonso's glosses are poetic—in fact, how they are lyrical—one way to begin is to ask what they are making. The answer is that these glosses perform Amphion's art by building a Castilian world that has a place in it for Alonso.[22] We see this world created on the page, as Alonso literally builds his own interpretations and sense into the *Coplas'* stanzas. A second process that takes place is more complex and requires a bit more explanation. It has to do with intersubjectivity, the interplay of the self and the social entailed in glossing, as a writer immerses themself, body and mind, in rhythms and attitudes set by an existing poem, played on someone else's lyre.

Shared Measures

Glossing is a term used to describe a variety of practices. What unites them is a shared rootedness in meaning-making that is ongoing, collaborative, and extended diachronically, across time. The extended title of Alonso's glosses includes a reference to a work "composed and created by" Alonso de Cervantes.[23] We can interpret the phrase in a variety of ways, but it points to the arrangement of materials (composing), as well as the act of conceiving of them and realizing them (creating). A writer uses a line or a fragment from an existing text and expands on it in verses or paragraphs that reflect on it seriously, parodically, or otherwise. Alonso presents himself as serious in his work with the *Coplas*; and his remarks on the project shape an account of how, as he works with the poem, it begins to work on him. He remembers that he is a man of action (not indolence), he remembers that he has skills and a passion for law (even if no one in Portugal acknowledges them), and he regathers himself as a writer. Society has a place for writers, as well as structuring principles that organize how they fit into the larger whole. For example, they should be obedient to their models ("ser obediente a la proposición y ejemplo").[24] They should also follow the custom of sending their work out to more accomplished princes and lords for review: "porque siendo costumbre de los que escriben elegir para enderezar sus cosas: a los príncipes y señores de sus tiempos mas cumplidos hallan" (as it is the custom of those who write to choose as someone

The Lyre and the World 33

to emend their writings princes and great lords of their time, the most accomplished that can be found). Alonso turns this latter obligation to his advantage:

> . . . A quien yo con mas justa razón devo enderezar y dirigir esta mi pequeña obra si no a vuestra . . . señoría donde son notorias y resplendentes las gracias dotes y virtudes de que los mucho las merecieron son siempre loados . . .[25]

> (. . . To whom should I with the greatest reason prepare and send this, my little work, but to your . . . lordship, in whom the gifts of grace and many virtues are notorious and shine forth . . .)

The tone and the content of these passages convey that the act of glossing restores Alonso to himself, in an operation that is poetic and subjective, yet quite different from what we encounter in, say, Petrarch, Wyatt, or Garcilaso de la Vega. While these poets use the lyre as an instrument to elaborate on the conceit of a transcendent, private self, in Alonso's hands, the lyre generates social relations. As he glosses Manrique's stanzas, Alonso sinks himself into the cadences and belief system of a seigneurial Castile, whose ethos, the Spanish community has agreed, is realized in the verses of the *Coplas*. The structuring codes and attitudes of this world—its walls, if you will—include the reciprocal obligations that Alonso invokes as he writes to the duke. Thus glossing creates the viable grounds for readmission into Spanish society. The two-part process at work here corresponds to Eric Hayot's paraphrase of ideas found in Heidegger and Jean Luc Nancy about the concepts of the world and the work of art:

> The work and the world name a self-enclosing, self-organizing, self-grounding process. This process is neither act nor event, subject nor object; it is the ground of activity, eventfulness, subject- and object-hood, and of procession. There is no common word for what the work and the world share, unless it is "world" itself. . . . But . . . "world" means also . . . the world, this world, the natural, actual, living world of human history.[26]

In a world conceived of in this way, "subjectivity" can be construed not only in terms of inner landscapes of perception, desire, and feeling, but also as a situation and a condition, the capacity to "make things happen" as the "subject of a verb."[27] This is what Alonso does, seizing the opportunity presented by this possible claim on the duke's attention—"possible" because dubious; Alonso has, after all, been banished—embedding a quick description, delivered in passing, of how "[p]or la cruel sentencia

34 Chapter One

que siendo vuestro corregidor en la vuestra villa de Burgillos contra mi . . . sin culpa de vuestros vasallos ni la mía fue dada" (by the cruel sentence your magistrate in your town of Burgillos delivered against me . . . through no fault of your vassals or my own).[28] This confidence in one's authority to lay claim to cultural patrimony and make use of it, the idea that certain poems and verses are available for everyone and anyone who claims membership in the patria, is a crucial dimension of *musa lyrae sollers* and, indeed, of lyric culture—at least up to the watershed of the post-Romantic lyricization of poetry. Amphion, in particular, represents for premoderns and early moderns the fact that participating in a community's meaningful verse and song forms is something everyone can do.

The outcome of this participation is dubious, of course. Spain, ultimately, is not a world Alonso creates. He can compose poetry in its most prestigious and powerful cadences, exercising Amphion's art in a bid to charm himself back into the collective. But Amphion's lyre builds polities, not democracies. The ultimate decision regarding who can inhabit a world and make things happen there lies with political authorities such as the duke. It seems that Alonso's suit was unsuccessful. Marino cites a complaint filed in Portugal, in 1512, against a judge named Cervantes who "would probably write better *coplas* than *sentenças* [sentences]."[29] Apparently, Alonso found a way to restart his career in exile. However, his glosses did not reincorporate him into the Spain he longed to rejoin.[30]

Lyre and World

Alonso prepared his glosses at a time of transition between new and old worlds in Europe. His prologue is dated 1501. Columbus had already landed on the island he named Hispañola, and the Spanish colonial project was underway. But Spain was not yet the global power it would become under the Hapsburgs. While the wholeness of the Christian, seigneurial world that the *Coplas* memorializes no longer existed (if, indeed, it ever had existed), the country was still an Iberian kingdom ruled by the Castilian and Aragonese monarchs Isabella and Ferdinand.

Over the course of the sixteenth century, "world" would become an increasingly active concept, not only on the Iberian Peninsula, but for Europeans more widely. Ayesha Ramachandran explains the flourishing of early modern poiesis, which she defines as "artful making," as motivated by "a new recognition of . . . existence in a radically uncertain world where we must create our own order."[31] This uncertainty was prompted in part by the experience of grappling with the jolts and dissonances unleashed in the lives of people of all walks of life in the wake of 1492. Roland Greene similarly points to the world-fracturing impact of the Spanish encounter with the Americas, which opened fissures in classical knowledge as an idea of an "entire," "singular," "corporeal," and "natural" world was challenged by evidence of powerful competing realities, concepts, and beliefs, rooted in previously unknown territories. "For the succeeding two or three generations," Greene argues, "the word and concept of the world seemed in play everywhere."[32] The essay that unfolds from his claim furnishes illuminating contexts for a spectrum of tropes and fictions found in early modern writing from the sixteenth century and the first half of the seventeenth century.

The lyre is one of these tropes. Horace's remarks on *musa lyrae sollers* open the way for a powerful Renaissance metaphor: the lyre represents the human capacity to intervene in nature, for a finite period of time, be that period short or long. Songs and poems of various kinds constituted one among a wide range of practices by which people managed the uncertainties and gaps in comprehension opened up by global modernity. More specifically, "lyric," as an emergent category of cultural production, furnished two concepts to help people negotiate a shifting world: the Orphic lyre, an instrument associated with law giving (Horace) and the generation of a transcendent self (Virgil, Ovid),[33] and the lyre of Amphion, whose melodies and harmonies mediate relationships between the individual and the social. In both cases, the Orphic and the Amphionic, the lyre rendered lived, political worlds that were only partially under a person's control somewhat manageable, at least in play.

The readings in this chapter present some representative examples of how we might approach sixteenth-century lyric as the art of *musa lyrae sollers*. I will be tracking how writers deploy culturally specific verse and song forms—octosyllables and hendecasyllables in Spain; huitains and alexandrines in France; heroic couplets, common meter, and blank verse in England—as a means of gaining a purchase on the worlds around them. I have selected poems in which writers practice the world-making and world-dismantling art of Amphion, deliver laws in the manner of Orpheus, or engage in the collaborative making and the social participation accomplished through activities such as glossing and translating, two categories of verbal production that tend to fall outside the bounds of what criticism and scholarship acknowledge as lyric. As we will see, they fall well within the category of Horace's lyric art.

Heroic Measures

"To Penshurst" (1616), by the English poet Ben Jonson, draws on the Renaissance Amphion directly. On one hand, an elegiac tribute to a house, Penshurst, the home of Robert Sidney and the traditional seat of the Sid-

36 **Chapter One**

ney family, the poem is also an exercise in lyric poetics.[34] Jonson (1572–1637) was familiar with the myth of Amphion, and in "To Penshurst" draws on it by presenting architecture and poetry as related practices capable of making worlds. Here, this activity is epitomized by the Sidney house. In lines 1–8, Jonson's lyric speaker presents the structure as both an "ancient pile" that is aligned with nature in ways that modern buildings, "built to envious show," are not and, synechdochically, an example of the civilized, social structures that humanity can create when their aims are modest, and when they work in concert with nature to produce works of substance:

> Thou art not, Penshurst built to envious show,
> Of touch or marble; nor canst boast a row
> Of polished pillars, or a roof of gold;
> Thou hast no lantern, whereof tales are told,
> Or stair, or courts; but stand'st an ancient pile,
> And, those grudged at, art reverenced the while,
> Thou joy'st in better marks, of soil, of air,
> Of wood, or water; therein thou art fair.[35]

"Pile" is a deliberate archaism here. Jonson contrasts the world of Penshurst, the world of the Sidneys, with a contemporary England beset by influxes of new wealth and an accompanying profligacy (buildings detailed with marble or gold), as well as simmering religious, social, and political conflicts that will eventually erupt in the English Civil Wars. The subtext of "To Penshurst" is Jonson's nostalgia, his wish that a fracturing English society might similarly be made whole again by recalling the rich tradition of its poets. To this end, he composes a robust and compelling poetic music: 102 lines arranged in 51 heroic couplets (iambic pentameter, rhymed AA, BB, CC, etc.), in which Jonson praises the house and its walls "of the country stone, / reared no man's ruin, no man's groan" (lines 46–47). The final lines of "To Penshurst" make the moral distinction between past and present clear: "Now, Penshurst, they that will proportion thee / With other edifices, when they see / Those proud, ambitious heaps, and nothing else, / May say their lords have built, but thy lord dwells" (lines 98–102). Between the first mention of those other houses in lines 1–8 and their second appearance, in line 99, however, Jonson creates forty-seven couplets, ninety-four lines of substantial and well-designed verses that describe the natural abundance of the estate: "Thou hast thy walks for health, as well as sport, / Thy mount, to which the dryads to resort, / Where Pan and Bacchus their high feasts have made // ... // Thy sheep, thy bullocks, kine, and calves do feed" (lines 11–22), and the generosity and goodwill of its lords: ". . . the same beer and bread, the selfsame wine, / This is his lordship's shall be also mine" (lines 63–64).

While "To Penshurst" is a poem about a great house and the community it anchored, then, it is also a poem about Amphionic lyric composition, the art of building in song. Jonson's assembled heroic couplets emulate hewn blocks in their extension, mass, and regularity, and their close rhyme functions both as mortar that affixes verse to verse and as one of the animating forces that move a reader through the poem to experience as a coherent whole. Jonson deploys additional important devices, anaphora and other patterns of repetition of words such as "Of," "Thou," "Thy," at the openings of lines. These lyric resources contribute to the sense of totality, as does enjambment, in lines 2–3, for example, which sends the eye, the breath, and the mind from one line to the next, emulating, onomatopoetically, the experience of the eye as a person looks down a row of rounded pillars. This early enjambment also inaugurates the dual function of the couplets, which are both discrete units (building blocks) and the mechanism by which the structure coheres.

We receive plenty of formal cues, as readers, that in "To Penshurst" Jonson is working with the concept of Amphion's lyre. The underlying politics of the poem are similarly shaped by conceits that Renaissance humanist writers drew from the myth. An extended section of the poem presents the surrounding families, farms, orchards, and forests as fodder that feed the stately house. The lyric speaker tells us that no man was ruined or groaned out loud as he contributed to building Penshurst. Yet the life of the house, its hospitality and liberality over time, requires the steady consumption of the fruits of the land, the labor of its inhabitants, and even the inhabitants themselves. In lines 48–55, the speaker recalls:

> . . . all come in, the farmer and the clown,
> And no one empty handed, to salute,
> The lord and lady, though they have no suit,
> Some bring a capon, some a rural cake,
> Some nuts, some apples, some that think they make
> The better cheeses bring them, or else send
> By their ripe daughters, whom they would commend
> This way to husbands . . .

The image of the harmonious, self-enclosed, self-nourishing world of "To Penshurst" is shadowed and undercut by its economics. In the manner of archaic polises found in Ovid, for example, Penshurst flourishes at the expense of the less powerful.[36] The notably chilling detail here is the inclusion of daughters in the catalog of rural products. Jonson's fluid verses

38   **Chapter One**

absorb the human predations and human costs of this world to generate a compelling hymn to an idealized, harmonious, natural ethos.

"To Penshurst" is thus an accomplished example of poetic world-making that addresses the uncertainties of seventeenth-century politics, both English and global, with a harmonious vision of a world remade by the lyre. This is a world anchored by the figure of England's prince of poets, Philip Sidney, and his family house, an England composed of communities that enjoy the produce of a well-managed estate. As a work, "To Penshurst" creates a world in and of itself. Jonson's heroic couplets build up the house, its environs, and its visitors, all of which behave in accordance with the poem's governing ethos of abundance and good order; this ethos in turn furnishes the rationale for the poem's form, the rhyming couplets that assure no statement or image or comparison will expand to hollow itself out in the manner of the vain houses "built to envious show" in lines 1–5. Jonson's couplets and pentameter keep language and the expanding English world in check, at least in this poem.

The Spanish Orpheus

"To Penshurst" is a striking example of Renaissance Amphionic poetics. Jonson deploys his heroic couplets to hold together a world whose fissures provide evidence, just beneath the surface, of the ceaseless forming and undoing of social compacts, regardless of the skill with which a poet plays the lyre. The "Ode ad florem Gnidi" demonstrates a similarly expert grasp of the nature, purpose, and poetics of *musa lyrae sollers*, although this time the poet, Garcilaso de la Vega (ca. 1501–1536), plays the lyre of Horace's Orpheus. One of Spain's most celebrated poets, Garcilaso de la Vega is synonymous with early modern poetry. In life, he represented the ideal of the Renaissance man: skilled with both the pen and the sword, he was a nobleman who died young in battle. With Juan Boscán, he translated *The Book of the Courtier* from Italian into Castilian. The "Ode ad florem Gnidi" (henceforth referred to as the Ode) contributes to Garcilaso's reputation. He composed the poem in the Italian *lira*, a stanza few Castilian writers attempted because differences between the stress patterns and cadences of Italian and Castilian make it difficult to work with. Garcilaso's success with the form attests to his talent for verses as well as to residencies in Italy, where he moved in the erudite, lettered circles frequented by Italian humanists and imperial courtiers. For our purposes here, the Ode draws attention because of its opening conceit:

Si de mi baja lira
tanto pudiese el son que en un momento

aplacase la ira
del animoso viento
y la furia del mar y el movimiento;

y en ásperas montañas
con el süave canto enterneciese
las fieras alimañas,
los árboles moviese
y al son confusamente los trujiese . . .[37]

(If the sound of my lowly lyre / were so powerful that in one moment / it
could soothe the ire of the raging wind / and the movement of the furious
sea; // and in the harsh mountains / with its soft song / gentle the fierce
beasts, / and move the trees, / beguiling them with confusing rhythms,
that they might draw near . . .)

In stanzas that allude to passages in the *Metamorphoses* and the *Georgics*, the
lyric speaker in this poem casts himself as a present-day Orpheus.[38] Both
ancient writers describe the powers that Orpheus's song wields to tame
wild beasts and forest the Thracian hillsides. The Orphic dimensions of this
poem reach beyond Ovid and Virgil, however, to extend to Horace, who
furnishes both the poem's form (the ode) and its key structuring conceits.
The singer recognizes his belatedness with respect to archaic and mythic
powers; his use of the imperfect subjunctive in the opening lines indicates
his self-consciousness about attempting the great feats of archaic times
and his decision to focus on the more modest aims of *musa lyrae sollers*.[39]
Having acknowledged this point, he also recognizes that his powers, limited as they may be, invest him with the Orphic authority to deliver societal
laws. Thus, the song he composes delivers a lesson about gender politics
to a female inhabitant of the city who fails to recognize the codes and texts
that shape her male- and Spanish-dominated world. In stanza 3, the lyric
speaker declares that *were* he able to wield the archaic lyre, he would do so
to persuade the poem's beautiful addressee to accept his friend's advances:

. . . solamente aquella
fuerza de tu beldad sería cantada,
y alguna vez con ella
también sería notada
el aspereza de que estás armada . . .[40]

(. . . only the power / of your beauty would be sung, / and, once in a while, /
that severe disposition / with which you arm yourself would be noted . . .)

40 Chapter One

The central portion of the poem seeks to rouse the lady's sympathy by elaborating on his friend's suffering. In stanzas 8–10, the speaker describes:

> Por ti, como solía,
> del áspero caballo no corrige
> la furia y gallardía,
> ni con freno la rige,
> ni con vivas espuelas ya l'aflige;
>
> por ti con diestra mano
> no revuelve la espada presurosa,
> y en el dudoso llano
> huye la polvorosa
> palestra como sierpe ponzoñosa;
>
> por ti su blanda musa,
> en lugar de la cítara sonante,
> tristes querellas usa
> que con llanto abundante
> hacen bañar el rostro del amante . . .[41]

(Because of you / he does not tame the fury and temerity / of the wild horse / he does not control it with the rein / nor afflict it with the lively spur; // because of you, he does not brandish / the swift sword with deft hand, / and on the uncertain plain / he flees from the dusty arena / as if it were a poisonous snake; // because of you his gentle muse, / instead of the sonorous zither, / sings sad dirges / which with abundant sighs / wash this lover's face in tears . . .)

The final third of the poem warns of the perils that await a woman who spurns a would-be lover. In stanza 14, the speaker reminds the lady of the myth of Anaxarete: if she continues to harden her heart against her suitor, she may, like Ovid's example in book 14 of the *Metamorphoses*, find herself turned to stone.[42]

> Hágate temerosa
> el caso de Anaxarete, y cobarde,
> que de ser desdeñosa
> se arrepentió muy tarde,
> y así su alma con su mármol arde.[43]

(Cower before / the example of Anaxarete / who repented too late / for her disdain, and thus her soul burns, trapped in marble.)

As in "To Penshurst," Garcilaso generates a world by means of lyric devices in the Ode. This world is simultaneously an aesthetic artifact (a poem) and an actual place and site of politics: Naples, as it is dominated and transformed by Spanish power. Garcilaso manipulates the intricate patterns of the *lira*, interlacing them with codes, allusions, and rules imported from Spain. In stanzas 8–10, for example, he manages the form's play of hepta- and hendecasyllables to intertwine descriptions of the friend's excellence and his falling away from that excellence. His elevated vocabulary conveys the friend's earlier heroism, while patterns of assonance and consonance enhance Garcilaso's images on a sonorous level, in a kind of onomatopoeia: a horse straining at the bit (stanza 8), a sword whirling through enemy forces (stanza 9), laments flooding from a grief-stricken muse (stanza 10). The anaphora that sets the passage off from the rest of the poem ("Por ti . . . Por ti . . . Por ti . . .") further highlights Garcilaso's dexterity.

As the Spanish Orpheus engages world-making, however, he is also engaging in world destruction. The lyric speaker and his fellow Spanish courtiers disrupt an existing social order and change the conditions of belonging and exclusion by imposing new behavioral codes and gender norms. The new conditions catch the Neapolitan woman off guard, and she makes two mistakes: she rejects a Spanish suitor but, more importantly, she fails to recognize that her world has changed. Naples is still called Naples, and the city occupies the same geographic territory as the Naples she knew as home, but Spanish courtiers have remade it on new terms shaped by imperial power. In this new formation, the "No" spoken by a local woman of rank and privilege is rendered, if not inaudible, certainly devoid of force. Perhaps surprisingly (or perhaps not), this highly self-conscious work of Renaissance artifice reveals the gendered operation of empire as it imposes its steady work of dislocation and dispossession on the native inhabitants of a space the occupier takes as his target.[44]

"La lira de Garcilaso contrahecha"

Garcilaso concludes his Ode. However, the world-making, law-giving music of the Ode continues to resonate throughout the community of Spanish courtiers. The parody "A un buen caballero y mal poeta: La lira de Garcilaso contrahecha" (To a good gentleman and bad poet: Garcilaso's lyre undone) by the Spanish courtier Hernando de Acuña (1517–1580) repro-

42 Chapter One

duces Garcilaso's prosody, his framework of allusions, and the world he creates. The two poems differ only in their details: the Ode is set in Naples, whereas Acuña creates an allegorical Apollonian court. The two writers also target different identities for exclusion, as Garcilaso takes aim at a woman and Acuña seeks to marginalize a fellow courtier. But both poems turn lyric aesthesis to the same political ends.

The word *contrahecha* can be translated in a number of ways. In Spanish, it means "imitation from nature," but it also means distorted or perverted. Acuña works with all these meanings in his parody, which is simultaneously a virtuoso work of *imitatio* and a merciless attack on a fellow courtier, Jerónimo de Urrea (1510–1573).[45] In stanzas modeled closely on Garcilaso's opening *liras*, Acuña reviles Urrea's lyre, whose music would drive a sane person mad:

De vuestra torpe lira
ofende tanto el son, que en un momento
mueve al discreto a ira
y a descontentamiento,
y vos sólo, señor, quedáis contento.[46]

(The sound of your clumsy lyre / offends so greatly, that in an instant / it moves the judicious man to ire / and unsettles him, / and you alone, sir, are left content.)

In stanza 2, the speaker says that wild beasts would be moved to laughter were the gentleman's songs to sound out through the forest:

Yo en ásperas montañas
no dudo que tal canto endureciese
las fieras alimañas,
o a risa las moviese
si natura el reír les concediese.

(I do not doubt that in the harsh mountains / such a song would harden / the ferocious beasts, / or move them to laughter / if laughter were permitted them by nature.)

And so on. Point for point, Acuña composes "To a Good Gentleman" following the formal pattern of Garcilaso's Ode, reshaping the stanzas' meaning to assail what he portrays as Urrea's perverse failures in nearly every task that Renaissance culture assigns to poets: the praise of heroes

("¡Ay de los capitanes en las sublimes ruedas colocados, / aunque sean alemanes, / si para ser loados / fueran a vuestra musa encomendados!" [Alas! for those captains / who occupy the high spheres, / even the German ones, / if they have been commended to your muse / for praise!]; stanza 4); the praise of women ("Mas ¡ay, señor, de aquélla / cuya beldad de vos fuere cantada! / que vos daréis con ella / do verse sepultada / tuviese por mejor que ser loada" [But oh, sir, pity the lady / whose beauty you sang! / You have given her reason to prefer / that her name be buried rather than praised]; stanza 5); providing solace to the condemned ("Triste de aquel cautivo / que a escucharos, señor, es condenado / que está muriendo vivo / de versos enfadado, / y a decir que son buenos es forzado" [Sad indeed is the captive / who is condemned to listen to you, sir, / and is withering away / from your vexing verses / and is compelled to praise them]; stanza 7); and the invention of songs that please Apollo ("el pecho contra Apolo empedernido, / y a su pesar cantando, / de que él está sentido / y el coro de las musas muy corrido" [your heart hardened against Apollo, / and singing in a way that troubles him, / that saddens him / and leaves the choir of muses quite distraught]; stanza 14). Indeed, the good gentleman's songs could drain the color from a meadow of flowers, as in stanza 6:

Que vuestra musa sola
basta a secar del campo la verdura,
y al lirio y la vïola,
do hay tanta hermosura,
estragar la color y la frescura.

(All on her own, your muse / can dry up the green of a field / and corrupt the color and the freshness / of the lily and the violet, / wherein there is so much beauty.)

These faults are especially grievous because of the poem's setting, which is not Naples but Parnassus; that is, not occupied territory but a mythical domain presided over by Apollo and inhabited by the Muses— and also by courtiers, since Parnassus is a common allegory of court in the sixteenth and seventeenth centuries. The good gentleman's perverse insistence on composing lyrics that please no one but himself is thus a kind of lèse-majesté. Moreover, he appears to escape reproof for flouting his sovereign: "Por vos, como solía, / no reprehende Apolo ni corrige / la mala poesía, / ni las plumas rige, / pues la vuestra anda sola y nos aflige" (Because of you, / Apollo no longer chastises nor corrects / bad poetry, / nor

44   Chapter One

does he govern the pen, / thus your muse wanders along her own path and makes us suffer"; stanza 8). On all these grounds, the lyric speaker calls for his peer's dismissal from the mountain:

> Si yo poeta fuera,
> viendo la cosa ya rota y perdida,
> a Apolo le escribiera,
> pues que de sí se olvida,
> que reforme su casa o la despida.
>
> Que no ha sido engendrada
> la poesía de la dura tierra,
> para que sea tratada
> como enemigo en guerra
> de quien se muestra amigo y la destierra.

(If I were a poet, / seeing that the matter is broken beyond repair, / I would write to Apollo / to say that he is forgetting himself, / that it is time he get his house in order or let the man go. // For poetry did not spring forth / from the hard ground / to be treated / like an enemy on the battlefield / by someone who appears to be a friend but sends her into exile.)

This expulsion makes sense according to the poem's surface conceit. Obviously, a bad poet does not belong on Parnassus. It also corresponds to the processes of world-making and world exclusion that Garcilaso builds into his Ode.

A historical detail intersects with the poetics of "To a Good Gentleman" here. Urrea disappears from court records in the 1560s, perhaps in the wake of a secret investigation into allegations of sodomy.[47] Rumors about Urrea's sexuality inform a subtext of Acuña's attack in "To a Good Gentleman," most notably in the play with the idea of a "bad poet." In book 10 of the *Metamorphoses*, Ovid recounts that when Orpheus lost Eurydice the second time, he turned away from the love of women and wooed young men: "Orpheus even started the practice among the Thracian / tribes of turning for love to immature males and of plucking / the flower of a boy's brief spring before he has come to his manhood."[48] In framing Urrea as a poet who plays Garcilaso's lyre *contrahecha*, Acuña points to this later phase of Orpheus's desire. The image of a muse who drains the color from a meadow of flowers elaborates the conceit. Subsequently, having established the association between Urrea and Orpheus as lovers of boys, Acuña weaves double entendres across his stanzas: the good gentleman's state is "broken and lost" ("rota y perdida"; stanza 12);

his poetry is flaccid or diseased, without a sound bone in its body ("hueso sano"; stanza 9).

The allusions are clear. The question is how to interpret them. "Sodomy" was a vague allegation whose prosecution was carried out unevenly, often as a blind for the settling of a civic, religious, ethnic, or personal conflict.[49] Iberian Christians invoked it as evidence of the corrupt nature of people of the Jewish and Islamic faiths. Baltasar Fra-Molinero shows that the othering of Black men often included variations on the same discourse.[50] As he develops his case for the legitimacy of his actions in the Yucatán Peninsula, Hernán Cortés cites sodomy and cannibalism among the region's inhabitants.[51] Carina Johnson calls attention to pamphlets created and circulated by Dutch printers that elaborated on what European readers would consider deviant practices, adding illustrations recycled from other publications to attract readers. Johnson also observes that during this same period, people who moved across and between cultures, such as diplomats and merchants, were often targets of rumors about sexual excess.[52]

Of course, it is possible that Urrea *was* shunned from court because of his writing. Decisions he made about verse form and stanza provoked mockery and embarrassment among fellow courtiers. Among the double entendres Acuña incorporates in "To a Good Gentleman," the lyric speaker reminds the gentleman:

> Por ley es condenado
> cualquier que ocupa posesión ajena,
> y es muy averiguado
> que con trabajo y pena
> el oro no se saca do no hay vena . . .

> (The law condemns / the man who occupies a place that is alien to him / and oft has it been proven / that despite effort and suffering / gold will not be mined where there is no vein . . .)

Again these lines suggest sodomy, as Acuña intimates that Urrea is putting parts of himself where they don't belong. The lines also speak to poetic composition, however. *Vena* can mean "vein," as I have translated it above, in keeping with Acuña's principal metaphor of the gold mine, a source of profit. *Vena* also means inspiration, though, and Acuña has strong opinions about Urrea's verses and his muse. In "To a Good Gentleman," he points specifically to Urrea's translations. In stanza 9, he cites the bad poet's "miserable, frenzied translation" (aquella triste traducción furiosa):

46   Chapter One

Por vuestra cruda mano
aquella triste traducíon furiosa
no tiene hueso sano,
y vive sospechosa
que aun vida le daréis más trabajosa.

(Penned by your rude hand, / that miserable, frenzied translation / does
not have a sound bone in its body, / and it lives in fear / that you may give
it yet another afterlife that is even more troubled.)

The stanza refers to Urrea's version of *Orlando Furioso* (1549), the first rendering of Ariosto's poem into Castilian. Acuña was not alone in disparaging the project. Urrea's translation was roundly mocked in erudite circles, and as late as 1605, the priest in *Don Quixote, Part I,* delivers the tactful opinion that Urrea "might have been better off not attempting the task."[53]

We cannot know the circumstances of Urrea's disappearance from court records. But "To a Good Gentleman" tells us something else; namely, the power of lyric forms to enact politics. The parody draws structure and authority from the Ode, but Garcilaso's poem also hands Acuña a powerful instrument with which to transform insiders into outsiders, stripping away their worlds. In this way, *musa lyrae sollers*—here represented by the Ode and "To a Good Gentleman"—reproduce in verses the work that sixteenth-century lawyers, scholars, rulers, canons, and bishops were carrying out to parse degrees of humanity, dignity, and personhood as part of the process of creating an early modern Christian world structured by imperialism, colonialism, gender, mercantilism, and extractivism.

The Task of the Courtier

A conflict around a separate project, Urrea's translation of the French lyric *Le Chevalier délibéré*, lays bare the stakes of poetry, lyric, and verse as Acuña, Urrea, and their circles perceived them.

Le Chevalier délibéré was composed by Olivier de la Marche (ca. 1422–1502) in 1483. La Marche was a loyal knight and retainer of Charles V's ancestors Charles the Bold (his great-grandfather) and Mary of Burgundy (his grandmother). *Le Chevalier délibéré* presents these two famed aristocratic Burgundians as mirrors of Christian perfection and virtue. Over the course of 338 stanzas of French huitains (octaves of octosyllabic verse), the poem recounts the journey and adventures of a knight, "La Marche," who, on the threshold of old age, sets out for a tournament held in the forest of Atropos (Death). His encounters with allegorical figures such as Appetite, Desire, Time, Good Counsel, Fresh Memory, and Understanding provide a template both for the good Christian life and for a good death, which La Marche indicates is represented most fully by the demise of his beloved and sorely missed friends.

A lively and engaging poem, *Le Chevalier délibéré* is not upon first reading especially significant. But it was important to the Hapsburg family, and Charles V regarded it as an heirloom. La Marche deploys a complex of rhetorical and poetic strategies, weaving Christian allegory with a memoir of the lives of his masters to realize a vision of a chivalric Burgundian world that is lost as Philip the Good, Charles the Bold, and Mary of Burgundy are taken by death. As Susie Speakman Sutch and Anne Lake Prescott show, *Le Chevalier délibéré* ultimately positions the three Burgundian aristocrats as signs of God's eternal majesty.[54] Charles V was trained to this tradition. Indeed, in his youth, he is rumored to have created the prose translation of *Le Chevalier délibéré* that Acuña worked from. At the end of his life, he brought two copies of the poem with him into retirement: the French version penned by La Marche and a version Acuña set into Castilian verse: *El cavallero determinado, traduzido de la lengua Francesa en Castellana, por Don Hernando de Acuña, y dirigido al Emperador Don Carlos Quinto Máximo, Rey de España nuestro Señor* (The resolved gentleman, translated from the French language into Castilian by Sir Hernando de Acuña and dedicated to the Emperor Sir Charles V, His Majesty the King of Spain). The book was printed in 1553 by Johannes Steelsius. Urrea also prepared a version of the poem. Titled *Discurso de la vida humana y aventuras del caballero determinado traduzido de frances por Don Jerónimo de Urrea*, this work was published in 1555 by Martin Nutius.[55]

The two Castilian-language translations of *Le Chevalier délibéré* intertwine political identity and lyric form. During the 1550s, Charles V was preparing to abdicate in favor of his son Philip II. This was the first dynastic transfer of power for the Spanish Hapsburgs, and the family and their councillors prepared it carefully. References to the divinely willed transit of Burgundian majesty to Spain are ubiquitous in art and literature produced around this time, and Charles V appears to have commissioned Acuña's translation as part of the ceremony. Acuña's task with *Le Chevalier délibéré*, then, was to re-create this valued piece of Hapsburg patrimony in Castilian verse and, in so doing, expand the allegory to encompass Spain.

The front matter of the book supports this project. A letter penned by Charles V himself, composed in French, describes the book's contents, which he forecasts will include both an account of a journey Philip II took through his future domains and Acuña's *Cavallero determinado*. This pairing would have been consistent with a plan to incorporate *Le Chevalier délibéré* into propaganda surrounding the transfer of rule, although in the actual event, the poem and the travel account were published separately.

48 **Chapter One**

However, the vocabularies of vassalage, fealty, and majesty that suffuse both Charles V's letter and the letter Acuña penned himself, in which he presents his work to his liege, enhance the chivalric character of the volume and contribute to the mood of joyous solemnity the Spanish Hapsburgs promoted during the transition of rule from father to son. That Charles V wrote in French similarly reinforces the Burgundian connection, as by this point in his career he was fully capable of writing in Spanish. French reinforced a sense of continuity between present-day Spain and fifteenth-century Burgundian France.

The logic that links Hapsburg Spain to La Marche's France is therefore a logic of allegory, kinship, and resemblance. The dukes of Burgundy are a category that includes Charles V—certainly, this is the view he and his aunt and regent, Margaret of Austria, maintained—and the Spanish Hapsburgs thus fit within the cosmos La Marche designed. This idea shapes Acuña's praxis, which he anchors in rhyme's power, via the reproduction of identical sounds, to override other kinds of differences. In a preface to his poem, he explains:

> Hizose esta traducción en coplas Castellanas, antes que en otro genero de verso, lo uno por ser este mas usado y conocido en nuestra España, para quien principalmente se tradujo este libro. Y otro porque la rima Francesa, en que el fue compuesto, es tan corta, que no pudiera traduzirse en otra mayor sin confundir en parte la tradución, comprehendiendo dos y tres coplas en una, o poniendo de nuevo tanto subiecto que fuera en perjuicio de la obra, y assi lo traduzido va una copla por otra; y lo que en ellas se añade, es en partes donde no daña.

> (This translation was made in Castilian *coplas*, instead of in another kind of verse, first because they are the most frequently used and the best known here in Spain, for whom this book was translated, principally. And next because the French rhymes in which it was composed are so close that I could not translate it into another, longer line without partly confusing the translation, gathering two or three verses into one, or putting things in new ways often enough that the work would be placed in jeopardy, and thus the translation comes rhyme by rhyme; and what is added to them is in places where it will not cause harm.)[56]

According to Acuña, the French huitain furnishes La Marche with the means to accomplish a double act of poiesis: the generation of a poem whose rhyme scheme secures perfect integrity. This poem in turn inscribes the coherent Burgundian world. To accomplish this poem-world's transit,

Acuña recognizes that he must deploy the lyre to Spanish ends, directing the melopoeia generated by patterns of rhyme worked across short lines to draw the knight and his poem between worlds, from Burgundian France to Castilian Spain, unscathed.[57] At least, this is how Acuña sees things. Sutch and Prescott analyze in detail the significance of the "deformations" that *Le Chevalier délibéré* undergoes on its journey. Most important, of course, Acuña grounds the poem by modifying elements that might not make sense to the Spanish audience for whom it is prepared. By situating his version of *Le Chevalier délibéré* in an actual place, Acuña violates the rules of allegory. However, in his view (and in that of Charles V), because it is La Marche's rhymes that perform the world-making here, it is possible to take license with content. Acuña sets his *coplas* into *quintillas*, paired five-line stanzas of octosyllabic verse (that mirror La Marche's own eights), arranged in a regular pattern of rhyme, in this case: ABABACCDDC. But he makes an important modification in La Marche's opening. A comparison illustrates Acuña at work:

LA MARCHE, *LE CHEVALIER DÉLIBÉRÉ*
Ainsi que a l'arrière saison (A)
Tant de mes jours que de l'année (B)
Je partis hors de ma maison (A)
Par soudaine achoison, (A)
Seul a par moi fors de Pensée (B)
Qui m'acompaigna la journée (B)
Et me vint en remembrance (C)
Le premier temps de mon enfance.[58] (C)

ACUÑA, *EL CAVALLERO DETERMINADO*
En la postrera sazón (A)
del año y aun de mi vida (B)
una súbita ocasión (A)
fue causa de me partida (B)
de mi casa y mi nación. (A)
Yendo solo mi jornada (C)
a mi memoria olvidada (C)
despertó mi pensamiento (D)
renovando el tiempo y cuento (D)
de la mi niñez pasada.[59] (C)

Acuña carries the musicality of La Marche's French into the Castilian tongue. His style is serious but engaging, with accents and rhymes em-

50   Chapter One

ployed to add movement, music, and onomatopoeia to the lines. For example, Acuña emulates and even enhances La Marche's assonances in lines 7–10: "a mi memoria olvidada / despertó mi pensamiento / renovando el tiempo y cuento / de la mi niñez pasada."[60] This skillful formal work allows him to intervene in the nature of the knight's quest, building in an idea of geographical and political place via his insertion of the word *nación* in line 5.[61] La Marche's *Le Chevalier délibéré* presents a primarily spiritual and psychological journey. Acuña grounds the vision, thereby preparing the way for a *translatio imperii* that reveals, rather than violates, the allegory's world. Therefore, in a lyric composed in Latin and addressed to Acuña's readers, Juan Cristóbal Calvete de Estrella celebrates the "golden" Spanish verses that wield the power to transcend the limits of death and keep Burgundian majesty alive:

> Lector candide, quid stupes triumphos,
> Quos dura Atropos egit an perisse
> Credis, quos canit hoc brevi libello
> Pimplaque, chori, et decus Gradivi
> Fernandus? vetat hoc Camoena dulcis,
> Et rhythmi liquor aureusque fulgor
> Hispani . . .

> (Candid reader, are you struck dumb by the triumphs / won by hard Atropos? Do you believe that they have died, / those whom Hernando, honor of the chorus of the Muses and of Mars, celebrates in this little book? / That end is prevented by this sweet song and the fluid rhythms, the golden brilliance of his / Spanish . . .)[62]

In contrast, Urrea openly breaks with this world to anchor his poem more firmly within a world cut to the dimensions of human concerns: on the one hand, the caballero's standing among men; on the other, the bothersome human fact of old age and death, events for which all men and women must prepare. For Urrea, what is most striking and valuable about *Le Chevalier délibéré* is not the poem, but the skills exhibited by its poet:

> . . . porque la material de envejecer y morir es pesada y enojosa, ponse la por agradables figuras, en estilo tan de cavallero como el fue, porque la dulçura del verso, y primor de la invención, engañe al dañado gusto de aquellos que andan desabridos con la vejez, y no quieren leer historia de muerte, como si la una destas dos cosas no viniesen de venir . . . por tratar el libro material grave lo he traduzido en verso grave, assi como tal historia requiere.

The Lyre and the World   51

(. . . because the matter of aging and death is burdensome and troubling, he puts it in agreeable figures, in the style befitting to a knight such as himself, so that the sweetness of the verse and the charm of his imagination beguile the injured taste of those who are displeased by the fact of age and do not want to read about death, as if either of these things were not to arrive . . . because this book treats of serious matters, I have translated it in serious verse, as the story requires.)[63]

Grossman describes a poem as "founded on the infinite plurality of worlds which cannot also appear."[64] The characterization is apt for Urrea's and Acuña's competing translations of *Le Chevalier délibéré*. Urrea's androcentric world fully eclipses Acuña's chivalric one. What takes place is not simply a question of two translators' different choices about how to treat the same literary object. Urrea translates a completely different poem from the one La Marche composed and that Acuña and Charles V stretched and re-formed to include Spain. In Urrea's poem-world, the creator is human, a poet who creates the efficacious metaphors that communicate core truths and frames them in the cadences that resonate with the surrounding world. In this case, the form is the Italian hendecasyllable, which Juan Boscán and Garcilaso de la Vega introduced into forward-looking, cosmopolitan circles of the Spanish nobility earlier in the century. Urrea employed the hendecasyllable in his translation of *Le Chevalier délibéré*, which proceeds at a stately pace in stanzas of terza rima, a lyric form suitable "for serious matters . . . as the story requires":

En la postrer sazón del mes y año, (A)
y de la juveníl flor de mi vida (B)
me sacó de mi casa un caso estraño. (A)
Por súbita ocasión acontecida (B)
dejé la patria, y el contento estado, (C)
siguiendo una ventura desabrida (B)
solo yendo caminos desusado.[65] (C)

When it was introduced into Castilian letters, the hendecasyllable raised objections on two grounds. First, writers who employed it appeared to break with a history, a tradition, and an identity memorialized for centuries in either the heavily metrical, twelve-syllable lines of Castilian *arte mayor* or in *romances* (ballads) and other *coplas* of *arte menor* (the art Acuña employs). Traditionalists among the Spanish nobility celebrated poems such as *Laberinto de la fortuna* (The labyrinth of fortune) by Juan de Mena (1411–1456) and the *Coplas por la muerte de su padre* (Rhymes on the death of his father), which we have already discussed, poems that rep-

52   Chapter One

resent the ideals of the Castilian warrior past. To turn away from these meters and the history they enshrined was a betrayal. Famously, Cristóbal de Castillejo, a noble cleric and retainer in the Viennese court of Ferdinand I, Charles V's brother, called Garcilaso and Boscán anabaptists.[66]

Second, traditionalists argued that the hendecasyllable reads like prose. Sixteenth-century Spanish hendecasyllables prioritize rhythm and wit over meter, and the longer lines weaken the power of rhyme. In a letter that accompanies a book of hendecasyllabic poetry that Boscán dedicates to the Duchess of Soma, he describes the dispute:

> Los unos se quejaban que en las trobas de esta arte los consonantes no andaban tan descubiertos ni sonaban tanto como las castellanas; otros decían que este verso no sabían si era verso o si era prosa, otros argüían diciendo que esto principalmente había de ser para mujeres y que ellas no curaban de cosas de sustancia sino del son de las palabras y de la dulçura del consonante.

> (Some complained that in songs of this art, the beat and rhyme were not as clear, nor did they sound as loudly as Castilian ones; others said of this verse that they did not know if it was verse or prose, others argued saying that this was principally something for women and that they do not worry about matters of substance, but only the sound of the words and the sweetness of the rhyme.)[67]

His defense of the Italian form indicates the extent to which conflicts about poetics in the imperial court were struggles between old and new worlds, the stance and resonance of traditional Castilian caballero and the sprezzatura and understatement of the courtier.[68] In Boscán's view, the former group is hardly worth acknowledging:

> ¿[Q]uién ha de responder a hombres que no se mueven sino al son de los consonantes? ¿Y quién se ha de poner en pláticas con gente que no sabe qué cosa es verso, sino aquel que calzado y vestido con el consonante os entra del golpe por el un oído y os sale por el otro? Pues a los otros que dicen que estas cosas no siendo sino para mujeres no han de ser muy fundadas, ¿quién ha de gastar tiempo en responderles?

> (Who needs to respond to men who are not moved except by beat and rhyme? And who needs to enter into debates with people who do not know what verse is, unless, shod and clothed in rhyme, it crashes into one ear and leaves through the other? As for those who say that these are only

things for women, and therefore not important, who needs to waste time responding to them?)[69]

Spanish Renaissance court poetry is rife with examples of lyrics whose overriding purpose is to enact coterie politics. Ignacio López Alemany calls attention to the political and social significance of a subcategory of sonnets known as the *sonsoneto*, a form aristocrats used that turns the tables on humanists and *letrados* (studious men and women, not always of noble rank) who arrive at court from all regions of the empire, threatening the privilege enjoyed by members of the traditional aristocracy.[70] If the sonnet (*soneto*) is an important modern lyric form that was aligned with Renaissance humanist practices, cosmopolitanism, and, as Boscán writes, good taste and good judgment, the *sonsoneto* undermines those aspects of the form by producing poetry that is wasteful and frivolous (as the duplication of sounds in the word "*son*soneto" suggests). These poems frame overtly trivial, ephemeral messages, very often intended to speak to a select audience, rouse a collective sense of identity, and enhance a sort of caste animus against the *letrado*-other.

Urrea participates in dislodging the chivalric world and contributes to elaborating the habitus of the modern Spanish caballero: a subject, a man, and a Spanish knight, in the manner of the Castilian heroes of the past, but a man of the present as well, one whose rhythms and cadences identify him with humanist advances in human knowledge, art, and skill. This is the kind of knight Juan Martín Cordero celebrates in a prefatory sonnet to the poem. The immanent Christian knight-chevalier has finally come to the world in his material form. We know him by his style and patterns of speech:

> Determinate tu, Determinado
> Caballero por nombre, y valeroso,
> A salir que te vean animoso
> . . . .
> Urrea te hizo hablar tan gravemente
> Como conviene que hable un caballero
> Determinado a todas aventuras.
> Urrea te levanta entre la gente,
> Y te quiere poner como primero
> Que menosprecies las desaventuras.

(Resolve yourself, oh Resolute Knight, / so called by name, and called so also for your valor, / come forth, so they can see your great spirit // . . . //

54   Chapter One

Urrea caused you to speak in the grave style / that suits a knight / resolute before all adventures. / Urrea exalts you among men / and seeks to establish you as first among them / you who are not daunted by misadventure.)[71]

The different lyric poetics that Acuña and Urrea employed in their translations of *Le Chevalier délibéré* "meant the world" in the erudite circles of Spain's power elite in the 1550s. The contest here was not solely or simply one between ancients and moderns. Lyric properties—rhythm, rhyme, sonorous patterning—were both the site of and the weapons in a proxy battle as Spanish subjects struggled over the identity of a Hapsburg Spain that was just taking shape. As "To a Good Gentleman" makes clear, from the perspective of writers and their communities, the two worlds could not coexist. These struggles were especially vigorous during the transition between the reigns of Charles V and Philip II but, notably, both Charles V and Philip II understood the value of stoking rivalries among factions at court. They kept the nobility occupied and facilitated both monarchs' strategies of absolute control.

Everyman's Lyre

Conflict over poetry and identity in early modern Spain was bound up with struggles for Christian hegemony on the peninsula. It was further shaped by politics in the wake of Spanish encounters with a "new world" in the Americas, as ruling elites addressed the challenges of accommodating a global empire to Spanish identity (and vice versa). Tensions regarding the nature of English identity during the same period often arose around the fraught question of religion. A chaotic era was inaugurated by Henry VIII's break with the Catholic Church (formalized in the Act of Supremacy in 1534). The act led to an extended period of cultural upheaval marked by the dissolution of English monasteries and convents, and the crown confiscation of their lands and wealth; the reign of Mary Tudor, from 1553 to 1558, who imposed the Catholic religion and persecuted Protestants; followed by the accession of Elizabeth I, who broke with the Catholic Church once again and reimposed Protestantism. Recent interventions by scholars of Anglophone poetry bring the painful, often violent, disruptions to specific communities and to the social order, more generally, to bear on English lyric. In particular, their work complicates ideas about meter and English identity by nuancing claims for the significance of both the English language and iambic pentameter during the period. For example, Anne R. Sweeney notes that in this era of religious conflict, Catholic youths who traveled abroad for their education were trained to deploy English to debate with English Protestants and both Latin and local vernacular languages to pursue their training and plan with each other how best to restore England to the Catholic faith.[72] With respect to lyric, the sixteenth century has long been considered a point of inflection in English poetry because of regularization of iambic pentameter in Richard Tottel's 1557 *Songes and Sonnettes* (better known as *Tottel's Miscellany*).[73] Scholars such as Lucía Martínez Valdivia and Beth Quitslund call the cultural and social influence of *Tottel's Miscellany*—and iambic pentameter, more generally—into question by highlighting the powerful social and cultural role common meter played during this period.[74] Common meter consists of quatrains of alternating lines of iambic tetrameter (eight syllables) and iambic trimeter (six syllables). A long-line version of this form is the "fourteener," which combines two lines of common meter into a single line divided into two hemistichs (eight plus six). The fourteener contains a noticeable caesura after the eighth syllable and thus sounds like common meter. Another related form, poulter's measure, is formed of couplets whose first line contains twelve syllables (six beats of iambic meter), whereas the next one consists of fourteen (seven iambs).

The effect of these meters can be hypnotic. When we read them now, conditioned by modern pedagogies and theories of lyric, their pronounced beat, powerful caesuras, and long lines rapidly become tiresome (Sutch and Prescott refer to the "dismal" fourteener).[75] Meter competes with "sentence sense" and often wins. But John Thompson reminds us that important sixteenth-century writers such as Gascoigne and Surrey assigned value to the fourteener and to poulter's measure.[76] Moreover, Martínez Valdivia points out that common meter wielded tremendous impact beginning in the 1540s, as Thomas Sternhold and John Hopkins chose it as the verse form for their *Certayne Psalmes Chosen out of the Psalter of David, and Drawen into Englishe Metre* (1547/48). Though *Tottel's Miscellany* marks a threshold in English lyric analogous to the one laid down by the publication in Spain of *Las obras de Juan Boscán y algunas de Garcilaso de la Vega, repartidas en cuatro libros* (The works of Juan Boscán and some by Garcilaso de la Vega, divided into four books)—both volumes represent the incorporation of Italian humanist language reform into emerging vernacular poetics—Martínez Valdivia points out that Sternhold and Hopkins's *Certayne Psalmes* was the best-selling book in early modern England. Moreover, the English Church appended Sternhold and Hopkins to the Book of Common Prayer in the 1560s. Therefore, "every English man, woman, and child was expected to know and recite or sing the poems on a monthly, weekly, or even daily basis. The best efforts of critics who scathingly dismissed the quality of the verse, or of the composers and poets who repeat-

56 **Chapter One**

edly offered readers new music and new words, were to no avail: the words and melodies popularized by Sternhold and Hopkins stubbornly remained in use well into the nineteenth century."[77]

This historical information identifies common meter with the social role of *musa lyrae sollers*. Here, the beat is the form by which "oracles were delivered," according to Horace, "and the economy of life pointed out."[78] The origin of the sobriquet "poulter's measure" illustrates the point, as George Gascoigne is said to have coined the name, explaining that when a person purchased two dozen eggs from English egg sellers, vendors often put fourteen eggs in the second batch. These examples suggest how literally *musa lyrae sollers* performed social functions in the premodern and early modern periods.[79] The emergence of iambic pentameter, common meter, and their related longer-verse forms to positions of new cultural and political prominence in the sixteenth century demonstrates the worldmaking power of lyric forms.

When Stephen Bateman (ca. 1542–1584), librarian to the archbishop of Canterbury, set about translating Acuña's *Cavallero determinado* into English, he employed fourteeners. Thus, as *Le Chevalier délibéré* continued its journey through early modern courts and related centers of power such as the Roman and the English churches, it carried on the work of Amphion's lyre. Each of the three iterations of *Le Chevalier délibéré* we have considered thus far—La Marche's French poem, Acuña's translation or versification of that poem, and Urrea's translation and re-worlding of Acuña's version—inscribes a distinct totality. Acuña interrupts La Marche's cosmos by anchoring it geographically in France and Spain. In doing so, he contributes to the Spanish Hapsburg world that Charles V, Philip II, and their councillors sought to create, and inscribes *Le Chevalier délibéré* in that world in the form of the *Cavallero determinado*. Urrea dislodges the chivalric world and replaces the Burgundian aristocrat with the Spanish caballero or knight. He thereby re-creates the poetic world of the modern Spanish courtier, a world formed by hendecasyllables drawn from Italy, now naturalized into Renaissance Spain. Bateman adapted the poem for the Protestant every person who sought to mend their ways, embrace the True Religion, and eschew the temptations of worldly error (including popishness). In his dedication to Sir William Damsell, Bateman writes: "I thought it good to dedicate this my simple and unlearned travail, who having nothing else on your worship to bestow, called the Trauailed pilgrim, wherein I have painted forth the fond devise of man, and the strange Combats that he is daily forced unto, by means of this our feeble nature, showing also how every degree should, or at the least ways ought, to frame themselves, and so advisedly to watch that we be found vigilant watchmen, aspecting the great and second coming of our lord Jesus."[80]

Bateman was a committed Protestant and reformer, the author of *A Christiall Glasse of Christian Reformation* (1569) and the book of exegesis *Bateman upon Bartholomew* (1582). *The Trauayled Pilgreme, Bringing Newes from All Parts of the Worlde, Such Like Scarce Harde of Before* (London, 1569) is an unacknowledged translation. Bateman mentions neither Acuña nor La Marche, although numerous details of his poem suggest that Acuña's *Cavallero determinado* was its source.[81] Sutch and Prescott speculate that *Le Chevalier délibéré* may not have been well known in England and that mention of prior iterations of the poem were not therefore necessary. This may be the case, although *Le Chevalier délibéré* and Acuña's *Cavallero determinado* were objects of value and prestige throughout Europe, both because of their association with powerful aristocrats and because of their woodcuts. Moreover, *Le Chevalier délibéré* enjoyed popularity among the English aristocracy. It is therefore difficult to determine whether (or who among) Bateman's readers knew the French and Castilian versions of *Le Chevalier délibéré* and whether or not they understood it to be a translation.

More significant for our purposes is the impact of Bateman's decisions about how to convey the poem from Spain to England, from Castilian verse into an English form. As we have seen, verse form carries cultural and political significance; and in this instance, fourteeners transform what to this point has been a Catholic narrative into the habitus of the English True Religion. Bateman's choice of common meter reshapes the poem's world and its contents. For example, La Marche, Acuña, and Urrea present a knight-caballero, a member of the Burgundian and Spanish nobility. Bateman's protagonist is a "writer" and an "Author" who joins his readers as a fellow pilgrim and who contributes to their quest to join with Christ.[82] This shift in emphasis is signaled by the poem's title, which draws the idea of a journey into the foreground with the play on "travail" and "travel." Though Bateman will also show his readers how to prepare for a good death, the inward spiritual journey plays a part in this process for Protestants that it does not play in Catholicism. In Protestantism, individuals make their way toward the truth of Jesus Christ. It is the responsibility of a Protestant to measure and consider experience and attend to the promptings of conscience, whereas Spanish Catholic orthodoxy emphasizes emulating models and engaging in displays of Church doctrine. Bateman's poem opens by sermonizing, with a brief review of the book of Genesis: "The mighty Jove celestial, when he first took in hand / That Chaos huge, he made to fall, and formed so a land, / Wherein he set and created, all things as now we see . . ."[83] This opening material is abbreviated, for as the author-pilgrim admits, "It were too long all to recite." However, verses we can identify as drawn from *Le Chevalier délibéré* and *Cavallero determinado* do not appear

58   Chapter One

until line 37, and Bateman continues to interrupt the narrative with sermons and lessons:

> IN *Hyems* force, both trée and herbe doth vade as rest of life,
> On sudden then to me appeard the state of worldly strife:
> As I thus going all alone (one) did to me appeare,
> Awake, quoth he, from pensive mone, of me have thou no feare.
> Both he and I togither went, as friendes a certaine space,
> Till at the last I did repent, my former time and case,
> Then stepped I forth full suddenly, as one bereft of glorie,
> And to my minde I did apply to note therof some storie.
> As afterwardes there shall be seen, with such advised heed.
> The state of life I will beginne, thus haue I full decreed.
> Consider first both life and wealth, be mindefull still thereof,
> For that will bring most perfect health, so shall at thee none scoffe.
> If that forgetfulnesse endure, no hope there is of gaine,
> Where state decreaseth be thou sure, bereft from ioy to paine,
> The time once past, needes must consume the pleasant orient smell
> Of tree and herbe that growes on ground, as proofe full well can tell.
> Likewise all trees that fruite doth beare, in light they show a shade,
> And time once past straight will appeare, at all things needs must vade,
> So likewise those that vainly spende, their lives they care not how,
> The wrath of God on such attendes, and age of force must bow.
> The trée that once cleane withered is, can be by no meanes greene,
> No more can Age be youngwise, it never hath bene seen,
> Conceive therefore full well in minde, and youthfull time so spende,
> That when Death comes thou be not blinde, to late then to amende . . .[84]

Reading these fourteeners may stir a lulling effect as we are caught up in the singsong pattern of language; however, the fact that the Anglican Church adopted common meter as a key form of collective prayer indicates this effect may be by design. It draws La Marche's protagonist—formerly a Burgundian knight, now any Christian—into the English Protestant habitus. Thus, just as Acuña deploys *quintillas*, thereby extending divinely willed Burgundian majesty to Spain, and just as Urrea changes octosyllables for hendecasyllables to create a poem that resonates with the Renaissance Spanish nobleman, Bateman deploys verse form to accomplish his purpose. And like Acuña and Urrea before him, Bateman makes significant changes to the poem's content; he not only introduces speeches and sermons but trades Hapsburgs for Tudors and draws in a second narrative theme structured in terms of the Prodigal Son. As with each version of the poem, however, its meaning and its ethos are encoded in its verse, and the forms of the verses, the music they sound, stir their selected publics and draw them into the poem's world, in whatever texture and resonance the poet has given it. In this way, *The Trauailed Pilgrime* participates in the same lyric art, the Amphionic lyric poiesis, that La Marche enacts with *Le Chevalier délibéré*.

Amphionic Renewals

Thus far, I have focused on how the lyric culture of *musa lyrae sollers* foregrounded verses and specific poem forms as sites for the mediation of worlds and the negotiation of identities. This chapter closes in the key of renewal, with a brief consideration of the Amphionic power of scholarship.[85] In recent decades, critics have undertaken projects of creative dismantling of a more or less stable picture of Renaissance Europe that has structured early modern studies. Close readings of poetic form, undertaken with a sense for the Renaissance lyric culture of *musa lyrae sollers*, contribute to the work of recovering the vibrant co-presence of worlds. Lyric devices shape polities and mediate people's relationships to those polities, as we have seen throughout this chapter. Two final examples—drawn from the work of Miguel Ángel Vázquez, on Morisco poetry, and Nicholas R. Jones, on *habla de negros* (Africanized Castilian)—are representative of what the practice I would characterize as Amphionic reading can bring to decolonial studies.

The Castilian poetry written by Muslim Spanish Moriscos in the sixteenth and seventeenth centuries presents what at first appears to be a paradox: poems that praise Mohammed and memorialize core teachings and practices of the Islamic faith, composed in lyric forms such as the sonnet and the romance that are associated with Christian Spanish Renaissance culture. In a brief but compelling analysis of this body of work, Vázquez makes the point that it is in all ways Spanish poetry. It was written by people who made their home in Spain until they were forced into exile, and many of them wrote in a highly polished, erudite sixteenth-century Castilian, creating poems that demonstrate their thorough grasp of Spanish poetic expression.[86] That the content of these lyrics falls outside the boundaries of modern notions of Spain, Spanishness, and Golden Age lyric invites us to revisit how we read, think about, and teach Spanish poetry—and from there, early modernity more broadly construed.

The Christian conquest of the Iberian Peninsula was completed in January 1492, when the armies of Isabel I of Castile and Ferdinand of Aragon defeated those of the Nasrid ruler Boabdil (Muhammad XII) in Granada. This event was followed, in rapid succession, by the expulsion of Spain's Jewish population (declared in March 1492, with a final departure date that

60   Chapter One

July), and the beginning of over a century of successive laws and policies that codified the repression of Spanish Muslims and, increasingly, Christians of Muslim descent. Charles V outlawed Islam in Aragon in 1526 (the religion was outlawed in Castile and Navarre earlier in the century), and harassment of Christian Moriscos was pervasive throughout the 1500s. A 1567 edict issued by Philip II forbid Muslim cultural traditions such as dress, dance, games, and key social practices. Furthermore, the edict declared documents such as contracts and deeds recorded in the Arabic language null and void.[87]

The category of the "Morisco/a" arose as anti-Muslim sentiment intensified in the early decades of the sixteenth century. It was an ill-defined ethnic category whose objective was principally that of othering. It was capacious enough to both ensnare and blur the specificities of a wide range of identities, peoples, and bodies that Christian Spain sought to exclude, exploit, or subject to a combination of the two.[88] But Moriscos were Spanish, at least until the final expulsions that took place over the years 1609–14.

Islamic Spanish lyrics performed the cultural work of *musa lyrae sollers* by memorializing key historical events and preserving important practices and tenets for the cultural memory.[89] For example, Vázquez discusses the Spanish version of the Arabic *Kitab al-Anwar* by the writer Abu al-Hasan al-Bakri, which Mohamed Rabadán completed in 1609, with the title *Discurso de la luz*. The introduction to the poem explains why the poet has chosen to set the work in verse: "Es el verso reclamante / que aviva el entendimiento / y hace que con más juicio / la memoria removemos" (Resounding verse / is what quickens understanding / and leads us to recall / with greater discernment).[90] The form he chooses is the romance, which is the lyric form often used to commemorate events and celebrations in the popular cultural memory. Vázquez also calls attention to an anonymous sonnet on the expulsion of the Moriscos. In keeping with a widespread topos of the period, the poem presents the expulsion as God's punishment to Spanish Muslims, who have lost their way as a people. In signing the order, Philip III saves them from further sin.[91]

> Dios, que a los suyos padeciendo mira
> muerte en la vida y en el cuerpo infierno,
> por pecados de padres sin gobierno
> o por la causa que a su globo admira,
> alza la ardiente espada de su ira,
> y como criador y amante tierno
> no es, siendo eterno, en la venganza eterno
> que al descanso, piadoso la retira.
> Del Faraón de España ablanda el pecho,

y a su pesar les da en el mar camino,
que stá de verdes flores prado hecho;
y en su vuestro ingenio raro y peregrino,
dándole luz de Dios tanto provecho,
que ya no sois mortal sino divino.

(God, who sees the suffering of his people / how they are the living dead, from birth, hell embodied, / for the sins of their undisciplined fathers, / or perhaps to strike wonder throughout the globe, / raises the shining sword of his ire, / and, as he is not a tender and loving creator, / being eternal, wields its vengeance eternally / rather than retiring it, piously, to rest. / This softens the heart of the Pharaoh of Spain, / and in sorrow he offers the people a route through the sea, / transformed into green and flowered fields; / and this rare device, passing strange, / works so much for the benefit of God's light, / that you [Sire] are no longer mortal, but divine.)[92]

The complex syntax and solemn tone of this sonnet display the writer's grasp of the Spanish baroque poetic style. The power dynamics the poem stages are also representative of Golden Age Spanish poetry, whose aesthetics are shaped by Counter-Reformation Christian doctrine and absolutist monarchic power. The poet represents Philip III as an intermediary between an erring Morisco humanity and a wrathful God. In so doing, he draws an analogy between the Spanish monarch and Christ, who intervenes with God on behalf of humankind. The poem thus pays homage to the Spanish monarch, perhaps reflecting the necessity many Morisco subjects perceived to flatter their persecutors. At the same time, however, the corpus of poetry that builds Muslim culture and knowledges into Castilian verse and poem forms furnishes evidence of a Morisco *musa lyrae sollers* that is not other to Spanish culture, but an active part of it, even as the poets she inspires are violently dislocated from their homes on the Iberian Peninsula.

Jones focuses on the Castilian *villancico*, a kind of song composed of *coplas* (stanzas of short lines, hexasyllables or octosyllables), punctuated by an *estribillo* (refrain). Variable in format (e.g., the ratio of *coplas* to *estribillos*), these songs are highly rhythmic and danceable, and stage dialogues between voices. The verses usually employ assonant rhyme. The *villancico* is the object of a good deal of critical interest, as its flexibility as a form and its basis in dialogue furnishes views into the makeup of communities.[93] For example, Church authorities used *villancicos* to inspire community in the context of religious festivals (*villancicos* still circulate today, in Spanish and Latin American music, most notably as Christmas carols). Civic celebrations also included performances of *villancicos*. The composers of

62   Chapter One

villancicos often used Amphionic techniques to accomplish this work of creating belonging, employing music and rhythms that would appeal to a specific group of people who would be in attendance at a mass, a ceremony, or an event: drum rhythms, dances, bells, flutes that helped shape a habitus that resonated with a diverse public that included members of the political and cultural elite, through men and women who worked as laborers and servants, and enslaved people. In essays on the *villancicos* of Luis de Góngora and Sor Juana Inés de la Cruz, Jones focuses attention on the significant subgroup of *villancicos* that is composed in *habla de negros*. Jones revisits the place this poetry holds in accounts of early modern Spanish cultural production, and he offers alterative readings that reveal the poems as they draw Black African life and Black personhood into presence.[94] For example, the very existence of these poems indicates that white Christian architects of the ceremonies and celebrations that included *villancicos* thought that Black African and African-descended people were a population they needed to engage. Jones points to Black populations of significant size in sixteenth- and seventeenth-century Spain and Mexico, and shows how the *villancicos* furnish evidence of their contributions across a broad band of sectors of society. Just as important, for our purposes here, Jones discerns key tropes and motifs of Black personhood in this poetry. For example, antiphonal poems frame personal and social relationships among speakers, show their capacities to care for each other in private relationships, and act in and on public spaces as they move through them.[95]

Armed with Jones's readings, it becomes possible to dismantle some barriers that have blocked many critics from engaging with this important and valuable body of work.[96] One of these barriers is the language that Spain's white poets put into the mouths of their Black interlocutors.[97] It is possible to read Africanized Castilian as othering discourse. Particularly as writers such as Góngora and Quevedo deployed it, this language can appear to be pure artifice, an exoticizing touch that is a feature of baroque aesthetics.[98] Rather than letting ourselves be distracted by these evidently problematic features of *habla de negros* poetry, Jones reminds us that we can shift our focus. When we read this poetry through non-European frames of reference—for example, as art that was created in a Spain which served as a key site of African diaspora—the intentions of Spain's dominant castes recede in importance. What comes into view instead are the ample signs of meaningful lives lived by social and cultural contributors. Vázquez and Jones call attention to poems and to reading practices that have the capacity to restore and renew entire sixteenth- and seventeenth-century worlds. This kind of scholarly and critical work represents the essence of Amphionic rereading.

Mercurial *Translatio*

[CHAPTER TWO]

Amphionic Lyric Poetics from
Du Bellay to Trevor Joyce

Amphion reshapes lyric tradition. Restored to his place alongside Orpheus as one of two divine patrons of *musa lyrae sollers*, he broadens the scope of lyric-making by joining poems and *poleis* as twin products of the lyre. While this way of conceptualizing lyric poiesis is marginalized in nineteenth- and twentieth-century literary criticism, in the early modern period, Amphion and Orpheus inspire writing that ranges from the descriptive to the proscriptive regarding intersections between poetry and politics. In *L'Art Poetique* (1674), Nicolas Boileau describes a lyric harmony that mediates divine forces, re-creating their orderly designs on earth:

> De là sont nés ces bruits reçus dans l'univers,
> Qu'aux accents dont Orphée emplit les monts de Thrace,
> Les tigres amollis dépouillaient leur audace;
> Qu'aux accords d'Amphion les pierres se mouvaient,
> Et sur les monts thébains en ordre s'élevaient.
> L'harmonie en naissant produisit ces miracles.

> (Thence were born the strains that resounded through the universe, / Orpheus filled the Thracian mountainsides with their meters, / and tamed fierce tigers, calming their ferocity. / By Amphion's melodies stones were stirred / and on the Theban mountains they raised themselves into order. / The birth of harmony produced these miracles.)[1]

Other writers, as we have seen, mobilize Horace to more immediate ends. George Puttenham elaborates on Amphion as a figure for the power of political leaders who "mollify stony hearts" and "lead by sweet persuasion."[2] For Garcilaso de la Vega, to play Orpheus's lyre is to set out, via virtuoso

64   Chapter Two

patterns that astonish and charm, social codes that confer and withdraw privileges of agency and personhood in Spanish-occupied Naples.[3]

Among these theoretical and practical engagements with Horace's poetics, *Les Antiquitez de Rome* (The ruins of Rome) by Joachim du Bellay warrants sustained consideration. The sequence, which was published in 1558, is a striking experiment with the affordances and limits of lyric discourse. Du Bellay—a member of the French "Pléiade," a group of Renaissance humanist poets dedicated to linguistic and poetic reform—draws together two emergent verbal technologies: the lyre, as understood by Horace, and the Petrarchan lyric sequence, an assemblage of sonnets and songs whose poems work on their own as discrete lyrics, but which also generate worlds and narratives when read as a coherent whole.[4] The Petrarchan sequence accomplishes an Orphic feat. Poets who work with the device successfully transcend death by sublimating the erotic energies stirred by a worldly object of desire (most often, a physically beautiful woman) to create a poetry that secures them eternal fame (more dubiously, this immortality extends to the beloved object of desire as well).[5] The witticism that animates the *Antiquitez* substitutes Amphion for Orpheus. As Petrarch was able to deploy lyric to Orphic ends, might a skilled poet, armed with knowledge of Horace and Petrarch, create a sequence that transforms the violent energies men use to heave great boulders and build Theban walls, sublimating them, by means of the Neoplatonic powers of the lyre, into a stable form of political power, lasting imperium? Such a project would entail, as it does in the *Canzoniere*, the conversion of base appetites into their purer, celestial forms. In this case, the appetite in question is not sexual desire, as in Petrarch, but the bloodlust that begins to simmer when energies that people once directed to inspire collaborative projects of civilization building have no productive outlet. Once a city is built and its great walls are raised, people begin to turn against each other in internecine quarrels. Violence that city planners thought they had closed out emerges within. This natural animus that rouses human collectives is what Du Bellay sought to tap and transform, by means of the lyre, into a powerful and eternal French poetry that would secure the imperium of a Renaissance Christian state.

Historically, the ambition is destined for Orphic failure. Du Bellay took up the myth of Amphion for literary reasons, as he was an avid student of Horace, but the increasingly agitated atmosphere of religious conflict in France played out what Amphion tells us about the ceaseless motion of political formations, which make and unmake themselves, rhythmically and constantly.[6] To seek to arrest this natural process is in fact to turn away from Amphion and look instead toward Orpheus, who shows poets how to recast the failure of their heroic struggles against the laws of nature as at least poetic triumphs. And by the latter part of the sixteenth century, France descended further into conflict and eventually all-out civil war.

Furthermore, when later writers take up the *Antiquitez*, they do so inspired by Du Bellay's skills with Petrarchan-Orphic voicing. Works such as Edmund Spenser's *The Ruines of Rome* (published 1591), the sonnet "Buscas en Roma a Roma ¡oh peregrino!" (You seek Rome in Rome, oh pilgrim!)—in which Francisco de Quevedo (1580-1645) imitates *Antiquitez*'s sonnet 3, "Nouveau venu, qui cherches Rome en Rome"—and the poems from the *Antiquitez* that Henry Wadsworth Longfellow (1807-1882) includes in his project in literary nation-building *Poems and Places* (1876-79) use the sequence as a succession of exercises through which to develop their voices as imperial poets and singers of empire. These are schoolroom exercises (indeed, Spenser probably wrote *The Ruines of Rome* when he was a student), and there might not be much more to say about the *Antiquitez* in its afterlives, were it not for the transformative impact of Trevor Joyce's 2014 *Rome's Wreck*. A "translation," the cover of the book tells us, of Spenser's *Ruines of Rome*, *Rome's Wreck* delivers a wry critique of Spenser, of English imperialism (Joyce is an Irish poet), and of Renaissance poetry as an art that is inextricable from imperium: both ruins and the poets who, inspired by the rubble of destroyed cities and civilizations, fashion grandiloquent, melancholy lines to memorialize the terrible inevitability of destruction.

As a translation from English to English, the stakes of *Rome's Wreck* are not anchored in differences between national languages. Rather, the gulf breached is one that Ann Laura Stoler describes as separating a sovereign subject, who casts a "wistful gaze of imperial nostalgia" on "ruins"—objects such a viewer identifies as signs of the "fragility of power and the force of destruction"—from the persons and the communities that inhabit those landscapes continuously over time. This latter population experiences the empire builder's ruins as "debris," accumulations of remnants and fragments that constitute "the material and social afterlife of structures, sensibilities, and things."[7] Debris corresponds to the temporality of empire lived as a continuous present, a social and political "formation" in which things made in the past—be they material objects, social hierarchies, political treaties and pacts, or economic systems—persist, in whatever disguised or degraded form.[8] Debris must be navigated, and it may be repurposed. The world of *Rome's Wreck* can be described as littered with this debris. By setting Renaissance poetry at its center, the sequence exposes a link between the economic boom and crash brought about by the interventions of foreign direct investors in the late 1990s and early 2000s with the Renaissance, and with Spenser's "View of the Present State of Ireland" (1596). Joyce's sequence therefore performs more than the Or-

66   Chapter Two

phic revivification of a sixteenth-century poetic text. Played on Joyce's lyre—a lyre I will be arguing here descends from Amphion—the *Antiquitez* is turned back on itself to expose an underside: an unromantic view of empire's long-lived predations. In this way, *Rome's Wreck* accomplishes a mercurial feat of Amphionic resignification. Moreover, in a mercurially reversible process, its reverberations reshape the *Antiquitez* across its lives and afterlives, from the sixteenth century to our own day.

Les Antiquitez de Rome

The historical and political circumstances surrounding the composition of the *Antiquitez* are well known. In 1553 Du Bellay traveled to Rome in the company of his older cousin, Cardinal Jean Du Bellay. Jean Du Bellay had been charged with overseeing the removal of antiquities from Roman soil to France. Joachim served as his secretary and witnessed the labor of excavation, documentation, and transport of architectural fragments, the "antiquities" he references in the sequence's title. The *Antiquitez* is structured by the conceit that though the material remains of ancient Rome are lifeless ("Rome n'est plus . . . Le corps de Rome en cendre est dévalé" [Rome is no more . . . The body of Rome is returned to ashes]),[9] the animating spirit of Roman imperium lives on ("le demon Romain / S'efforce encore" [. . . the spirit of Rome still strives]).[10] If this spirit is to be awakened, however, its *translatio* to France will not be accomplished by simply transporting the great piles of rocks the Roman and French workers struggle to move to a new site in France ("Ces grands monceaux pierreux" [Those great stony piles]).[11] It will travel by means of language and, specifically, in writing: "[S]es ecripts, qui son loz le plus beau / Malgré les temps arrachent du tombeau, / Font son idole errer parmy le monde" (. . . her writings, which in spite of time wrest her fairest praise from the grave, keep her specter wandering throughout the world).[12] The thirty-three sonnets that make up the *Antiquitez* represent one experiment in this kind of transmediation—power, materialized in stone and, subsequently, in language. Du Bellay also develops the idea in the *Défense et Illustration de la Langue Française* (Defense and celebration of the French language), his 1549 treatise on the French language and Renaissance humanist linguistic reform. As Richard Helgerson discusses in his introduction to his translations of Du Bellay's work, the *Défense* and the *Antiquitez* are informed by the same ideas about language and power, and it is illuminating to read them together.[13] In the *Défense*, Du Bellay writes:

> Le tens viendra . . . que ce noble et puyssant Royaume obtiendra à son tour
> les resnes de la monarchie, et que nostre langage (si avec Françoys n'est de

tout ensevelie la langue Françoys) qui commence encor'à jeter ses racines, sortira de terre, et s'élèvera en telle hauteur et grosseur, qu'elle se pourra egaler aux mesmes Grecz et Romains . . .

(The time will perhaps come . . . when this noble and powerful kingdom will in its turn seize the reins of universal dominion and when our language (if with Francis the French language has not been wholly buried), which is just beginning to put down roots, will spring from the ground and grow to such height and girth that it will equal the Greeks and the Romans themselves . . .)[14]

A play on words in this passage calls attention to the logic that underwrites both the *Défense* and the *Antiquitez*. Du Bellay deploys the harmonious coincidence between the name of François I (1494-1547) and "françoys," the word for the French language, to structure a prophecy of French power. That the words sound as similar as they do is a sign from God of the perfect alignment of François I and his line—including his son, Henri II, who ruled France during Du Bellay's time—with the spirit of their realm.[15] Henceforth, the French language will be both the sign and the efficient cause of imperium. Furthermore, French humanists such as Du Bellay assume the responsibility of perfecting their understanding of ancient Roman writings in order to bring the fruits of their scholarship to bear on royal programs to modernize French culture and politics. Du Bellay presents this ambition to Henri II in the dedicatory sonnet of the sequence:

Ne vous pouvant donner ces ouvrages antiques
Pour vostre Sainct Germain, ou pour Fontainebleau,
Je les vous donne (Sire) en ce petit tableau
Peint, le mieux que j'ai peu, de couleurs poëtiques.

Qui, mis sous vostre nom devant les yeux publiques,
Si vous le daignez voir en son jour le plus beau,
Si pourra bien vanter d'avoir hors du tumbeau
Tiré des vieux Romains les poudreuses reliques.

Que vous puissent les Dieux un jour donner tant d'heur,
De rebastir en France une telle grandeur
Que je la voudrois bien peindre en vôtre langage:

Et peult-estre, qu'à lors vôtre grand' Majesté
Repensant à mes vers, diroit qu'ilz ont eté,
De vostre Monarchie un bienheureux presage.

68   Chapter Two

(Unable to give you these ancient works for your Saint Germain or for your Fontainebleau, I give them to you, Sire, in this little picture, painted, as best I could, with poetic colors, // Which, placed before the eyes of the public under your name, if you deign to view it in its best light, will be able to boast of having pulled from the tomb the dusty remains of the ancient Romans. // May the gods one day give you the good fortune to rebuild in France such greatness that I would willingly paint it in your language, // And perhaps then your great majesty, remembering my serves, would say that they have been a blessed omen of your universal dominion.)[16]

Du Bellay invokes a French language imbued with the representational and expressive powers of other key Renaissance arts: architecture, painting. It is further enhanced by Du Bellay's classical knowledge and his linguistic expertise. Finally, however, it is strengthened by the lyre, which is the instrument Du Bellay uses to generate this particular verbal creation. The conceit that structures the *Antiquitez* is the ceaseless pattern of flourishing and decay that governs civilizations and states ("le temps destruit les Republiques" [time destroys states]; Sonnet 8),[17] a natural law that might be interrupted by skilled players of the lyre, which permits them to tap into divine powers. Thus, following Horace—albeit, in a mythic register that differs significantly from Horace's arch, cosmopolitan tone—Du Bellay assigns his lyric speaker two lyres, Orpheus's, which he invokes in Sonnet 1, and Amphion's, to which Du Bellay alludes in Sonnet 2. In Sonnet 1, the lyric speaker intones with a vatic voice that can raise spirits from the dead:

Divins Esprits, dont la poudreuse cendre
Gist sous le faix de tant de murs couverts

Si des humains la voix se peut étendre
Depuis ici jusqu'au fond des enfers,
Soient à mon cri les abîmes ouverts,
Tant que d'abas vous me puissiez entendre.
Trois fois cernant sous le voile des cieux
De vos tombeaux le tour devocieux.

(Divine Spirits, whose dusty ashes lie under the weight of so many ruined walls (but not your praise, which lives in your fair verses and will never walk beneath the earth), // If a human voice can reach from here to the depths of the underworld, let the abyss open to my cry so that from far below you may hear me.)[18]

Sonnet 2 is structured by a poetic topos with which Amphion frequently associated: a succession of powerful cities and monuments whose glory has been eclipsed by time:

Le Babylonien ses hauts murs vantera,
Et ses vergers en l'air, de son Ephesienne
La Grece descrira la fabrique ancienne,
Et le people du Nil ses points chantera.

(The Babylonian will boast of his high walls and hanging gardens; Greece will describe the ancient construction of its Ephesian temple; and the people of the Nile will sing their pyramids.)[19]

Sonnet 2 elaborates on a play between a fearsome, violent past and its heir, a sound and orderly present, in which rulers exercise a kind of power built on solid foundations. This topos, the archaic polis that is emended and set in order by its successor, the well-designed empire, is a feature of imperialist discourse. An influential example for Renaissance humanists appears in Book 15 of Ovid's *Metamorphoses*, where the philosopher Pythagoras chants a litany of civilizational flux:

. . . We see times change and civilizations
rise and fall. Yes, Troy was great in her riches and people;
for ten long years she was able to spend the blood of so many
sons in her cause; but now she is humbled and all she can show
for her glorious wealth is ancestral barrows and ancient ruins.
Sparta was highly renowned and so was powerful Mycénae;
so flourished the cities of Cecrops at Athens and Theban Amphion . . .[20]

He goes on to predict the rise of Rome:

And now word goes that Dardánian Rome
is rising; close to the river that's born in the Ápennines, Tiber,
foundations are being laid of a mighty city and empire.
Rome is changing her shape as she grows. Sometime in the future
she'll form the head of the boundless world.[21]

Pythagoras's harangue contains the seeds of an argument that proponents of empire mobilize continually as they justify their conquest and dismantling of existing communities and societies: Roman power is established on secure foundations. Laws and principles guide the exercise of

70   Chapter Two

violent domination, thereby containing the natural human instinct for violence and directing physical force to civilizational ends, such as raising a city. This idea is implicit in the myth of Amphion as Euripides and Plato recount it: Hermes/Mercury foretells that in legend and lore the king will displace Zethus as the builder of Thebes. Du Bellay draws on it in the *Antiquitez*, which develops an image of a Rome as an archaic, pagan polis, an entity that rises to power and destroys itself in accordance with the law of nature. This Rome serves as a foil to the Christian French state whose foundations are laid by God, acting from Heaven, and on the ground through the efforts of the Valois kings and their humanist courtiers and councillors.[22] In Sonnet 25 of the *Antiquitéz*, Du Bellay invokes the lyres of Orpheus and Amphion directly. His lyric speaker questions his own poetic powers as they might be measured against "la harpe Thracienne," which awakens "[c]es vieux Cesars . . . [q]ui ont basty cette ville ancienne" (those old Caesars . . . who built this ancient city), and "celle Amphionienne," which animates "d'un accord plus heureux . . . [d]e ces vieux murs les ossements pierreux" (with a happier harmony the stony remains of these old walls).[23] Sonnet 2, however, introduces the theme from the start, invoking Amphion and indicating the use that Du Bellay will make of the myth in the *Antiquitez*. Like Amphion, France's Christian king will raise a majestic and permanent city by transforming human nature—whose excellence is marred by pride, arrogance, and a thirst for violence—into the stuff of imperial power. The thirty-one sonnets that follow invite the reader to consider the greatness of Rome at its height and to confront the awesome spectacle of its self-induced fall, as the great city galls Heaven by competing with it ("antique orgueil, que menssoit les cieux"; Sonnet 27)[24] and, restless in peace, animates mutinous rage among its citizens ("anima contre soi d'un courage mutin"; Sonnet 22).[25] In Sonnet 16, the lyric speaker compares the fall of Rome to cataclysmic natural spectacles: churning seas, a violent storm, the progress of a raging fire:

Comme l'on void de loing sur la mer courroucee
Une montagne d'eau d'un grand branle ondoyant,
Puis trainant mille flotz, d'un gros choc abboyant
Se crever contre un roc, où le vent l'a pousée,

Comme on void la fureur par l'Aquilon chassée
D'un sifflement aigu l'orage tournoyant,
Puis d'une aelle plus large en l'air s'esbanoyant
Arrêter tout à coup sa carriere lassée:

Et comme on void la flamme ondoyant en cent lieux
Se rassemblant en un, s'aguiser vers les cieux,
Puis tumber languissante: ainsi parmy le monde

Erra la monarchie . . .

(As one sees from afar on the angry sea a mountain of water cresting with violent motion, then, pulling along a thousand waves, crashing with a huge shock, break against a rock on which the wind has flung it, // As one sees the fury driven by Boreas whipping up the storm with a deafening roar, then, with a broader wing sporting in the air, suddenly cease its wearied course, // And as one sees the flame rising from a hundred places, gathering itself in one, flare up toward the heavens, then fall back spent, so throughout the world // Wandered empire . . .)[26]

In Sonnet 20, Rome is like a storm cloud that

Des vapeurs de la terre en l'air se soulever,
Puis se courbant en arc, à fin de s'abrever,
Se plonger dans le sein de Thetis la chenue,

Et montant derechef d'où elle estoit venue,
Sous un grand ventre obscur tout le monde couver
Tant que finablement on la voit se crever
Or' en pluie, or' en neige, or' en gresle menue.

(. . . rises in the air from earth's vapors, then bending in an arc, to slake its thirst plunges into the bosom of gray-haired Thetis, // And, rising once again to the place from which she had fallen, covers the whole world under her great dark belly, until at last she bursts open, now in rain, now in snow, now in fine hail . . .)[27]

Sonnet 18 develops the theme from a different angle. Here, the speaker reflects on the iterations of Roman imperium as it took shape within human communities: initially, humble farmers; subsequently, wealthy city dwellers, followed by imperial armies who succumbed only to the will of Heaven. References to *l'annuel pouvoir* and *six mois* refer to stages in the Roman Republic; the consuls of Rome held office for a year, dictators for six months (with the exception of Caesar). Augustus created the position of emperor, whose reign was perpetual:

Chapter Two

Ces grands monceaux pierreux, ces vieux murs que tu vois,
Furent premièrement le cloz d'un lieu champestre:
Et ces braves palais dont le temps s'est fait maistre,
Cassines de pasteur ont esté quelquefois.

Lors prendrent les bergers les ornemens des Roys,
Et le dur laboureur de fer arma sa dextre:
Puis l'annuel pouvoir le plus grand se vid estre,
Et fut encor pus grand le pouvoir de six mois:

Qui, fait perpetuel, creut en telle puissance,
Que l'aigle Imperial de luy print sa naissance;
Mais le Ciel s'opposant à tel accroissement,

Mist le pouvoir en mains du successeur de Pierre,
Qui sous nom de pasteur, fatal à ceste terre,
Montre que tout retourne à son commencement.

(These great stony piles, these old walls that you see, at first enclosed country fields, and these brave palaces, which time has overthrown, were once the cottages of shepherds. // Then the shepherds assumed the ornaments of kings, and the rough plowman armed his right hand with steel. Then the year-long power became greatest, and still greater was the power of six months, // which, made perpetual, grew to such strength that from it the imperial eagle was born. But Heaven, opposing such increase, // placed that power in the hands of the successor of Peter, who, under name of pastor, a name linked by fate to that land, shows that everything returns to its beginning.)[28]

In the final lines of the poem, Heaven sets Roman power under the dominion of Peter, the first pope. The stanza thus transfers Rome into the Christian cosmos, where it becomes not an active, feeding polis but a sign.[29] Du Bellay thus introduces the idea that Christianity may set the foundations for an eternal French city whose power is aligned with the will of Heaven, not in competition with it. He leaves the answer to this question open. Sonnet 32, the concluding poem of the sequence, laments:

Si sous le ciel fust quelque eternité,
Les monuments que je vous ay fait dire,
Non en papier, main en marbre et porphyre,
Eussent gardé leur vive antiquité.

(Were there any eternity under heaven, the ancient monuments of which I have made you speak would have survived intact not on paper but in marble and porphyry.)

If eternal imperium can be wrought, the feat will be accomplished by the lyre:

> Ne laisse pas toutefois de sonner
> Luth, qu'Apollon m'a bien daigné donner:
> Car si le temps ta gloire ne desrobbe.

> Vanter te peuls, quleque bas que su sois,
> D'avoir chanté le premier des François,
> L'antique honneur du people à longue robbe.

(Do not for all that cease playing, lute, which Apollo has deigned to give me, for if time does not steal away your glory. // You can boast, however, lowly you are, that you have sung, first among the French, the ancient honor of the long-robed people.)[30]

The *Antiquitez*'s Afterlives

Sonnet 32 is prescient. In Du Bellay's own time, the *Antiquitez*'s greatest achievement is poetic. Valois France is subject to the laws that govern all things of this world: decay, death, and the limits of human poetic accomplishment. Despite Du Bellay's ambitions for the French language, French unity unravels in the Wars of Religion.[31] However, the combination of Petrarchan and Amphionic poetics that Du Bellay forges in the sequence remains active. The *Antiquitez* becomes a site at which poets in Spain, England, and France who are sympathetic to empire and to the idea of imperial poets hone their skills with lyric poetics.

Francisco de Quevedo (1580–1645) prepared a translation of *Antiquitez*'s Sonnet 3, "Nouveau venu qui cherches Rome en Rome," as part of a number of reflections on the decadence that beset the Hapsburg Spanish empire in the late sixteenth century. His poem is simultaneously a statement of political disillusionment and a skilled example of Spanish baroque aesthetics, in which disenchantment or *desengaño* is a principal theme:

> A Roma, Sepultada en Sus Ruinas
> Buscas en Roma a Roma ¡oh peregrino!
> y en Roma misma a Roma no la hallas:
> cadáver son las que ostentó murallas

74   Chapter Two

y tumba de sí proprio el Aventino.
Yace donde reinaba el Palatino
y limadas del tiempo, las medallas
más se muestran destrozo a las batallas
de las edades que blasón Latino.
Sólo el Tibre quedó, cuya corriente,
si ciudad la regó, ya sepultura
la llora con funesto son doliente.
¡Oh Roma en tu grandeza, en tu hermosura,
huyó lo que era firme y solamente
lo fugitivo permanece y dura!

(To Rome, Entombed in Her Ruins: You seek Rome in Rome, oh pilgrim! /
and in Rome herself, you do not find Rome: / those superb walls are ca-
davers now. / The Aventine is his own tomb. / The Palatine hill is laid low
where once it ruled / and encrusted by time, medallions / commemorate
the destructive force of battles with the ages / more than the emblems of
the Latin Standard. / Only the Tiber persisted; if once his current / irri-
gated the city, now it mourns / this grave with its morbid song. / Oh Rome!
Of your majesty, of your beauty, / that which lasts disappeared, / and only
what is ephemeral remains!)[32]

Whereas Du Bellay opens the sonnet with enjambed lines: "Nouveau venu
qui cherches Rome en Rome / Et rien de Rome en Rome n'apperçois,"
Quevedo closes down line 2 with the exclamation "¡Oh peregrino!" The
consequences for rhythm of these two quite different openings shape
the ensuing poems. Du Bellay's sonnet balances verbal contents that refer
to ruins and destruction with a smooth, rhythmic flow propelled by assonances, elisions, and repetition:

Ces vieux palais, ces vieux arcz que tu vois,
Et ces vieux murs, c'est ce que Rome on nomme.
Voy quel orgueil, quelle ruine: et comme
Celle qui mist le monde sous ses loix,
Pour donter tout, se donta quelquefois,
Et devint proye au temps, qui tout consomme.

The fragment captures the process that inspires the French sequence as
a whole: the great city's self-destruction and reanimation. Quevedo inscribes finality with equal skill by erasing any theme of renewal (*nouveau*)
and substituting an aesthetics of desiccation, an effect he generates with
the speaker's rasping *s*'s and short *a*'s, both in the early lines and through-

out the poem. Perceived from the jaded perspective of Quevedo's speaker, Rome's ruin is as unambivalent and unambiguous as a vanitas painting, and it is memorialized by dead objects—rubble, eroded hillsides, dry streambeds—indicating the grim fate of all things of this earth, including Spanish imperial power.[33] The enhanced emotionalism of the Spanish version underscores the point. Quevedo transforms what is in the *Antiquitez* a series of prompts to reflection on Rome's rise and fall into a more dramatic and comprehensive statement of the ephemeral nature of all worldly things.

Edmund Spenser handles the sequence differently. Unlike Quevedo, he treats the lyrics *as* a sequence and translates thirty-two of the poems. Furthermore, it seems likely that he did this work when he was a student and developing his poetic voice. These contexts shape his approach to the *Antiquitez*, which he treats as a source through which to experiment with his stance as a poet of imperium. This transformation is signaled first and foremost by his omission of the dedicatory sonnet. In place of an opening frame, Spenser adds an epilogue, in which he praises "Bellay, first garland of free poësie." These interventions clear the way for Spenser to foreground his voice and implement his own lyric objectives with the sequence. In place of Du Bellay's intertwined Amphionic and Orphic strains, Spenser's sequence is decidedly Orphic, motivated by the desire to showcase the linguistic accomplishments of the translating poet:

SONNET 1

Ye heavenly spirits, whose ashy cinders lie
Under deep ruins, with huge walls oppressed,
But not your praise, the which shall never die,
Through your faire verses, ne in ashes rest;
If so be shrilling voice of wight alive
May reach from hence to depth of darkest hell,
Then let those deep abysses open rive,
That ye may understand my shrieking yell.
Thrice having seen under the heaven's veil,
Your tombs devoted compass over all,
Thrice unto you with loud voice I appeal,
And for your antique fury here do call,
The whiles that I with sacred horror sing
Your glory, fairest of all earthly thing.[34]

As a reflection of the changed status of the *Antiquitez* in its Spenserian form, William Ponsonby (1546?-1604) published the sequence as part of

76   Chapter Two

the *Complaints* (1591). His preface to the volume situates this collection in a manner consistent with Renaissance humanist ideas about poetry and lyric, justifying the publication of this assortment of "small poems" on the basis of the success of Spenser's epic, *The Faerie Queene*. Ponsonby's subsequent statements conform to the sixteenth-century concept of lyric as *musa lyrae sollers*. He tells us that the poems were previously "dispersed abroad in sundry hands, and not easy to become by, by himself; some of them having been diversly embezzled and purloined from him, since his departure over Sea." Ponsonby gathers them together, first, "for the better increase and accomplishment" of the reader's "delight" and, second, "for that they all seem to contain like matter of argument in them: being all complaints and meditations of the world's vanity; very grave and profitable." These are the ends of *musa lyrae sollers*, the art of the worldly and the day-to-day. In this context, Ponsonby carries out the work of Amphion as he assembles the discrete poems into a coherent whole. The association would not be amiss; publishers and printers saw themselves as makers of newly emerging French, English, Italian, and Spanish worlds, curating, collating, and printing collections of lyrics, with the stated object of shaping domestic culture and letters.[35] To Ponsonby's Amphion, Spenser plays a companion role as Orpheus. Both the *Complaints* overall and the contents of specific lyrics printed in the volume position Spenser as an heir in a lineage of lone singers, a tradition that leads from Orpheus to Sidney and is animated anew by Spenser's voice.[36] Spenser draws this link directly in remarks addressed to Mary Sidney, Countess of Pembroke, in a preface to "The Ruines of Time." This poem appears first in the volume, where it does the work of framing Spenser as the national Orpheus in lyric as well as epic. In the dedication, Spenser accepts the mantle of the poet who succeeds the great Sidneys:

> [S]ince God hath disdained the world of that most noble Spirit, which was the hope of all learned men, and the Patron of my young Muses; together with him both their hope of any further fruit was cut off: and also the tender delight of those their first blossoms nipped and quite dead. Yet since my late coming into England, some friends of mine (which might much prevail with me, and indeed command me) knowing with how straight bands of duty I was tied to him: as also bound unto that noble house, (of which the chief hope then rested in him) have sought to revive them by upbraiding me: for that I have not shewed any thankful remembrance towards him or any of them; but suffer their names to sleep in silence and forgetfulness. Whom chiefly to satisfy, or else to avoid that foul blot of unthankfulness, as I have conceived this small Poem, initialed by a general name of the world's Ruines: yet specially intended to the renowning of that

noble race, from which both you and he sprung, and to the eternizing of some of the chief of them late deceased.[37]

In the poem itself, Spenser unseats Rome as the archaic site of *imperium* by assigning Verulamium pride of place.[38] The substitution makes a claim for the archaic power of Britain as the destined seat of *imperium*. In lines 1–46, Spenser not only displaces but erases Rome. Synecdochally, the gesture also unseats France and Hapsburg Spain, since each of these countries has represented itself as Rome's modern heir:

> It chanced me one day beside the shore
> Of silver streaming *Thamesis* to be,
> Nigh where the goodly *Verlame* stood of yore,
> Of which there now remains no memory,
> Nor any little monument to see,
> By which the traveler, that fares that way,
> This once was she, may warned be to say.
> . . . .
> I was that City, which the garland wore
> Of *Britain's* pride, delivered unto me
> By *Roman* Victors, which it won of yore;
> Though nought at all but ruins now I be,
> And lie in mine own ashes, as ye see:
> *Verlame* I was; what boots it that I was,
> Since now I am but weeds and wasteful grass?
>
> O vain world's glory, and unsteadfast state
> Of all that lives, on face of sinful earth,
> Which from their first until their utmost date
> Taste no one however of happiness or mirth . . .

The feminine conceit, the image of a city as a woman, is more developed here than it is in, for example, Sonnet 4 of the *Antiquitez*. In his poem, Du Bellay plays with the fact that the French word for city is the feminine noun *cité*. Spenser elaborates on the connection to create a more fully imagined female figure (and, of course, Spenser writes seeking the favor of Queen Elizabeth). As a result, *Antiquitez* in Spenser's poem, the city participates in the human-centered perspective that shapes "The Ruines of Time," the *Complaints*, and, indeed, Spenser's idea of lyric overall.

Again, this is Orpheus's lyre at work. Whereas the *Antiquitez* represents an exercise in Horatian poetics that tests their usefulness to France, as a nation and a political unity, Spenser's and Ponsonby's impulses are less

78 Chapter Two

civic-minded. The *Complaints* subsumes Du Bellay's Amphionic sequence into Spenser's and Ponsonby's project of fashioning Spenser as England's dominant Orphic singer, and *The Ruines of Rome* is published as one part—part five—of a nine-part collection. This position, at the center of the opus, is an inflection point in the volume's architecture, to be sure. But the volume's design subordinates French accomplishments to those of Elizabethan and Spenserian England, and shifts Amphion out of place as a figure for lyric poetry and aligns him instead with the work of compiling and publishing another poet's songs.

Over time, the *Antiquitez* continues to supply a form and an array of lyric devices through which to realize the constellation of lyric phenomena, poetry-polis-self. This remains the case even after Amphion disappears as a point of reference for lyric and the art becomes associated primarily with Orpheus and Apollo. Henry Wadsworth Longfellow includes three poems from the *Antiquitez* in his massive anthology, *Poems and Places*. This work was published by James R. Osgood and Company as a set of thirty-one volumes issued over the course of 1876 to 1879. The anthology includes both an English-language version of Quevedo's "A Roma sepultada en sus ruinas," translated by Felicia Hemans, and in a section devoted to "Rome, Ruins of," an entry titled "The Ruines of Rome." The section contains Sonnets 3 ("Thou stranger, which for Rome in Rome here seekest"), 18 ("These heaps of stones, these old walls which ye see"), and 25 ("O that I had the Thracian poet's harp") from the sequence. Longfellow credits Du Bellay as author of the poetry and lists Spenser as the translator. An accomplished and prolific translator himself, Longfellow clearly subscribed to the notion of a fundamental distinction between an "original" composition and translation, and his treatment of the *Ruines* indicates that what he values in the sequence is an essence original to the French and conveyed into English by Spenser, to whom Longfellow assigns the role of medium. But these decisions also illustrate Longfellow's view that French *monarchie* and English imperium are interchangeable as relics of a distant political era, the age of empire from which the Enlightenment and liberalism have evolved and definitively eclipsed. Longfellow's projects substitute cosmopolitanism and the schoolroom for conquest and trade; furthermore, presented singly, the poems he selects from the *Antiquitez* demonstrate romantic themes—a modern wanderer's encounter with Rome's ruins; a great city's humble beginnings, its rise, and its leveling; the poet who yearns nostalgically to wield ancient lyric power.[39]

Poems and Places thus contributes to the wider project of nations, the masking of domination by means of refiguring it from heroic, divinely sanctioned, violent activity to a multivalent, pedagogical process carried out by social and political mechanisms that work on the "nobler" aspects of human nature—principally, the mind—and conceal, to the greatest extent possible, acts of coercion and physical violence. Longfellow's contributions to culture were first and foremost pedagogical. Collections such as *Poems and Places* accomplish the Amphionic work of gathering discrete and disparate fragments into a totality that can be read and digested by generations of students and intellectuals to come. The fragments included in its entries can be said to build erudite walls around a cosmopolitan, Anglo-American subject who sits comfortably at the center of a world whose distant reaches arrive to hand, by subscription, to be perused at his or her convenience.[40]

Ruins' Wreck: Trevor Joyce

In *Rome's Wreck*, the Irish writer Trevor Joyce confronts the imperialist rhetorics of Du Bellay and Spenser to demand that their poetry account for itself. Joyce subtitles the sequence *Translated from the English of Edmund Spenser's "Ruines of Rome."*[41] Such a translation is necessary, Joyce's lyric speaker indicates, because the rationale and the prestige of Spenser's *The Ruines of Rome* is entirely lost to the present. In the twenty-first century, and especially in the wake of the crash that followed upon a decade of exploitative investment on the part of individuals and multinational corporations, Spenser's poetry, with its grandiose voicing and its lofty, dissociated gaze upon ruins, lies "limp there in the dumps."[42] Why, Joyce's lyric speaker inquires, is it even there at all? Why does anyone care about ancient Rome, or the preservation of glory and imperium? In Sonnet I, the speaker challenges the "great ghosts" of Rome to answer for themselves as objects of reverence:

SONNET I

Hey, you great ghosts, you ash and deep
set dust that hefts the weight of walls,
your fame lives on in verse that won't
now leave you limp there in the dumps.
So, if a man's slight voice may sound
from here down to the ground of hell,
then let my cry knock deep gulfs wide
that you might yet just get my gist:
three times veiled by the sky I viewed
that route that rings your tomb with steps,
and like three times now ask out loud
(yes, hear me hit your pitch of rage),
to cut through the high filth and pick
you out and name you fine, most fine.

80 Chapter Two

From that opening, Joyce proceeds to rewrite Spenser's (and thus Du Bellay's) thirty-two sonnets in his own idiom. He follows the structure and pattern of *The Ruines of Rome* and the *Antiquitez*. However, Joyce's witty poetics work postmodern stances and attitudes into the Renaissance Horatian-Petrarchan structure, and *Rome's Wreck* ends up altering the sequence's timbre and sense to a significant extent.[43] Where Spenser is theatrical and uses an archaized English, Joyce's speaker is terse. Where Spenser is mellifluous, Joyce's speaker employs monosyllables and colloquial turns of phrase ("like three times now"). Furthermore, Joyce veers from both Spenser and conventions of the English sonnet by replacing English iambic pentameter with octosyllables of varying stress. He similarly eschews Spenserian and Petrarchan rhyme schemes to create acoustic patterns of his own devising.

Joyce acknowledges these differences by having his speaker refer to his "slight voice" (line 5). What is evident from the opening lines of Sonnet I is that this voice is anything but slight. In fact, Joyce's hewn monosyllables are resonant heirs to Du Bellay's *langue Français/François*. In Sonnet XXV, Joyce's speaker refers to a "high hard style":

> That bard of Thrace, give me his harp,
> and I'd stir from the sloth of hell
> those old Tsars, and the shades of those
> who built this town in days gone by;
> or him who raised the walls of Thebes:
> give me his lyre, I'd make quick work
> of these old walls' stiff joints . . .
> . . . .
> at the least, grant me a skilled pen:
> helped by some great ghost of words, I'd
> limn the lines of these fine halls; then
> say that which in me is, and build
> back up now in a high hard style . . .

What *Rome's Wreck* shares with the *Antiquitez* is a sense of lyric poetry as transmediated human force, energy converted by Romans into stone structures and by French humanists into rhetoric. This sense is lost in Spenser's lyric discourse, which points histrionically and insistently to the poet, at the expense of drawing on the wider context of imperial song-making: conquest accomplished by feats of eloquence and political devices—policies, contracts, writs, metaphors, narratives, and legalese—as much as by physical force. Du Bellay and Joyce each grasp the significance of this expanded field of empire-making. However, while

Du Bellay's Amphionic-Petrarchan poetics of the *Antiquitez* turn on a conceit in which people—their bodies, their violence, and their bravery—are sublimated into a transcendent and eternal poetic discourse, *Rome's Wreck* rejects an eloquence that builds up cities but distracts attention from the value of the people who are those cities' inhabitants.

The difference is particularly salient when we contrast Sonnet II of *Rome's Wreck* with the second sonnets of Du Bellay's and Spenser's sequences. In the *Antiquitez*, Sonnet 2 introduces the Amphionic theme of cities. In *The Ruines of Rome*, Spenser does not necessarily understand the significance of the sonnet's placement. Indeed, it does not appear that he understands the Horatian poetics of Orpheus and Amphion, as Du Bellay uses them. However, as a dutiful translator, he follows suit:

> Great *Babylon* her haughty walls will praise,
> And sharped steeples high shot up in ayre;
> *Greece* will the old *Ephesian* buildings blaze;
> And *Nylus* nurslings their Pyramids fair;
> The same yet vaunting *Greece* will tell the story
> Of *Jove's* great Image in *Olympus* placed . . .

The lyric speaker in *Rome's Wreck* rejects the poetic fancy that cities, archaic or modern, raise themselves to the charming music of the lyre. The monuments and structures of Babylon, Greece, Egypt, Crete, Rhodes were built by men:

> SONNET II
> Men spired up high in air, til pride
> and blab of tongues plunged them back down;
> Greeks rose to blaze some dame of hunt,
> then saw the Nile gods get the same,
> and so they told a tale more tall
> how in his home Jove larged it up:

A similarly important poem in the sequence, Sonnet 18—which traces Rome's rise through the successive civic forms of community, republic, dictatorship, and empire, before returning to the status of community— looks quite different in *Rome's Wreck* than it does in the *Antiquitez* or *The Ruines of Rome*. Joyce demystifies Du Bellay's "grands monceaux pierreux, ces vieux murs que tu vois" ("great stony piles, those old walls that you see"),[44] rendering them in pedestrian terms. They are "lumps of rock . . . failed walls." For Du Bellay's "pasteurs," with its Christian valence, Joyce employs "herds":

82 Chapter Two

SONNET XVIII

These lumps of rock, and these failed walls,
closed in at first just fields, and these
brave halls that time has brought to bend,
in the old days were plain huts of herds;
then those herds got tricked out like kings,
the wright armed his right hand with steel . . .

At stake here is not simply vocabulary but register, and an entire concept of the significance of Rome, a city built up from enclosed fields, and that remains, in *Rome's Wreck*, the dwelling place for "herds" of human beings. Joyce avoids both the allure of kingly ornaments ("ornemens des Roys," in Du Bellay; "kingly ornaments," in Spenser) and the Christian significance of shepherds and flocks to fix *Rome's Wreck* in the disenchanted world of day-to-day life. The poetics of *Rome's Wreck* thus give the lie to Hermes's prophecy to Amphion in Euripides and Plato.[45] In Joyce's sequence, cities are built by Zethus, not by Amphion. Moreover, the sequence brings into presence a fact Du Bellay labored to erase; namely, that within the imposed order and the regulated spaces created, supervised, and exploited by empires, people cope and go about their daily business as they always have, albeit in conditions of duress. *Rome's Wreck* remains attuned to this fact throughout the thirty-two sonnets that make up the sequence and in "Blockwork," the prose poem Joyce appends as a coda or a capstone to the project.

As evinced by Sonnets I and II, the speaker in *Rome's Wreck* approaches the ghosts of Rome as an outsider to Horace, to the charisma of imperial monuments, and to the idea of a *demon Romain*. This position inflects his utterances, which are cantankerous, rebellious, and irreverent, sometimes aggrieved, sometimes yearning—and all divergent from Spenser's portentous tones and his "shrieking yell." *Rome's Wreck* operates in the gap between an imperial world that recruits lyric poetry to its cause, as a mechanism to secure eternal power and fame, and the world that Joyce's speaker lives, thinks, and acts in, and the world he speaks to. This world is shaped by continuous vulnerability to the impacts of military and economic imperialism and extractivism. Thus whereas Du Bellay draws poetic power from myth and discourses of Christian empire, and Spenser draws his power from Du Bellay, the lyric speaker in *Rome's Wreck* draws his power and authority from his lived experience. For him, imperial cities are

. . . high, sad wrecks and views . . .
all fake but for the name, you tombs
that still hold safe the brief slight fame

of souls long gone up to their Gods;
. . . .
. . . tick tick, too bad
that bit by bit you end in ash,
scarce worth a laugh, you spoil our source . . .[46]

The self-imposed constraints that Joyce grapples with in *Rome's Wreck* (e.g., his monosyllables, arranged in octosyllabic lines) align the project with conceptual poetry, a movement Craig Dworkin has described as motivated by a revolt against lyrical tradition.[47] The laconic humor of Joyce's lyric speaker contributes to the poem's postmodern feel. We might say that Joyce's octosyllables are objective correlatives to an empire's subaltern subjects, while the roman numerals he employs to label his sonnets draw connections between the imperial Roman past, institutions that center and emulate that past, and the economic, social, and political crises of the present. The postcolonial poetics that shape *Rome's Wreck* extend a project Joyce has been elaborating for the past several decades. From his earliest work, published in the 1960s, Joyce has shown an interest in reworking existing poetry from a variety of cultures and traditions into new forms, remaking them for new contexts. In an incisive reading of Joyce's more recent work, Robert Kiely argues that poems such as "Capital Accounts" (2007) and the chapbook *The Immediate Future* (2013) are shaped by the Irish experience of neoliberal economics. Joyce sets "the market" as the structuring center of poetic meaning in these works. In so doing, Kiely shows, he highlights how free market economics and globalization unsettle nations and states. Multinational corporations and foreign investment prompt questions regarding the "*meaningful* sense" in which "the money form . . . [is] tied to any particular nationality."[48] Among the consequences of this question, the relevance of nations (e.g., Great Britain), their acknowledged histories (e.g., British history), their cultures (e.g., the poetry and art of the English Renaissance), and the central place those national histories and cultures hold in the social imaginaries of their colonies and former colonies are thrown into question. *Rome's Wreck* extends that question to Renaissance lyric. In what meaningful sense is this poetry of value in a twenty-first-century Ireland whose relationships to England and Europe have always been and continue to be mediated by coloniality? Thus where Du Bellay's lyric speaker addresses the ruins of Rome, *Rome's Wreck* addresses the ruins of Renaissance poetry (and perhaps especially Renaissance humanists' awe of Roman rhetoric).[49] This challenge is evident from Sonnet I, with the lyric speaker's nonplussed reaction to Spenser's verses, and perhaps also in the moving tone of his concession, delivered at the end of that poem, that the great ghosts are "fine most fine." It

84 Chapter Two

also inflects poems such as Sonnet IV. Following are the three versions of
the poem composed by Du Bellay, Spenser, and Joyce.

DU BELLAY:

Celle qui de son chef les éstoilles passoit,
Et d'un pied sur Thetis, l'autre dessous l'Aurore,
D'une main sur le Scythe, et l'autre sur le More
De la terre, et du ciel, la rondeur compassoit:

Juppiter ayant peur, si plus elle croissoit,
Que l'orgueil des Geans se relevast encore,
L'accabla sous ces monts, ces sept monts qui sont ore
Tumbeaux de la grandeur qui le ciel menassoit.

Il lui mist sur le chef la croppe Saturnale,
Puis dessus l'estomac assist la Quirinale,
Sur le ventre il planta l'antique Palatin:

Mis sur la dextre main la hauteur Celienne,
Sur la senestre assist l'eschine Exquilienne,
Viminal sur un pied, sur l'autre l'Aventin.

SPENSER:

She, whose high top above the stars did soar,
One foot on Thetis, th' other on the Morning,
One hand on Scythia, th' other on the More,
Both heaven and earth in roundness compassing,
Jove fearing, least if she should greater grow,
The old Giants should once again uprise,
Her whelm'd with hills, these seven hills, which be now
Tombs of her greatness, which did threat the skies:
Upon her head he heap'd Mount Saturnal,
Upon her belly th' antique Palatine,
Upon her stomach laid Mount Quirinal,
On her left hand the noisome Esquiline,
And Cælian on the right; but both her feet
Mount Viminal and Aventine do meet.

JOYCE:

She, whose high tip did top the stars,
one foot stamped down the west, one dawn,
one fist in ice, one fast on sands,

Mercurial *Translatio*   85

both sky and earth bound in one round,
Jove feared, that if she grew yet fore
those greats he'd quelled might rise back up,
so he dumped hills on her, these ones,
that load her low so skies are safe:
the cap of crops helms her head,
two more lock down her guts and groin,
two pin her hand to left and right,
the last two splay her feet spread wide.
I've lost their names. So what? Which mean
the most, dead words or ones well known?

Which words mean what, and *how* do they mean, in Ireland, 2014? The question is motivated by the speaker's position on the receiving end of the ongoing cycles of promise and betrayal extended first by Great Britain, as the imperial power that dominated Ireland for centuries, and, second, by the multinational corporate entities that pumped money and influence into the country in the 1990s. Joyce's poetry sets imperialism and neoliberalism on a continuum. As the various promises extended by colonizers—assurances of spiritual salvation, civil stability, economic well-being—yield the disruptions, dispossession, and restricted opportunities that shape the world of the colonized, the rationale for keeping the language of imperium alive—for example, by memorializing the names of the Roman hills—erodes.

Having said that, for the speaker of *Rome's Wreck*, to wane is not to die out entirely. Just as in Sonnet I the speaker approaches Rome's great ghosts with curiosity—What are they about?—in Sonnet IV, he asks a genuine question: Which *do* mean the most? "Dead words"? "Ones well known"? Words such as "she," "stamp," "foot," "fist," "ice," "Jove," "head," "guts," "groin," "splay"? This is the language that matters to the speaker in Sonnet IV. He does not look back on Roman imperium with the mixture of awe, nostalgia, and rivalry displayed by writers who identify as imperial subjects. How could he? As an Irish poet, he is excluded from that subject position. When he looks at the ruins of Rome, Joyce's speaker observes not a sign of future empires, but the spectacle of patriarchal power and a ruler's fear of losing that power; a struggle between a proud woman and a god intent upon imposing his will; a conflict that results in a collection of body parts strewn across the landscape: head, fist, guts, groin, feet.[50] Joyce's speaker does not fetishize these body parts in the manner of Petrarchan lyric. He simply observes them as they lie, across tradition, pinned down or unceremoniously splayed.[51]

This is translation played on Amphion's lyre, in which the same po-

86   Chapter Two

etry that builds up an empire harbors the seeds and the energies to reverse course and nimbly dismantle empire apart from the inside. Joyce displaces Spenser's Orphic vates and rewrites the sequence to reveal "the best joint work / of earth and art and sky," which in *Rome's Wreck* is not a monumental city, but rather a community. In Sonnet V, the person or persons "you" might be fellow inhabitants of the landscape of *Rome's Wreck*, or they might be the reader: you, me. Whoever the addressee is or are, they have a role to play in the generation of meaning and a dwelling space built from Rome's rubble:

> You'd like to view the best joint work
> of earth and art and sky? Step up
> and let Rome show, though you must make
> the thing whole in your heart from parts.
> Rome is no more; but if these stones
> can yield us still some sight of Rome,
> we'll see a corpse charmed from the tomb.

Throughout *Rome's Wreck*, the miracle generated by the convergence of earth, art, and sky—the miracle engineered by the lyre—is neither the creation of an object, such as an eternal city, nor a continuously relevant and self-renewing poem or lyric sequence. Rather, it is the collaborative community, the extraordinary and also daily event of human beings applying themselves—body, mind, and heart—to collective effort. Joyce consolidates this point in the final poem collected in *Rome's Wreck*, "Blockwork," a stand-alone piece that Joyce describes as a "physical realization of *Rome's Wreck*." The piece is composed of four lyrical paragraphs, three of them of roughly equal length (eight lines, ten lines, and eight lines), followed by a slimmer portion (three lines). Visually, the proportions of the piece suggest a Spenserian sonnet. However, unlike a Renaissance sonnet, which is self-oriented, this poem is populated by great quantities of people, depicted singly and in groups. The contents of the first two sections run as follows:

> When men live in a large group which has lots and lots of linked
> bits, each with its own part to play in the whole, but that big
> whole breaks up, then the great frame that holds and helps all
> the men who are part of it gets weak, or goes for good. Man can't
> then look to it to save them from the threats this side of the wall,
> or that, from in or out, or to keep up road and rail, see drains are
> cleared and in ship shape, or make sure that food and such
> things they need get through.

Men, then, don't act as one, but break down to such small sets as
can still live hand to mouth, and we see group fight with group,
by word or deed, in place of a broad peace and a whole which
takes care of all that have their part of it. Such as stay on in towns
or other haunts of the great, use the big old halls and homes, the
kirks and courts in their own fresh way. Not much is built from
scratch, and what odd jobs they have a go at, just set the ins and
outs to rights, stop gaps, and fix the old to serve new ends. Great
rooms are cut in two, three, four. Fake walls, false fronts put up,
and space that was for all is made now serve a few . . .

Think of these stanza paragraphs as the anti-Spenser, the anti–Du Bellay, indeed, as the anti-Renaissance, with its insistence on a gulf that sep-
arates past and the present. In Joyce's account, walls, towers, towns, halls,
homes, kirks, and courts are teeming with people engaged in ongoing life—
persons—who live in large groups, break into small sets, live hand to mouth,
get into fights, find jobs, find new jobs, subdivide their spaces, adapt, exploit. Joyce does not deny the fatal rhythm. Civic structures, the "great
frame that holds all," still forms and breaks down over the course of "Blockwork." But unlike Du Bellay and Spenser, Joyce attends to people and communities, their care for safety, for "road and rail," for "food and such things
as they need to get through." Thus, whereas "Blockwork" ruminates on the
process by which a community coalesces, makes things, and fractures, as
"groups which used to act as one seem now not to know old friends"—that
is, as it follows the fated pattern—Joyce invites us to consider whether this
pattern, given that it is foretold in myth and has been played out again and
again over the course of history, warrants renewed attention in 2014. What
might be more instructive is some attention to a second phenomenon that
the rise and fall of empires entails: ongoing human adaptability, as people
find and "have a go at" odd jobs, "set the ins and outs to rights, stop gaps,
and fix the old to serve new ends," cut rooms down to fit more occupants; as
they, in the next stanza, "shift to rooms high up as the ground floors break,"
mine structures "for bricks and blocks of stone with which to build."

That the *Antiquitez* contains both worlds—the imperialist's vanquished
great polis and Stoler's "debris"-littered landscape, in which "[f]ine walls
and gates are wrecked, and mined for brick and blocks of stone"—may
help to explain why Joyce composed *Rome's Wreck*. Despite the speaker's
skepticism in Sonnet I, the "great ghosts" of Rome win him over to a kind
of faith in the powers of lyric. Amphion's mercurial music inspires boulders to build walls and also to dismantle them. Joyce's speaker discovers he
can repurpose Spenser's verses to create a new poem that confers recognition on the people he wants to recognize: the resourceful, agile, and prac-

88 Chapter Two

tical community of men and women, a body best invoked and addressed through sturdy monosyllables and witty short lines. This community recognizes the value of poetry, and its members are moved, like anyone else, by divine inspiration. They just don't make a fuss about it. Thus, where Du Bellay's lyric speaker laments, didactically, and Spenser's speaker releases his "shrieking yell," Joyce's poetic speaker "cut[s] through the high filth" and delivers his assessment of the divine forces that deliver the inspiration that spurs people to build poems, sequences, communities, and cities. They are, in the end, "fine, most fine."

Rome's Resonance

Rereading the *Antiquitez* in the wake of *Rome's Wreck*, we may find our attention drawn to the great quantities of people Du Bellay weaves into his sequence. In Sonnet 6, his speaker describes a Rome that at its height burgeoned with children:

> Ceste ville, qui fut plus que la Phrygienne
> Foisonnante en enfans, et de qui le pouvoir
> Fut le pouvoir du monde, et ne se peut revoir
> Pareille à sa grandeur, grandeur sinon la sienne.
> . . . .
> Qu'autre pouvoir humain, tant fust audacieux,
> Se vantast d'égaler celle qui fit égale
> Sa puissance à la terre, et son courage aux cieux.

> (This city, who bore more children than the Phrygian and whose power was the power of the world; and no greatness equal to her greatness, except her own, will ever be seen again. // [. . .] No other human power, however daring, to boast of equaling her who made her power equal to earth and her daring to the heavens.)[52]

In Sonnet 10, Rome

> . . . fut en sa jeune saison
> Une Hydre de guerriers, se vid bravement pleine
> De braves nourissons, dont la gloire hautaine
> A remply du Soleil l'une et l'autre maison.

> (. . . who was in her youth a Hydra of warriors, saw herself valiantly filled with valiant offspring, whose high renown spread from the rising to the setting sun.)[53]

Prodigious fertility is a sign of Rome's greatness, but Du Bellay's sequence takes a dim view of humanity as infants grow into a city's mature inhabitants. Rome's sons turn on each other and bring the city down, "murs ensanglantez par la main fraternelle" (walls, bloodied by a brother's hand).[54] The perspective here is aligned with imperial power, and thus with archaic gods and a cosmos structured by awesome displays of force. Such an order serves the monarchs and emperors who purport to imitate that model. In the world structured by this vision, human beings are a resource to be managed. They can be exploited, their labor extracted to build cities, or, as in Du Bellay's conceit, their force and violence can be tapped to invigorate the French language. Yet their independence, intelligence, and willfulness pose continuous challenges to imperium. Thus, in Sonnet 27, Du Bellay's speaker invites a reader to contemplate a Rome that rebuilds *itself*, independent of human contributions:

> Regarde apres, comme de jour en jour
> Rome fouillant son antique sejour,
> Se rebatist de tant d'oeuvres divines:
>
> Tu jugeras, que le demon Romain
> S'efforce encore d'une fatale main
> Ressusciter ces pouldreuses ruines.
>
> (Then observe how from day to day Rome, excavating her ancient abode, rebuilds herself with so many divine works. // You will judge that the spirit of Rome still strives with a fated hand to resurrect these dusty ruins.)[55]

Rome's Wreck deflates both this idea and the oratory and rhetoric that support it. This is evident from Sonnet I, when the speaker refers to the Roman spirits with the pedestrian "great ghosts." Subsequent poems continue to put the gods in their place. They are outsize, but decidedly worldly, figures; for example, in Sonnet VI, Joyce replaces the reverent names and descriptors used for the goddess Cybele, Du Bellay's "la Phrygienne" and Spenser's "Berecynthian Goddess," with a description of an unnamed she-god who "whelps" her broods:

> Think a she-god, quick in her cart
> of war and crowned with spired, all joy
> to have whelped a mess of gods . . .[56]

Later lines in the poem sharpen the speaker's point that gods have less to do with Rome's glory than do its citizens:

90 Chapter Two

> This town, who more than that gods' dam,
> won fame for fame of those she bore . . .

For better and worse, the Rome in *Rome's Wreck* is a human dwelling place, from ancient times to the present. Where Du Bellay and Spenser each personify the archaic cities listed in Sonnet 2 of the sequence, Joyce rewrites the poem to place emphasis on "men" who conceive of great and fearsome structures, build them, and tear them down through "blab of tongues":

SONNET II
Men spired up high in air, til pride
and blab of tongues plunged them back down;
Greeks rose to blaze some dame of hunt,
then saw the Nile gods get the same . . .[57]

Joyce repeats this gesture continually in the sequence, with the result that *Rome's Wreck* transforms a melancholy imperialist's rumination on ruins, the tombs of exalted great spirits of the past into a meditation on the lives that people cobble together for themselves as they make use of the materials at hand: rocks, powerful energies, the promptings of instincts—for reproduction, for forming communities, for violence, and for an "old pride" that makes people "mix it up with the high skies" (Sonnet XXVII). These instincts may extend to a desire for divine inspiration that, while it may not warrant the exalted place that Renaissance humanists and Christian empire-builders assign it, merits nonetheless a degree of acknowledgment.

In this way, across its afterlives, the *Antiquitez* bears out Wai Chee Dimock's observation that texts are "objects that do a lot of traveling: across space and especially across time. And as they travel they run into new semantic networks, new ways of imputing meaning."[58] Resonant readings and translations take cultural flux into account as a crucial dimension of the long and varied course of human existence that writing moves across and through. This flux is the justification for the attention and concern that Renaissance humanists devoted to refining practices of *translatio* and *imitatio*, as Thomas M. Greene demonstrated some time ago in his classic study *The Light in Troy*.[59] Amphion invites us to look again how Renaissance humanists wrote about the inexorable mutability of language and culture. As-yet-unidentified references to the demigod—Amphion himself, and also the play of Amphion and Zethus—may lead us to a more nuanced sense of how sixteenth-century writers thought about the lyre as a metaphor for political, social, and cultural power. Moreover, Amphion opens new pathways between early modern texts and a wide and varied field of twenty-first-century literary activity, the post-, de-, and anti-colonial translations of which *Rome's Wreck* is but one example.[60] It is possible to adduce dozens more works in which writers turn the lyre—which is to say poetic devices such as prosody, rhythm, harmony, verse form, song form, poem forms, register of diction, conceits of subjectivity—to the service of bringing social relations, communities and political formations, populations, and entire worlds that may elude notice in one iteration of a poem or a work into vibrant presence.[61]

How to Do Things with *Copia*

[CHAPTER THREE]

De la quilla a la gavia, ¡o extraña cosa!
Toda de versos era fabricada . . .

(From stem to stern, what a strange sight!
It was fabricated entirely of verses . . .)

—CERVANTES, *Viaje del Parnaso*

Miguel de Cervantes's *Viaje del Parnaso* (*Journey to Parnassus*, 1614) begins as an old soldier "of Greek and Roman valor" is approached by Mercury. The god requires help with a mission he has undertaken in service to Apollo. Phoebus seeks to assemble an army of Spanish poets to combat a mysterious squadron rising up to challenge him in the east. The soldier, whose fictional name is Miguel de Cervantes, is skeptical, but he agrees to discuss the mission on board Mercury's galleon. Upon boarding the ship, Cervantes is struck with wonder to find that "De la quilla a la gavia, ¡o extraña cosa! / Toda de versos era fabricada, / sin que se entremetiese alguna prosa" (From stem to stern, what a strange sight! / It was fabricated entirely of verses / without one single line of prose).[1] The mast of the ship is a canto, or an extended song composed in great verse (hendecasyllables, *verso mayor*, or alexandrines); the poop deck is composed of sonnets. The *crujías*, or the rails that lead from poop to prow, are fashioned of an extended elegy, because, the speaker tells us, elegy is the form in which one "rails" or laments against misfortune.[2] And so on: Cervantes compares the oars of the ship to *esdrújulos*, an onomatopoetic verse form that has a facility for speeding the movement of a poetic line (in the Spanish word *esdrújulo*, the *ess* sound of the first syllable slides into the assonances that follow it—es-**dru**-julo—just as oars propel a galley through the water). The parrels that attach spars and yards to the mast are made of *redondillas*, jocular, informal songs whose rhyme scheme "rounds them off" (*redondo* means "round" in Spanish, and the suffix *-illa* is a diminutive).[3] The lyric's name thus suggests the circular shape of these rings. The sundry crew, the *chusma*, are native Castilian ballads, or *romances*, which are bold, necessary, and can adapt themselves to any purpose: "Era la chusma de romances toda, / gente atrevida, empero necesaria, / pues a todas acciones

94   Chapter Three

se acomoda" (The sundry crew was made up of ballads / a brave people, and necessary, / for they suit themselves to any activity).[4]

This ingenious catalog of a ship's parts and their verse-form correlatives extends across numerous stanzas in chapter 1, and Cervantes adds to it as the poem proceeds. In the copious aggregate, the passages present a virtuosic display of Cervantes's knowledge of Castilian and Italian lyrics—knowledge he fuses with his thorough understanding of the parts of a ship. (Cervantes spent four years in the Spanish navy, and he wrote great quantities of lyrics over the course of his career.) What may be equally apparent at this point is the Horatian nature of Mercury's allegorical galleon, which is built, like Amphion's walls, of lyrics and people—the *chusma*—who handily go about the business of making the great vessel run. As the Spanish Hapsburg empire extended throughout the "terraqueous globe,"[5] as Ricardo Padrón puts it, the substitution of a ship for a walled city adapts the myth to the Spanish Hapsburg context of global empire.

As the *Parnaso* proceeds, however, this jocular allegory takes on a melancholy tone. The fictional Cervantes watches Mercury's galleon approach as he is brooding about the fate of this sea, once the site of the Battle of Lepanto (1571). The victory at Lepanto was a peak moment in the Hapsburg reign, one that set the valor of Spain's fighters and the glory of their naval war machine on display for all the world. Cervantes participated in that clash, and he recalls it in glowing, nostalgic terms throughout his writing.[6] But in the *Parnaso*, this Mediterranean that once burgeoned with heroic captains and soldiers is now clogged with poets. Quarrelsome poets, moreover, all of them clamoring to be included among Apollo's elite ranks. They bicker, shove, and make cases and excuses for themselves.[7] They bob in the water like flotsam. In chapter 2 of the poem, Cervantes watches in wonder as giant storm clouds disgorge contenders for Apollo's favor. Would-be poets rain down on the galley decks:

Tal que se imagine ver (¡lo soberana
Virtud!) de cada gota de la nube
Saltar un bulto, aunque con forma humana.
. . . .
Eran aquestos bultos de la lista
Pasada de poetas referidos,
A cuya fuerza no hay quien la resista.

Unos por hombres buenos conocidos,
Otros de rumbo y hampo, y Dios es Cristo,
Poquitos bien, y muchos mal vestidos . . .

(As you might imagine seeing it with your eyes (the supreme / human gift!) / from each drop from that cloud / sprang a bulky shape, human in form. / ... / Those shapes were the poets / from the lists aforementioned, / whose force no one can resist. // Some were well known as good men, / Others as freewheeling rascals, as Bob's your uncle, / A few well-, and many more poorly, dressed.)[8]

In chapter 5, a group of would-be Parnassians attacks by ship and is repelled by Neptune. Venus transforms them into pumpkins:

¡O raro caso y por jamás oido,
ni visto! ¡O nuevas y admirables trazas
de la gran reina obedecida en Gnido!
en un instante el mar de calabazas
se vio cuajado, algunas tan potentes,
que pasaban de dos, y aun de tres brazas[9]

(Oh what a strange sight, unheard of / or seen! Oh what new and striking designs / of that great queen they obey in Sicily! [Venus] / in an instant the sea appeared / clogged with pumpkins, some so great, / that they surpassed two, and even three arms' length)

Pulpy, starchy fruits such as squashes and medlars served as metaphors for fatuous speech in Renaissance humanist discourse.[10] Thus the opening of the *Parnaso* interweaves political allegory, Horatian poetics, and the specter of what for many sixteenth- and seventeenth-century thinkers constituted a grave abuse of imaginative writing; namely, the extravagant waste of language through the rhetorical activity of *copia*, the practice of crafting passages of language using an abundance of words. *Copia dicendi*, as Terence Cave explains, was a term Renaissance humanists used for a "rich, many-faceted discourse springing from a fertile mind and powerfully affecting its recipient."[11] In its positive valence, *copia* enhances the truth-disclosing powers of language. By heaping up a variety of words and phrases, it is sometimes possible to lead readers to understand a point, observation, or reality that eludes terse expression. In other cases, however, *copia* distracts from what is true, real, and good. It can make lies more convincing (as in the case of some of Mercury's deceptions). Just as significant, for Christian writers, verbiage elaborated for the sheer pleasure of spinning and smithing words, *verba* (language) empty of *res* (substance), distracts attention from the true purpose of language, which is to point humanity toward the contemplation of Christ and the miracle of God's love.

96 Chapter Three

Cervantes builds this contrast into the *Parnaso*. The galleon represents the "extraña cosa," the wondrous powers of *copia* as it facilitates the smooth, efficient operations of a well-ordered collective. *Copia*'s negative sense is represented by the multitudes of false poets, people who overlook the daily miracle of community that is inspired by *musa lyrae sollers* and instead compete with each other to seek individual recognition and favor as poets.[12]

Horace's theory of lyric thus serves as the bridge that joins two of Cervantes's abiding interests: the nature and purpose of poetry, on one hand, and the relationship of political regimes—in Cervantes's case, monarchic states and empires—to the human community, on the other. These questions are especially salient in late works, such as the *Parnaso*, *Don Quixote, Part II* (1615), and the posthumously published *Los trabajos de Persiles y Sigismunda* (1617).[13] As Anthony J. Cascardi points out, much of Cervantes's mature work turns the resources of literary discourse to the project of creating useful political writing:

> Cervantes looked to his humanist predecessors as well as to a host of contemporary genres (some literary, others not at all so) in order to craft a form of fiction that proposed a new, critical, and ironic set of relations among these terms, a form that neither accepted the distinction between "literature" and "politics" nor required their reconciliation.[14]

Don Quixote, in particular, Cascardi argues, addresses Plato's question regarding the place of literature within the state. In the *Parnaso*, Cervantes explores this question via Horace, who answered it for Romans via Orpheus, Amphion, and *musa lyrae sollers*. The demigods represent two necessary components of a polis: seers and eloquent political leaders (such as Apollo, who foresees trouble and summons forces, and Mercury, who carries out Apollo's order and gathers the right people for the job). Lyrics represent the third crucial element: people, who do the necessary work. Yet canny Cervantes, who thoroughly understood the *Ars Poetica*, liked Orpheus well enough but was clearly taken with Amphion. Mercury's poet attends to dimensions of lyric poiesis that exceed a ruler's control and create via the power of mass, great quantities of writing. This power was in evidence all around Cervantes. The Spanish empire was building itself up through writing as well as through military conquest. The production of expansive philosophical, philological, and political treatises; the piles of administrative documents necessary to the governing of large and diverse territories—all of these were necessary materials to the expansion and fortification of Hapsburg imperium. Equally important was Spain's thriving culture of letters. The ingenuity and wit of the galleon scenes in the *Parnaso* celebrate the phenomenon of wide-scale participation in creative verbal activity that yielded the cheerful production of Spanishness.

The title of this chapter alludes to John Austin's classic study *How to Do Things with Words*. However, following Cervantes's lead, my interest here is not the effectual power of individual speech acts (the power of Orpheus), but rather the social and civic power generated through the copious production of verbal and linguistic forms (Amphion). To make this argument, it is necessary to stay with Cervantes a bit longer, as a clearer view of the nature and stakes of lyric *copia* emerge when we examine a second Horatian set piece found in *Don Quixote, Part II*: the adventure of the Knight of the Green Coat.

The Knight of the Green Coat: Everything as It Should Be

The episode of the Knight of the Green Coat begins as Don Quixote and Sancho meet Don Diego de Miranda, the "Knight of the Green Coat," in chapter 16. Just prior to the encounter, they have skirmished with the Knight of the Wood (el Caballero del Bosque) and his squire (chapter 15). At the end of that episode, the Knight of the Wood is revealed to be no knight at all but rather Sansón Carrasco, a somewhat presumptuous student from Alonso Quexana's village who has conspired with the priest and the barber to bring Don Quixote/Quexana home. Both the false nature of the Knight of the Wood and the grandiose self-image that his defeat inspires in Don Quixote set the scene for the appearance of Don Diego de Miranda.

In contrast to Sansón Carrasco (and, perhaps, to Don Quixote), Don Diego is a figure of thorough integrity. This quality is signaled at first by the narrator's description of his dress, which is coherent in all details.[15] He wears a green topcoat with velvet trimmings and a matching cap. These "Morisco accessories" are perfectly coordinated. Don Diego's boots match his sword strap, and his spurs are not "gilded, but lacquered green, and . . . shone so brightly that, matching as they did the rest of his dress, they looked better than if they'd been coated in the purest gold."[16] Don Diego's skillful accessorizing furnishes insight into whom he represents in the world of *Don Quixote, Part II*. In conformity with Renaissance ideas about outward appearance and the inner man, the green enamel of Don Diego's spurs is well polished and modest, like the man himself, and like his household, as we learn slightly later on in the episode. Green is also the color of Islam, and Don Diego's ethnic identity is relevant to Cervantes's purposes in this part of the novel. In their first encounters, however, Don Diego impresses Don Quixote with his graciousness and his quiet self-assurance. Don Diego's personal integrity carries over to his house, which

98 Chapter Three

is neither opulent nor rustic. It is spacious, "in the village style," and it is his family seat. His coat of arms, carved in "rough stone," as opposed to the marble that adorns great houses, is found over the door to the house and also over the wine cellar and the buttery, which are well stocked.[17] All of these details contribute to the image of a household of established but moderate prosperity that accords with the Renaissance ideals of moderation and self-containment. Don Diego's family is well ordered and harmonious as well. His wife, Doña Cristina, and his son, Don Lorenzo, are courteous and know their roles and duties. Doña Cristina sees to their guest's needs, and Don Lorenzo entertains Don Quixote before dinner, as is expected of him.[18]

It is in this context, in a household that represents one of the most stable and prosperous social units to be found in either part I or part II of *Don Quixote*, that Cervantes introduces the theme of lyric poetry. He does so first as Don Quixote and Don Diego meet and get to know one another in chapter 16. As they ride together and exchange pleasantries, Don Diego laments that his son balks at studying law or theology, and instead has developed a passion for poetry:

> Será de edad de diez y ocho años; los seis ha estado en Salamanca, aprendiendo las lenguas latina y griega, y cuando quise que pasase a estudiar otras ciencias, halléle tan embebido en la de la poesía (si es que se puede llamar ciencia) que no es posible hacerle arrostrar la de las leyes, que yo quisiera que estudiara, ni de la reina de todas, la teología. . . . En fin, todas sus conversaciones son con los libros de los referidos poetas, y con los de Horacio, Persio, Juvenal y Tibulo; que de los modernos romancistas no hace mucha cuenta, y con todo el mal cariño que muestra tener a la poesía de romance, le tiene agora desvanecidos los pensamientos el hacer una glosa a cuatro versos que le han enviado de Salamanca, y pienso que son de justa literaria . . .[19]

(He's eighteen, and has spent the last six years in Salamanca, studying Latin and Greek, and when I wanted him to go on to the study of other areas of knowledge, I found him so enthralled with poetry, if that can be called knowledge, that I can't make him show any enthusiasm for law, which I would like him to study, or for the queen of all study, which is theology. . . . [A]ll his conversations are about the books of these poets and of Horace, Persius, Juvenal and Tibullus; he does not think very highly of modern writers, and despite the antipathy he displays toward poetry in the vernacular, his thoughts are now entirely turned to writing a gloss on four lines sent to him from Salamanca, I think for a literary competition.)[20]

The father is describing the fairly well-known generational phenomenon that accompanied the emergence of a social group known as the *letrados* in early modern Spain. These men were sons of well-to-do households whose families sent them to universities at Salamanca or Alcalá de Henares. Instead of preparing to enter traditional professions in law or in the Church, *letrados* turned their training in language and letters to securing positions as administrators in an increasingly bureaucratized imperial government.

A number of the young people encountered in *Don Quixote, Part II*, appear to be aspiring *letrados*. The aforementioned Sansón Carrasco is one example. Another is a young licentiate (chapter 19) and his cousin, "a humanist" whose primary activity is "composing books for publishing, all of them very beneficial and no less diverting for the nation."[21] Don Lorenzo appears to be following the path of the *letrado* as well, and although Don Diego expresses disappointment at his son's predilection for letters, his comments convey a degree of pride in a son who looks beyond the horizon of his parents' knowledge and embraces modern times. Don Quixote concurs. His advice to his newfound friend expresses optimism about young men and women who have been well bred and well raised by their parents:

> ... que vuesa merced deje caminar a su hijo por donde su estrella le llame; que, siendo él tan buen estudiante como debe de ser, y habiendo ya subido felicemente el primer escalón de las ciencias, que es el de las lenguas, con ellas por sí mismo subirá a la cumbre de las letras humanas, las cuales tan bien parecen en un caballero de capa y espada, y así le adornan, honran, y engrandecen como las mitras a los obispos, o como las gamachas a los peritos jurisconsultos. Riña vuesa merced a su hijo si hace sátiras que perjudiquen las honras ajenas, y castíguele, y rómpaselas; pero si hiciere sermones al modo de Horacio, donde reprehenda los vicios en general, como tan elegantemente él lo hizo, alábele ... con que no señale persona alguna; pero hay poetas que a trueco de decir una malicia, se pondrán a peligro que los destierren a las isla de Ponto. Si el poeta fuere casto en sus costumbres, lo será también en sus versos; la pluma es lengua del alma; cuales fueren los conceptos que en ella se engendraren, tales serán sus escritos, y cuando los reyes y príncipes ven la milagrosa ciencia de la poesía en sujetos prudentes, virtuosos y graves, los honran, los estiman, y los enriquecen, y aun los coronan con las hojas del árbol a quien no ofende el rayo . . .[22]

> (. . . you should allow your son to walk the path to which his star calls him; if he is the good student he should be, and if he has already successfully climbed the first essential step, which is languages, with them he will, on his own, mount to the summit of human letters, which are so admirable

100 Chapter Three

in a gentleman with his cape and sword, and adorn, honor and ennoble him, as miters do bishops or robes the learned jurists. Your grace should reprimand your son if he writes satires that damage other people's honor; you should punish him and tear up the poems; but if he composes admonitory sermons in the manner of Horace, in which vices in general are elegantly reproved, then praise him . . . as long as he does not point out a specific person; but there are poets who, for the sake of saying something malicious, would run the risk of being exiled to the Islands of Pontus. If the poet is chaste in his habits, he will be chaste in his verses as well; the pen is the tongue of the soul: his writings will be like the concepts engendered there; when kings and princes see the miraculous art of poetry in prudent, virtuous and serious subjects, they honor, esteem and enrich them, and even crown them with the leaves of the tree that lightning never strikes . . .)[23]

Don Quixote shows his knowledge of the *Ars Poetica* in this exchange, and his respect for Horace's advice indicates that he thinks it useful to present-day Spain. The laurel crown ("the tree that lightning never strikes") is awarded to writers who compose good and virtuous poetry that is also prudent and circumspect. Don Quixote supports this point with references to writers whose poetic achievements brought political disaster—notably, Ovid.

Orpheus, Amphion, Don Quixote, and Don Lorenzo

This early allusion to Horace and the *Ars Poetica* in the adventure of the Knight of the Green Coat opens the way into Cervantes's larger meditation on Amphion, Orpheus, and the nature and function of lyric poetry in 1615. Composed in answer to a call issued from "Salamanca," a name that designates both a principal Spanish city and Spain's most important university, Don Lorenzo's current poetic project is Amphionic and contrasts with a second kind of lyric that Cervantes introduces at the start of chapter 18. When Don Quixote and Don Diego arrive at Don Diego's house, Don Quixote's eyes fall on earthenware jugs from El Toboso. The vessels inspire him to thoughts of Dulcinea and, thence, of poetry:

> . . . tinajas a la redonda, que, por ser del Toboso, le renovaron las memorias de su encantada y transformada Dulcinea; y suspirando, y sin mirar lo que decía, ni delante de quién estaba, dijo:
>
> —¡O dulces prendas, por mi mal halladas,
> dulces y alegres cuando Dios quería!

¡Oh tobosescas tinajas, que me habéis traído a la memoria la dulce prenda de mi mayor amargura![24]

(All around there were enormous earthenware jars that, having been made in El Toboso, revived Don Quixote's memories of his enchanted and transformed Dulcinea, and, not thinking what he was saying or what company he was in, he sighed and said:

> "O sweet treasures, discovered to my sorrow,
> Sweet and joyous when God did will them so!"

Oh Tobosan vessels, which have brought to mind the sweetest treasure of my deeper grief!)[25]

Don Quixote draws the lines of poetry from the opening of Sonnet 10 by Garcilaso de la Vega, "the Spanish Orpheus":[26] "¡O dulces prendas por mi mal halladas . . . !"[27] Just as important as the reference, however, is the lyric work these lines enact, which is to accomplish the Orphic task of giving form to universal human feelings of desire and loss.

Cervantes continues developing the theme of Orphic and Amphionic lyrics throughout the adventure of the Knight of the Green Coat. When Don Quixote has recovered from his encounter with the Tobosan vessels and is waiting to join Don Diego, Doña Cristina, and Don Lorenzo at their family meal, Don Lorenzo arrives to entertain him. Don Quixote inquires: "Your grace's father, Señor Don Diego de Miranda, has informed me of the rare ability and subtle ingenuity which your grace possesses, and, in particular, that your grace is a great poet."[28] Don Lorenzo demurs:

—Poeta, bien podrá ser—respondió don Lorenzo—; pero grande, ni por pensamiento. Verdad es que yo soy algún tanto aficionado a la poesía y a leer los buenos poetas; pero no de tal manera que se me pueda dar el nombre de grande que mi padre dice.

—No me parece mal esta humildad—respondió don Quijote—; porque no hay poeta que no sea arrogante y piense de sí que es el mayor poeta del mundo.

—No hay regla sin excepción—respondió don Lorenzo—; y alguno habrá que lo sea y no lo piense.

—Pocas—respondió don Quijote—; pero dígame vuesa merced: ¿qué versos son los que agora trae entre manos, que me ha dicho el señor su padre

102 Chapter Three

que le traen algo inquieto y pensativo? Y se es alguna glosa, a mí se me entiende algo de achaque de glosas, y holgaría saberlos; y si es que son de justa literaria, procure vuestra merced llevar el segundo premio, que el primer siempre se lleva el favor o la gran calidad de la persona, el segundo se le lleva la mera justicia, y el tercero viene a ser segundo, y el primero, a esta cuenta, será el tercero, al modo de las licencias que se dan en las universidades . . .[29]

("A poet, perhaps," responded Don Lorenzo, "but by no means great. The truth is, I have a predilection for poetry and for reading good poets, but that does not justify calling me great, as my father has done."

"This humility does not seem a bad thing to me," responded Don Quixote, "because there is no poet who is not arrogant and does not think himself the greatest poet in the world."

"Every rule has its exception," responded Don Lorenzo, "and there must be some who are great and do not think so."

"Very few," responded Don Quixote. "But tell me, your grace, what verses are you at work on now? Your father has told me that they have made you somewhat restive and thoughtful. If it is a gloss, I know something about the subject and would like very much to hear it; if the verses are for a literary competition, your grace should try to win second place; first is always won through favor or because of the high estate of the person, second is won because of pure justice, and by this calculation, third becomes second, and first becomes third, in the manner of degrees offered by universities; but, even so, being called first carries with it great celebrity.")[30]

As a Salamanca-trained student of letters, Don Lorenzo recognizes the limitations of his abilities. Moreover, as a dutiful son who has been raised in Don Diego's exemplary household, he accepts a place in the middle of the pack among Spain's emerging writers and embraces his lot, that of contributing poetic labor to the modern Spanish state in the form of verses, composed in the Castilian language, on institutionally sanctioned themes. Don Quixote's advice to Don Lorenzo in the adventure of the Knight of the Green Coat bears out this understanding of the nature and stakes of the poetry contest. In a poetic situation whose parameters and meaning are determined by Amphion, politics dictates the meaning of "winning," and the equation turns out differently from what a reader trained to Orphic horizons might expect. The skills of the individual poet are subordinate in importance to his or her position in the greater social pattern.[31]

A second element of this exchange stands out as well. Cervantes has Don Quixote single out the poetry contest as the kind of poetic activity that might occupy a young man of Don Lorenzo's talents and bent. As we saw in chapter 1, glossing is a form of collaborative poetic generation, a way to share in the production and extension of social worlds. The poetry contest is similarly animated by collective spirit. Don Lorenzo's enthusiastic participation in these kinds of activities is an important dimension of his significance to the portrait of the Spanish empire that Cervantes creates in *Don Quixote, Part II*. A brief look at how poetry contests functioned in sixteenth- and seventeenth-century culture helps bring what Cervantes creates with Don Lorenzo more clearly into view.

You Are Invited!

Early modern poetry contests are associated with two origins.[32] Aurora Egido cites the Provençal *puys* that took place in closed, elite venues such as courts, universities, and private academies in the cosmopolitan atmosphere of fifteenth-century Aragon. On the other hand, Spanish, French, and English writers emulated the model of Italian academies, in which members tested their skills with a variety of set verse forms and themes. Poetic tournaments commemorated special occasions and events, and they play a role in the process of late medieval and Renaissance "courtierization"—the constellation of policies, practices, and royal orders and favors by which members of the traditional nobility, a group that identified with the warrior values of the militaristic past, were induced to abandon violence for politics.

Inmaculada Osuna Rodríguez observes that these events grew in importance with the gradual integration of participants from a wider range of social ranks over time. Certainly, by the time Cervantes wrote *Don Quixote*, poetry contests (*certámenes*) and tournaments (*justas*) existed independently of the more private kinds of poetry-writing events organized by academies and were well-organized civic affairs, sponsored by churches, civic organizations, wealthy patrons, and (as in the case of Don Lorenzo) universities. Contest announcements, frequently composed in verse themselves, were issued far and wide, often beyond the borders of the town or city in which the contest took place. They summoned contestants to turn their wits and their writing hands to the service of a larger cause: a town celebrating the anniversary of its founding, a church commemorating a patron saint, a vice realm witnessing the birth of an heir or the loss of a viceroy or vicereine, or celebrating the visit of an important dignitary. The announcers invited all members of the public to test their skills with a variety of lyric forms composed on set themes (for example, four stanzas

104 Chapter Three

on the theme of Saint Teresa's spiritual wedding to Christ and the golden nail he presented her as a gift).[33] On a larger scale, poetry contests were among the ceremonial and festive activities that kingdoms organized to commemorate the signing of a peace treaty or the formation of an alliance between states.[34] In the Americas, poetry contests and festivals were part of empire building and played a significant role in colonial culture.

Participants were given a set amount of time to prepare their submissions. Once poems were collected, they were posted publicly so that passersby could read them. The final ceremony prompted yet more poetry writing, as one or some of the contest officials prepared a *vejamen*, a long poem, usually satirical, that announced the names of the winners, and perhaps those who placed second and third.

The poetry generated by tournaments and poetry contests is notoriously difficult to read. First and foremost, it arrives to us in voluminous quantities. Tens, even hundreds of participants might assemble portfolios. Announcements generally stipulated a specific quantity of poems composed in a range of forms: a sonnet, nearly always followed by a gloss, followed by a variety of Castilian song forms and stanzas, including octaves, tercets, *liras*, *décimas*, *canciones*, *romances*, et cetera. The archive presents a nearly "unscalable mountain" of verse, in Egido's words. Moreover, she characterizes these poems as being of "inconsistent literary quality." What mattered to their authors and to contest judges was a writer's adherence to the contest guidelines and, perhaps (as Don Quixote advised Don Lorenzo), their social status. Egido characterizes the task of reading this work as "demoralizing" and cites the withering opinion of the poet and critic Dámaso Alonso: "The poet sings on themes handed to them (and sometimes these themes are quite extravagant) . . . and the competitors are all the middling writers, the followers, the obscurantists, those who have nothing to say and no one to listen to their verses."[35]

Does no one want to read this vast corpus of lyric production, though? And did no one back then? Perhaps a better way to describe the situation is that the questions that literary criticism trains us to ask are not helpful. Generic questions (e.g., *Is this a lyric poem?*) and evaluative questions that train attention on the individual poem as a work of art (*Is this a good poem? How is it a good poem? And where does it fail?*) do not serve us here. Thus it might be a good idea to look for other options for shaping a reading practice. Sixteenth- and seventeenth-century lyric culture offers those options, in the form of the bipartite art that is Horace's *musa lyrae sollers*, created by the two distinct lyres of Orpheus and Amphion. Amphion, in particular, encourages us to ask not whether a poem is "lyrical" or whether it succeeds or fails as an aesthetic object. Rather, Amphion steers us to consider what that poem is doing and what larger social patterns it might form part of. Where and how does a poem participate in acts of human world-making and polity-making that the myth of Amphion figures, as the king charms stones to build Theban walls?

Reading *Copia*

We can answer these latter kinds of questions when we bring them to bear on contest lyrics, because whether or not people did or did not want to *read* this poetry (there is no reason to think they didn't), we can say for certain, based on copious evidence, that people wanted to create it.[36] That is not a meaningless point. Great masses of people wanted to do this work, to create poems in response to prompts and challenges designed by contest and festival authorities. To "read" contest lyrics, to unlock what Cervantes views as their profound significance, it is necessary first to recognize and acknowledge this fact of widespread, eager participation, which points us to one of the most tender and vulnerable dimensions of humanity as a species: our enthusiastic desire to share in acts of coproduction that are sometimes—even often—labor-intensive, but whose burdens we bear cheerfully, in the spirit of community.[37] In this framework, the aesthetics of contest lyrics begin to make some sense. For example, consider the following stanzas, which open an announcement for a poetry contest hosted by the city of Valencia, in honor of Saint Vincent Ferrer, in 1615:

La santa sabiduría
quiere labrar un palacio
que con la esfera compitan
sus ricos y hermosos cuartos.

Y porque las cuadras piensa
vestir de admirables cuadros,
hacer la experiencia quiere
de los pinceles más sabios.

Por prueba primero
un soneto castellano
que de Vincente Ferrer
le pinta al vivo retrato;

y porque un topacio en oro
fue la vida de este santo,
al que mejor engrandezca
le ofrece en oro un topacio . . .

(Saint knowledge / seeks to build a palace / whose rich, beautiful rooms / compete with the heavenly sphere. // And because she seeks / to adorn its walls / with admirable paintings, / she seeks the experience / of the most worthy brushes. // As the first test / a Castilian sonnet / that paints the living portrait / of Vincent Ferrer; // and because a topaz set in gold / was the life of this saint / to he who elevates him best / she will offer a topaz set in gold . . .)[38]

The meter of the poem is lost in the translation, but readers who do not understand Spanish will still be able to pick up on some of the important devices that shape this *romance* and animate its motion. It is composed of octosyllabic verses arranged in an assonantal rhyme scheme, abab/cdcd/efef/ghgh. This rhyme carries momentum forward through the poem's fifty-six lines. The meter and rhyme accompany a fanciful narrative, in which a personified wisdom (la santa sabiduría), who is building a palace, finds she needs paintings (cuadros) to decorate the walls (cuadras) of its rooms (cuartos), and therefore convenes a poetry contest. The first challenge in this contest is to create a portrait of Saint Vincent Ferrer in sonnet form.

Every element of these stanzas is designed to charm. Their lilting melody lightens the spirit. The account of Saint Wisdom with her building plan is clever and delightful. The correspondence between the rooms she wants to decorate and the nicely rounded quatrains is accomplished. The poet brings each to a close with a neat correspondence of rhyme and punctuation, as periods and semicolons at lines 4, 8, 12, and 16 duplicate the closure of the stanza's rhyme. The witty wordplay and punning: the polyptoton of the "cua" words: "cuarto" (room), "cuadra" (which can mean block, as in block of stone; also, small room or cell), and "cuadro" (painting)—all are directed to the purpose of inspiring people to join in the game. Alliteration, punning, and polyptoton are fun! Poems aren't that hard to compose! A house of wisdom! Paintings, jewels, and prizes! Why not join in? Come build Saint Wisdom's house! Caught up in these stanzas' momentum, a reader is drawn further and further into the poem's world.

In this context, uses of aesthetic language that might lead us to judge this poem as tedious (the meter), naive (the wordplay), jarring (the confusing imagery and awkward phrases), and generally substandard emerge in a different light as evidence of a lyric that is doing its work, in the manner of Cervantes's stalwart, adaptable "chusma," say—or, behind Cervantes's conceit, Horace's *musa lyrae sollers*. Even the awkward maneuver in the fourth quatrain makes a certain kind of sense. The strain in the poem's flow as the poet heads in the direction of announcing the first challenge and the associated prize (a topaz set in gold, because Saint Vincent's life was "a topaz set in gold," which means what, exactly?) are meaningful, as they reveal poetic labor. The poet and the language itself are expending effort on behalf of us, the poem's readers and potential contest participants.

This "tell" is certainly unintentional, but it points nonetheless to a qualitative distinction between contest lyrics and, for example, the poetry of Renaissance sprezzatura, whose practitioners cultivate the art of masking or disguising effort in the interest of projecting the image of a self-contained, all-capable self. The contest announcement stanzas are up to something different. Timothy Hampton captures it in his discussions of "cheerfulness," an emotion, Hampton tells us, that does not bind the self away from the social group, but rather bridges a gap between our inside condition and our outside selves, thereby drawing us into community.[39] The cheerfulness inspired by singsong verse, pretty images, and the occasional catachresis that results from striving to frame and polish a serviceable conceit establishes the affective register of warm solidarity between poets and readers that Raymond Williams identifies as a key component of community. Affect is what distinguishes this kind of social formation from organizations structured from above, such as realms and states.[40] Lighthearted coproduction maintains internal social bonds and helps make a community amicable and tolerant.

Close reading has brought us to the revelation of this basic and powerful social fact. However, it would be a mistake to lose track of the wider context we began with in this section. The questions we were looking at have to do with the overwhelming quantity of sixteenth- and seventeenth-century contest lyrics and how to read the archive. The concept of *copia* invites us to consider whether the sheer abundance of this poetry might contain a truth to be disclosed on its own terms, truth that a focus on individual poems might not reveal. That is, if the massive archive of contest lyrics points us to the minor miracle that is the continuous, inspired proliferation of goodwill and collective spirit manifested by this abundance, is the close reading of individual poems consistent with its ethos?

Oren Izenberg steers us in a productive direction. Writing of a corpus of poetry that on first encounter seems significantly different from sixteenth- and seventeenth-century contest lyrics—the output of twentieth-century Anglophone Language poets—Izenberg proposes a thought experiment that is fruitful enough for our purposes to be quoted at length:

> Imagine . . . that the poem is only a single part of its author's projected life work . . . one that explicitly subordinates the unit of the poem to the . . . unfolding category of poetry. . . . And now imagine that there are thousands upon thousands of other poems by other poets that bear more than a passing resemblance to this poem. . . . Soon, the rising tally of similarities and

108 Chapter Three

> texts places impossible demands on our capacity and will to attend to the manifest differences between one poem and another, to articulate the fine distinctions of tone or affect. . . . Imagine language, in effect, without a speaker . . . under these conditions indifference and inattention to the specifics of what is being said is not only a plausible response; it is the strong response that such writing demands . . . these poems do not mean to be well understood, do not ask to be revisited with devoted care, do not even seek to be finely perceived. In the most general terms, they do not seek to become available for judgments of taste. And I will suggest that it is in this indifference as well that we register a significance sense in which . . . [this] poetry might be said to be social.[41]

The significant differences in context that separate the poetry Izenberg is writing about from early modern contest lyrics are indicated by the ellipses needed to adapt this quotation. Izenberg situates the project of "language without a speaker" among late twentieth-century writers who respond to modernity's "failures to value persons adequately—or even to perceive persons as persons."[42] This response takes the form of writers' "resisting their own will to formal mastery" and undermining the "moral exemplarity of their poetic vision" in favor of "regrounding" "the concept and value of a person" from individual consciousness and subjectivity to the collective, or what Izenberg discusses as the social.[43] Sixteenth- and seventeenth-century lyric culture made room for that kind of person, as I have been demonstrating throughout this book. *Musa lyrae sollers* recognizes the value of both literary and the social poiesis, accomplished by both select individuals and more inclusive groups. This is true even as active tensions and conflicts of interest were at work between early modern society's Orpheuses and Amphions (on one hand), and Zethuses—Cervantes's handy *chusma* (on the other).[44] We will examine those tensions and conflicts more closely momentarily. For now, what is useful is Izenberg's concept of a poetry whose "internal logic . . . is the open-ended algorithm of addition."[45] Like the examples of Language poetry Izenberg describes, contest lyrics "are *social* in that what they take poems to be examples of is the unique capacity to produce language altogether and thus to announce . . . the existence of something fundamentally human on which the very possibility of social life can be predicated."[46] There are promising connections to be developed between Izenberg's "algorithm" and early modern lyric culture.[47] As we have seen a number of times in this book, sixteenth- and seventeenth-century societies acknowledged the role that verse and song forms play as sites for collaborative co-creation of culture and communities. The accounts of poetry contests that often appear in the front matter of printed collections of contest lyrics pro-

How to Do Things with *Copia*   109

vide further evidence of how thoroughly ideas of *musa lyrae sollers*, Orpheus, and Amphion informed lyric culture. These narratives present contests and festivals as significant venues for the building up of community spirit among people from all walks of life, represented at their most human: creative, resourceful, embodied men and women who cheerfully respond to summons and embark on co-creating meaningful forms.

Making Lyric Communities

A description of the poetry festival in honor of St. Teresa of Ávila, hosted by the city of Córdoba in 1615, presents a strikingly clear example of how lyrics create communities, a phenomenon that Europe's Christians often understood as a process guided by divine grace. The narrative account of this festival describes that, as news of the beatification spread through Spain:

> Concurrieron . . . en el Convento de San Joseph de Carmelitas Descalzos, sin prevención alguna, mas no sin traza del Cielo, las mas diestras, y aventajadas de la capilla de esta Ciudad, que no dio pequeño motivo, a los Religiosos de alegría, y de agradecimiento, y a los músicos de una devota admiración, considerando su paseo, y entretenimiento convertido misteriosamente al servicio, y gloria de la Santa . . .[48]

> (There arrived . . . in the Convent of Saint Joseph of Discalced Carmelites, with no obstacle whatsoever, indeed, by design of Heaven, the most skilled and outstanding members of the parish of this city, which gave not a little cause for joy and gratitude on the part of the Religious, and to the musicians, who watched with rapt admiration, as the procession and entertainment was mysteriously converted to the service and the glory of the Saint . . .)

From its earliest moments, the festival is converted into a sign of divine grace.[49] As the account proceeds, the poetry contest becomes the efficient cause of the formation of the community that this holy occasion inspires. In the passage quoted below, excitement and curiosity about the specific challenges that are included in the contest announcement draw people out into the streets, through the city, and into the chapel of the Convent of Discalced Carmelites, where the announcement will be posted:

> Satisfizo el de la Madre Priora al deseo, y voto de todos, dando principio a la fiesta con la publicación de un cartel desafío, que en nueve varios certámenes provocaba los eruditos ingenios, a que en elegantes, y cultos, ver-

110   Chapter Three

sos, assi Latinos como Castellanos, celebrasen las grandezas de nuestra Castellana Santa. Hízose domingo siete de Septiembre: y este día a la una de la tarde salieron del convento de San Joseph los atabales, y trompetas de la Ciudad a caballo con sus libreas, paseando las principales calles dellas, y previniendo a los que avía de asistir a la solemne publicación, y paseo del desafío, rematando la vuelta en las madres descalzas de donde se había de comenzar la publicación. Pobláronse a la seña de estos instrumentos la Iglesia, calle, y ventanas de damas, coches, y caballeros, cuyas orejas apenas hirió esta voz, cuando sus espuelas los caballos, en que se presentaron con lucidos aderezos al puesto señalado, puesto que conformes a la gravedad, que la ocasión pedía. Aguardose largo rato al mantenedor que había de llevar el cartel, granjeando con esta tardanza la curiosidad, admirar espaciosamente la mucha, que había en la iglesia, y altares, y recrearse todos con la maravillosa fragrancia, que muchas cazoletas, y pebeteros despedían, en cambio de la enfadadosa que concursos grandes en tiempo de tanto calor, como hacia, suelen causar.[50]

(It satisfied the Mother Prioress's desire, and the will of all, to give a start to the celebration with the publication of a posted list of challenges, in which nine varied contests spurred erudite wits, in elegant and cultured, verses, written in Latin as well as in Castilian, to commemorate the great accomplishments of our Castilian Saint. They set it for Sunday the seventh of September: and this day at one o'clock in the afternoon from the convent of Saint Joseph proceeded the kettledrummers and the trumpeters of the city, on horseback with their liveries, parading through the main streets, and notifying all that they should join the solemn convocation and the progress of the [contest] announcement, the procession concluding at the convent of the discalced nuns where the announcement would begin to be read. The Church, street, and windows were filled with ladies, gentlemen, and knights, whose ears were hardly pierced by the noise before they put spur to their horses, astride which they presented themselves with shining adornments at the appropriate place, in conformity with the gravity that the occasion demanded. Everyone waited a long time for the man who carried the announcement poster, increasing, by means of this delay, the curiosity, the admiration of the abundance contained in the church and on its altars, and delight in the wonderful fragrances that many dippers and cauldrons gave off, in place of the bothersome [scent] that large processions, in time of so much heat, usually cause.)

The final detail in this passage—the author's reflection on the smell and press of bodies on a hot day and the fact that no one minds them— underscores the social power of gaiety and goodwill, energies that facilitate the knitting together of a collective, to the beat of kettledrums, the melodies of the trumpets, and the jingle of spurs and tack. People bear the long wait to hear the challenges in a frame of mind keyed to pleasure and curiosity. So your neighbor uses excessive amounts of onion in their gazpacho. Who cares? Smell the incense. When the cartel-bearer finally arrives, he posts the first challenge, and the community processes out to the church, where he posts the second challenge. The third challenge is hung in front of the town council hall, and so on. In this way, the social activity of collective poetry-making overwrites and leavens these buildings' conventional functions as spaces used for the exercise of religious and political authority. The poetry contest remaps the city as a constellation of sites that prompt lyric participation, to the accompaniment of music and fireworks, in a carnivalesque atmosphere that draws on Amphion's art at its most playful and communitarian.

A striking feature of accounts of poetry contests is how clearly their writers understand the social poiesis these happenings inspire. Some accounts take it as a matter of course that to generate great quantities of poetry, in community, is meaningful. Others associate the events with Orpheus and Amphion directly. In religious contexts, the summoning of a community by means of poetry links the contests to heavenly designs (as above, in the case of the festival for Saint Teresa). Narratives that describe civic and privately sponsored poetry contests also present these events as significant in ways that extend beyond the poems themselves and have more to do with the power of collective participation. The account of a contest Don Miguel Thomás sponsored in 1625 in honor of the memory of his aunt, Sor Catharina Thomasa Mallorquina, is an example. Coproduction, on a mass scale, taps greater forces of poiesis as human collaboration falls into rhythm with God's designs and produces resonant signs of His favor. Don Miguel's account is notable both for the elaborate conceit he works around the myth of Orpheus, and for the matter-of-fact assumption that the poetry generated in poetry contests is associated with special powers, in the same way that, for example, precious and semiprecious stones have special properties.

Don Miguel published the proceedings of this contest, including a collection of the lyrics that participants submitted, in 1636. The cover of the volume features a crowned figure—he looks like a king—playing a harp, surrounded by smaller figures of men and women playing musical instruments (fig. 4).[51] The contest announcement develops an elaborate conceit around the powers of Orphic music. Stanza 3 links the power of the collective poetic enterprise undertaken by contest participants to a metamorphosis that could stem the rocks the Maenads threw as they assailed Orpheus:

4. Cover of *Certamen Poético, en honor de la venerable madre Sor Catharina Thomasa Mallorquina, Monja canóniga reglar de San Agustin, Mantenido en la isla y ciudad de Mallorca, en la Sala de la Congregación de los Cavalleros, en el Colegio de Monte Sion de la Compañía de Jesús* (Barcelona: Gabriel Nogués, 1636). Biblioteca Nacional de España. Photograph by the author.

How to Do Things with *Copia* 113

Las piedras viles con que le hizo tiro
La vil canalla del horrible Averno
Por si mellar pudiesse su firmeza;
En piedras ya de resplandor eterno
Trocadas brillan todas, ya el zafiro
La orna con jaspe de mayor fineza;
Ya de pies a cabeza
Cuajada de esmeraldas, de diamantes
sardas, jacintos, toda joyería
aljófar, perlas, toda argentería
nácares de riquísimos cambiantes,
y con braveza tanta
a Dios más prenda, al enemigo espanta.[52]

(The vile stones with which / the vile rabble of horrid Avernus / sought to chip away at his resolve / are now changed for stones of lasting splendor; / they all shine, the sapphire / adorns [this resolve] along with the finest jasper; / and from feet to head / encrusted with emeralds, with diamonds / carnelian, zircon, all variety of jewels / freshwater pearls and round pearls, all variety of silver / rich, changeable nacre / and with such a bold display / of tokens from God, the enemy is frightened.)

The announcement continues in prose to present each challenge in terms of a precious stone. There are thirteen tests in all: twelve set competitions (the narrator tells us that their number corresponds to the twelve "rocks" of the Church, the apostles), plus a final round. Participants will compete in creating ballads, hexameters, octaves, epigrams, sonnets, elegies, *redondillas* (which they could prepare in Castilian or in the Mallorcan tongue), a Latin ode, glosses, sapphics, hieroglyphs, songs, and odes. In the last round, competitors prepared a lyric form of their own choosing. The relationship of each stone to one of Catharina's excellencies or holy accomplishments is described in prose sections that lead up to the prompt for a poem. For example, chrysoberyl is described as "verde, con su resplandor de oro, aunque no es transparente: su fineza, y natural color a oscuras le deja mejor conocer. Propio símbolo de la obediencia ciega, cual ejercitó milagrosamente Thomasa . . ." (green, with the gleam of gold, although it is not transparent: its delicacy and its natural color stand out best in the dark. It is an appropriate symbol of blind obedience, which Thomasa exercised miraculously . . .).[53]

The richly imagined framing of this contest, with its interwoven conceits of stones in various states of metamorphosis (the stones that killed

114   Chapter Three

Orpheus, transformed by the poetry contest; stones with inherent meanings on their own, to which the author of the contest announcement adds Catharina's excellences; the poems the contest generates, which build a monument to Catharina's holiness)—all point to the lyric culture of *musa lyrae sollers*. Contest lyrics function like stones that charm and build walls here. Collective lyric-making creates densely elaborated imaginative worlds that also build up cultures and societies.

Lyric Labor

I refer to "society" and "culture" above, and not to "community," because unlike the account of the Cordoban festival, Don Miguel's narrative shows little interest in community. He demonstrates little care for the human dimensions of the contest. He refers to the great number of participants who joined in, but Don Miguel interprets their quantity as evidence of the favor God shows Sor Catharina. Both Don Miguel and the authors of supporting materials in the front matter of the volume[54] build a case that Sor Catharina's "cosas," the qualities of character and the holy deeds that are signs of her holy status, "son de tanta estima, y alabar, que merecen el desvelo, y despabilo, de los más agudos ingenios de Oradores, y Poetas, para ser dignamente predicadas, y cantadas" (are so estimable, and so laudable, that they warrant the sleepless nights and wakefulness of the keenest wits of Orators and Poets in order to be suitably evangelized and sung).[55] Through this excellence, Sor Catharina's life glorifies Mallorca. Don Miguel's celebration of his aunt becomes a case for the island's value as a component of the Spanish empire. The group states that they are printing the collected poetry "de gloria a España; de palma a su Patria; de lustre a la Religión; de ejemplo a los fieles; y de cumplida alegría al Mundo" (to the glory of Spain, from Palma [de Mallorca] to the patria; to add luster to Religion, as an example to the faithful, and to the greater joy of the World). Don Miguel elaborates on this idea at the conclusion of his prologue, when he advises readers of the volume's significance:

> . . . el leerlo, toca a todos, pues debemos todos alabar a Dios en sus santos, principalmente a los moradores de la Isla, y devotos desta prodigiosa virgen, como mas vecinos a ellas, cuyo cuerpo tienen . . . para que las alabanzas de Dios en ella suenen en nuestros oídos, de varios modos, y se nos comunique la gloria del Hacedor sumo, y protección de esta maravillosa virgen, a cuyos pies pongo este pequeño trabajo en nombre mío, y de mi patria, y de los que con grande devoción, y alegría, han celebrado sus alabanzas, animado el Clarín sonoro con el Poético aliento.[56]

How to Do Things with *Copia*   115

(. . . to read it, touches all, for we should all praise God through his saints, and principally to residents of this Island, and who are devotees of this prodigious virgin, as they are close neighbors of hers and possess her body . . . such that the praise of God in her resounds in our ears, in various ways, and communicates to us the glory of the supreme Creator, and the protection of this marvelous virgin, at whose feet I lay this small work in my own name, and in the name of my fatherland, and in the name of those who with great devotion, and joy, have celebrated her praises, as the Poetic spirit inspired the sonorous Clarion.)

This passage captures with remarkable clarity the ambivalence of early modern poetry contests, which on one hand served as powerful forces for generating community, and on the other were orchestrated by patrons, sponsors, and organizing committees that arrogated to themselves the privilege of using the events for their own ends. The contests and festivals thus stage a tension between community (created through social bonds and affective relationships) and society, whose organization is imposed from above.[57] As a figure for lyric both as it is created by people and as the art itself creates within the social conditions of oligarchic or autocratic regimes, Amphion holds space for both dimensions of these contests. There is nothing unusual or unique about the complete disjuncture between how different players experience and understand the events. The paradox is as old as the dilemma of Amphion and Zethus.[58] Kings perceive one kind of activity taking place: walls are being built for them. Contest participants experience something different: a sense of making and belonging. Charmed and cheerful, they move together to create those walls of their own accord, by making poems in forms that encode the culturally specific resonances discussed in chapter 1.

Don Miguel's language reflects this fundamental fact about the polity. He acknowledges the community of poetry makers who have celebrated Catharina's spirit with music animated by poetry. His words register the presence of community as it is created by the contest, and he imagines the benefit the volume will bring to the people of Mallorca, who live in proximity to Catharina and her body. However, in contrast to the account of the Cordoban festival, for example, community is not valuable in and of itself in this narrative. Don Miguel and his circle perceive both the contest and the book they publish as commodities that will bring both Mallorca, as an island, and themselves, as the contest sponsors, fame and recognition on the part of the mainland *patria*, Spain.

Other contest organizers were even more narrowly focused on personal gain. Don Bernardo Catalá de Valeriola (1568–1608) sponsored three contests. One celebrated his wife, one his tomb, and one his house.

116   Chapter Three

In a prologue to the volume he assembled from the resulting lyrics, Don Bernardo explains that his principal motivation for sponsoring the contests and gathering the lyrics to be printed "fue desear que los santos mis patrones que no pueden ser engrandecidos con mi pluma (por no ser Poeta) lo sean por las ajenas, que con dulzura, y destreza dicen a mi cuenta algunos loores . . ." (was that I desired that my patron saints, who cannot be praised with my pen (since I am not a Poet) are praised by the pens of others, who with sweetness and skill say praises on my behalf . . .).[59] The dedication to the volume does not mention his patron saints, however. Instead, Don Bernardo presents it to Don Francisco Gómez de Sandoval y Rojas, the powerful Duke of Lerma, in terms that underscore his serene lack of interest in the community he convened:

> Debese a los felices ingenios desta ciudad (que por mi devoción compitieron en estas Justas Poéticas) el premio de consagrar a Vuestra Excelencia sus trabajos, que es el galardón más crecido que se les puede dar. Este será para ellos único, y verdadero agradecimiento, y para mi gran gloria, pues publico, por este medio, el deseo que tengo de servir a Vuestra Excelencia, en cuya grandeza hallarán estas obras ajenas, la merecida protección, y la mia el acostumbrado favor y acogimiento.[60]

> (The happy wits of this city (who for the cause of my devotion competed in these Poetry Tournaments) well deserve the reward of having their work consecrated to Your Excellency, for this is the greatest prize that can be given them. This will be for them a unique and genuine pleasure, and for me a great glory, for I publish, by this means, the desire I have to serve Your Excellency, in whose grandeur these their works will find the protection they merit, and my own [work] the accustomed favor and acceptance.)

Accounts such as Don Miguel's and Don Bernardo's show us that the two distinct spheres inhabited by contest organizers and contest participants intersect where social and political worlds come up against each other. When they do, those in power have the ability to look away from the communities that sustain them. At the same time, there is no reason to discount or ignore what took place on the community side. The neighbors on Mallorca created a celebration in honor of a local saint, one whose body resides in their home space, on their island. Saint Teresa's celebrants marched, stood, and got too hot over the course of a long afternoon, and they were excited, eager, curious, and—crucially—tolerant. Guided by the festive atmosphere, they allowed themselves to be distracted from the potential annoyances posed by close proximity, celebrating instead a joyous community event.

The House Don Diego Built

What is Cervantes about, then, with his lyric allegories? What does he point us to with the ingenious fabrication that is Mercury's ship, with the teeming would-be Apollonians bobbing around in the Mediterranean, and with Don Diego and Doña Cristina, those thoughtful parents, living their peaceable, quiet lives in the Spanish countryside and raising their cheerful, confident, *letrado* son? What does *copia* reveal to us about the greater significance we might discover in these images and scenes?

In Cervantes's late writing, especially, poetry and song are especially tender sites for the negotiation of human existence and regimes of power. When people engage in the kinds of collective activity that the myth of Amphion describes, when they charm themselves or allow themselves to be charmed into position as willing collaborators in a larger civic project, that willingness itself is poetry's most valuable product. The power that human beings have to build working, harmonious collectives was, for Cervantes, miraculous. The misuse or abuse of that power was for Cervantes a sign of appalling corruption. Thus in the *Parnaso*, Cervantes lampoons would-be Don Bernardos, men who mistake the nature and purpose of poetry, and who enjoy positions of power and privilege that allow them to treat the lyre as a mechanism for the cultivation of status and fame harvested from the labor of others. In the satirical *Parnaso*, false poets—with their poverty of imagination regarding anything beyond their private interests, with their inflated and mistaken senses of their own skills, and with their lack of interest in turning what skills they do possess to productive social ends—pose obstacles to the smooth functioning of the Spanish state. At one point, Mercury is forced to jump from his galleon, grab a fishing net, and scoop them off the decks and hull so the ship can proceed through the churning water.[61]

In *Don Quixote, Part II*, the stakes are graver, since the Knight of the Green Coat episode highlights the political catastrophe that was the expulsion of the Moriscos, a process that reached its culmination in 1614. The expulsion subtends the novel, which raises continuous questions about kings, leadership, communities, and politics, from the prologue forward.[62] The climax of these ruminations appears in chapters 54 and 63, as the characters Ricote and Ana Félix recount, with compelling eloquence, their experiences in the wake of the edict. In the interest of securing the survival of his family, Ricote recalls, he buried the household valuables in a hidden spot before departing from his town. He did so under the gaze of his neighbors, a group that includes Sancho Panza, before setting off to explore Europe in search of a new place to establish a home. Ana Félix recounts the suffering and confusion she and her mother endured as two

118   Chapter Three

Christian women pressured by family and friends to travel to Morocco. Like their historical counterparts, Ana and her mother were forced to practice Islam despite their ignorance of Arabic, of Muslim culture, and of the religious faith of an Algeria that was for them an alien place. Ana's narrative is marked by pathos and also by Christian stereotypes. She describes *turcos* (Ottomans) who are wily and fickle. They pursue wealth and power in the interest of gratifying their opulent and sybaritic tastes, and Ana fears for the safety of her chaste and loyal suitor, the Christian Don Gaspar Gregorio, who draws the attention of a powerful Turkish man. She determines that her lover can best elude notice by disguising himself as a woman. This unsettling detail of Ana Félix's account underscores her identity as a conservative Spanish Christian. In this way, the scene points to what Cervantes viewed as the miserable irony of the expulsion of the Moriscos, a political intervention by which Spain rid itself of some its most loyal and successful inhabitants: men, women, and children such as the virtuous and pious Ana; the courageous, practical, and good-humored Ricote (first introduced as he extends hospitality to Sancho); and, before them, Don Diego and Doña Cristina, whom Cervantes skillfully introduces early in the novel, and who represent conscientious, circumspect, and hardworking Spanish subjects whose world is on the brink of disaster. Despite their devoted Catholic practice, despite their habit of keeping to themselves, despite the care with which they cultivate a virtuous life, and, finally, despite having raised a son whose dream is to labor in service to the empire, they may at any moment find themselves cast into the streets, subject to the same humiliation and dispossession suffered by Ricote and his family.[63]

What does *copia* reveal to us here? Sixteenth- and seventeenth-century lyric *copia* harbors the capacity to reveal "the most basic unit of social life . . . the most fundamental object of moral regard": the human person, as this person joins into community, and to create not only poems but sociality itself.[64] Against this backdrop, Amphion points us to the equally inescapable political fact of orators, politicians, and monarchs who enjoy the prerogative of deciding, at whim, whether to look at or look away from the communities they convene and inspire, to acknowledge or ignore the humanity of those communities' members. We can glean this information from a single text, for example, *Don Quixote, Part II*. It comes into vibrant presence when we sit attentively with great masses of verse and song, allowing their abundance to resonate with us.

Amphion in the Americas

[CHAPTER FOUR]

S'io avessi le rime aspre e choicce
come si converrebbe al tristo buco
sovra 'l qual potan tutte l'altre rocce . . .

(If I had the harsh and clacking rhymes such
as befit
the dreadful hole toward which all other
rocks point their weight . . .)

—DANTE, *Inferno*, Canto 32

Amphion shapes the colonial Spanish-American imaginary. From the beginning of the conquest of what sixteenth- and seventeenth-century Europeans refer to as a "new" world, the myth of Amphion provides figures, patterns, and what appears to be a heaven-sent narrative for a project that apologists represent as a modern epic achievement: the full-scale destruction of one world and its replacement by another.[1] *Musa lyrae sollers*—which, as we have seen, is both an active trope in the early modern imaginary and a descriptor for the work that lyric poetry performs for sixteenth- and seventeenth-century culture—contributes to the colonial project as well. It does so in two ways. Heaps of poems build up stacks of Spanish material, in the form of accumulations of poems. Moreover, world-obliterating and world-initiating speech acts such as the Treaty of Tordesillas (1494) and the Requerimiento (Requisition) issue from Amphion's lyre.[2] To the communities summoned to receive it, the Requerimiento was gibberish. Spanish conquistadores delivered it in advance of invasion and occupation; however, even as they cultivated native interpreters to communicate their words to the communities they addressed, the utterances were unintelligible. The Requerimiento invoked the authority of kings and queens, saints, the pope, "the Catholic faith." What might these words mean to people who have never encountered the Christian world? But this gibberish signaled the arrival of world-destroying force and mass extinction; of looting, rape, arson, murder, smallpox; of kin and community members inveigled and coerced to turn against each other. At the conclusion of the struggle, people were left to grope their way through spaces studded with settlements and cities from which they were thoroughly marginalized, landscapes that ceased to make sense to them, and in which they themselves no longer figured simply as human persons worthy of inclusion, dignity, and care.

120   Chapter Four

The *Cartas de relación* (Letters of relation) of Hernán Cortés set forth a methodical procedure of the razing of an existing world to allow for the construction of another. His narrative leads later writers to describe him in terms of Amphion. As scholars point out, the conquistador presented his mission in the Yucatán not as *rescate*, the barter and trade that captains and merchants had been carrying out in the Americas for decades, but *población* (settlement).[3] The first *Carta* opens in the collective voice of the city council of the newly founded Veracruz, which informs the monarch of what they have observed in their initial forays inland. The Yucatán is rife with cities, markets, and communities organized into political forms that lend themselves to conquest and control by a powerful monarch, even one who is as distant from Mexico as Charles V is: "[V]uestras majestades sepan la tierra que es, la gente que la posee y la manera de su vivir y el rito y ceremonias, secta o ley que tienen, y el feudo que en ella vuestras reales altezas podrán hacer y de ella podrán recibir." ([Y]our majesties will come to know what kind of land this is, the people who possess it, and their manner of living and the rites and ceremonies, the doctrine and the laws they have, and the fealty in which your majesties may hold it and gain from it.)[4] For this reason, Cortés's companions explain, they have taken it upon themselves to petition their captain, Cortés, to abandon the charge assigned him by Diego Velázquez and embark on a new project:

[L]e requerimos que luego se cesase de hacer rescates de la manera que los venía a hacer, porque sería destruir la tierra en mucha manera, y vuestras majestades serían en ello muy deservidos, y que así mismo lo pedíamos y requeríamos que luego nombrase para aquella villa que se había por nosotros de hacer y fundar, alcaldes y regidores en nombre de vuestras reales altezas.[5]

([W]e asked him to cease to barter in the manner we had come to undertake it, because that activity would destroy the land in many ways, and your majesties would be greatly disserved by that, and at the same time, we asked and petitioned him that he name mayors and magistrates, for this city he would create and found for us, to serve in the name of your royal majesties.)

As Margo Glantz observed long ago, in the *Cartas*, "poblar es fundar una ciudad" (to settle is to found a city).[6] Moreover, Cortés and his companions will build this city over one that already exists. Cortés describes the Yucatán as a place whose inhabitants organize themselves into orderly political units.[7] The *Cartas* emphasize this feature, which Cortés portrays as common to the Aztec empire, to the Tlaxcalans, and to the smaller city-states they encounter such as Chalchihuecan and Cempoal. When it comes to cities, the Yucatán, according to Cortés, is superior to Africa and rivals even Italy and Spain. Regarding the city of the Tlaxcalans, Cortés writes:

[E]s muy mayor de Granada y muy más fuerte y de tan buenos edificios y de muy mucha más gente que Granada tenía al tiempo que se ganó, y muy mucho mejor abastecida de las cosas de la tierra, que es de pan y de aves y caza y pescado de ríos y de otras legumbres y cosas que ellos comen muy buenas. Hay en esta ciudad un mercado en que casi cotidianamente todos los días hay en él treinta mil ánimas arriba. . . . Hay casas donde lavan las cabezas como barberos y las rapan; hay baños. Finalmente, que entre ellos hay toda manera de buena orden y policía, y es gente de toda razón y concierto, y tal que lo mejor de África no se le iguala.[8]

([I]t is much larger than Granada and much stronger, and with such good buildings and with many more people than Granada had at the time it was won, and it is by far better provisioned with products of the land, which is that of bread and fowl and game and river fish and other vegetables and things they eat, all very good. There is a market in this city in which nearly all day long, every day, there are upward of thirty thousand people. . . . There are houses like barber shops where they wash people's heads and shave them; there are bath houses. Finally, among them there is all manner of good order and protocol, and this is a people of reason and harmony, and one that is not matched by the best of Africa.)

Moreover, as Stephanie Merrim has observed, both Cortés and Bernal Díaz del Castillo, author of the 1575 *Historia verdadera de la conquista de Nueva España* (True history of the conquest of New Spain), pay as much attention to the systems of political authority they observe (or imagine they observe) at work on the peninsula as they do to the region's buildings. Merrim cites each writer's evident fascination with the supervision of the great market at Tenochtitlán. Here is Cortés, marveling at its sophistication:

Hay en esta gran plaza una gran casa como de audiencia, donde están siempre sentadas diez o doces personas que son jueces y libran todos los casos que en dicho mercado acaecen, y mandan castigar los delincuentes. Hay en la dicha plaza otras personas que andan continuo entre la gente, mirando lo que se vende y las medidas con que miden lo que venden; y se ha visto quebrar alguna que estaba falsa.[9]

122   Chapter Four

(In this great plaza there is a great hall that is like a court, where ten or twelve people are always on duty as judges, and they weigh all the cases that might arise in this market, and they order punishment for delinquents. There are other people in the plaza who walk among the people, watching what is sold and the measures used to weigh what they sell; and I saw one smashed when it was false.)

Johnson discusses the nature and stakes of a "reform" of description that early modern humanists undertook in the fifteenth and sixteenth centuries.[10] As Cortés picks out resemblances and differences, his discourse conforms to new representations that favor observation and comparison. In this instance, however, the rhetorical strategy of framing unfamiliar things by comparing them to known things opens the way for a violent disjuncture between life as it was lived on the ground in the Americas and the ideals and ideas Europeans had about the region. In the passage quoted above, Cortés shapes a constellation of commerce, space, and authority that conforms to the Renaissance ideal of how spaces might be planned to guide people into orderly and harmonious behavior—ideals many writers develop with reference to Amphion. Merrim identifies this aspect of Cortés's narrative strategy with Renaissance interest in the Greek idea of the polis. The repeated formula Cortés uses as he describes these cities (that they contain sophisticated buildings, are governed by laws, and have systems of authority in place to supervise human activity and uphold those laws) conform to Aristotle's theory of the structure.[11] However, Cortés's narration is motivated less by his desire to please humanists than it is by his desire to impress Charles V with the value of the Yucatán as spoils. Merrim describes the *Cartas* as framing a scriptural economy, "a record for rather than of." They "suggest the ready perfectibility of the Indians and offer them up as merchandise to be seized."[12]

Ángel Rama similarly describes the image of the Yucatán that Cortés and his company sent overseas as an example of the Foucauldian "ordered city," a society composed of linked, smoothly functioning sites for the generation, manufacture, circulation, and consumption of raw materials and products. The vision is simultaneously material—in that it is made up of actual buildings, streets, courts; judges, administrators, laborers, and consumers—and a product of Renaissance humanism and Neoplatonic abstractions.[13] In a well-known passage, Rama argues that humanist cultural and political reformers encountered obstacles to their attempts to remake European cities in terms of their interpretations of Plato and the ancients; that, moreover, as news of Spanish overseas discoveries circulated, they seized on the possibilities presented by a tabula rasa.[14] In this way, the Spanish-American "city"—urban centers as well as larger political units, such as the vice realm—is fundamentally paradoxical: it is a construct that is inspired by what Cortés perceives as the sophisticated civilization of the Yucatán (on the heels of Cortés, Francisco Pizarro and Diego de Almagro will write about Peru in similar terms), a civilization he deliberately destroys. Adding to the paradoxes, early modern discourse on the conquest and the building up of the colonial and vice-regal cities of the Americas presents these feats as accomplished both on the footprint and the remains of the vanquished civilization and, simultaneously, on "virgin" territory, in empty space.[15]

Amphion furnishes lyrical and rhetorical solutions to these contradictions. In a manner we began to examine in chapter 1, with respect to "To Penshurst," poets informed by Renaissance humanism drew on Amphionic music to harmonize exploitation and dispossession, weaving them into a greater vision of orderly, profitable life enjoyed by a benevolent ruling class or caste. In the "Epístola a Belardo" (1619?), the anonymous Peruvian "Amarílis" deploys lyric devices such as tone, rhythm, and rhyme to naturalize Spanish violence as a brief, distant episode that marked a moment of glory for Spain and cleared the way for the rise of a peaceable, if somewhat frivolous, Peru.

> En este imperio oculto que el Sur baña,
> más de Baco pisado que de Alcides,
> entre un trópico frío y otro ardiente,
> adónde fuerzas ínclitas de España
> con varios casos y continuas lides
> fama inmortal ganaron a su gente;
> donde Neptuno engasta su tridente
> en nácar y oro fino,
> cuando Pizarro con su flota vino,
> fundó ciudades y dejó memorias
> que eternas quedarán en las historias.[16]

(In this hidden empire, bathed on southern shores / traversed by Bacchus more than by Hercules, / between a cold tropic and the one that burns, / where the famed forces of Spain / in campaigns and continual battles / gained immortal fame for their people; / where Neptune plants his trident / in mother-of-pearl and fine gold, / where, when he arrived with his fleet, / Pizarro founded cities and left memories / that will live eternally in the stories of our history.)

Amarílis embeds this account of war, conquest, and settlement in a sea of classical metaphors, and she deploys an elaborate visual register of tropi-

124   Chapter Four

cal landscapes and glittering sea foam. The imagery and allusions support the poem's rich lyric music. The poem is composed in *estancias*, a Spanish song form that Renaissance writers adapted from Dantean and Petrarchan *canzone*. The form balances invention with regularity: a poet chooses a pattern of verses and a rhyme scheme of their own invention (here, hendecasyllables with one six-syllable line). Subsequent stanzas repeat the form. In the selection quoted above, enjambment between the eighth and the shortened ninth lines of the stanza is a particularly effective device with which to lead into Pizarro's arrival with his flotilla. Line ten ("cuando Pizarro con su flota vino") reasserts the tonic rhythm of the hendecasyllables as the stanza proceeds toward closure. The result is a smoothly flowing account of conquest, destruction, and rebuilding.[17]

Rhetorically, the myth of Amphion accommodates itself to messianic Christianity and contributes to a discourse that opens the way for defenses of the conquest and destruction of civilizations. Monarchs in England, France, and Spain incorporate Christianity into their projects of imperium. For example, François I promotes himself as the "Most Christian King," Henry VIII declares himself the Supreme Head of the Church of England, and Charles V of Hapsburg Spain exercises his authority and privilege as both the Spanish monarch and the Holy Roman emperor. Spain casts violence as a necessary phase in a divinely willed plan of salvation for the Americas. Bernardo de Balbuena (ca. 1562–1627) draws an explicit connection between Christian conquest and the myths of Amphion and Thebes. In a prefatory letter to his 1604 paean to Mexico, *La grandeza mexicana* (The grandeur of Mexico), the bishop draws connections between Cortés and Amphion, between Mexico and

> . . . Tebas, edificio y fundación de Cadmo y unos pocos compañeros suyos, y después ampliada y fortalecida por el músico Anfión, quien a fuerza de la suavidad de su arpa la ennobleció de muros y edificios . . . en que quedó hecho un retrato a esta gran ciudad de México, fundada como de nuevo por el valeroso Hernán Cortés . . .[18]

> (. . . Thebes, built and founded by Cadmus and a few of his companions, and later amplified and fortified by the musician Amphion, who by means of the sweetness of his harp ennobled it with walls and buildings . . . this is the very portrait of the great city of Mexico, founded as if anew by the valiant Hernán Cortés . . .)

Cadmus enables Balbuena to harmonize Thebes with biblical logic here. Thebes's initial founder, Cadmus, created the city by sowing the teeth of Mars's dragon. At the end of his human life, he and his wife were transformed into snakes.[19] Because the myth is rife with serpents, it is easy to adapt it to Christian ends. Mars's dragon draws in soldiers and armies. Furthermore, Balbuena, who in his youth received a strong humanist education, extends the conceit by drawing on Renaissance theories of architecture. Thus he presents Cortés as accomplishing a twofold Amphionic intervention in the Yucatán. The conquistador routs the legacies of the serpent from the territory (legacies present in the form of un-Christian lives lived by the region's inhabitants). He creates a new city with a building program that conforms to Neoplatonic Christian principles, in that it guides inhabitants to behave in ways that reflect God's designs. In the same prefatory letter, Balbuena explains:

> Y habiendo muerto la serpiente de la idolatría de aquellos mismos dientes que le quitaron, esto es, de sus ritos y fuerzas bárbaras, renacieron hombres nuevos en la fuente del bautismo, con que quedó mejorada en todo, creciendo después sus edificios y calles tan por orden y compás, que más parecen puesta por concierto y armonía de música que a plomo y machinas de arquitectos.[20]

> (And the serpent of idolatry having died by those same teeth he removed, that is, from the rites and barbaric forces, new men were born again in the baptismal font, with which all was improved everywhere, and its buildings and streets grew up with such good order that they seem to be placed by the concert and harmony of music [rather] than by the plumb line and architectural machines.)

While Balbuena describes Mexico as having been liberated from idolatrous practices of one sort, the city is rooted in another powerful fault line—the greed that inspires the city's prodigious growth:

> . . . sordo ruido y tráfago entretiene
> el contratar y aquel bullirse todo
> que nadie un punto de sosiego tiene.

> Por todas partes la codicia a rodo
> que ya cuanto se trata y se practica
> el interés de un modo de otro modo.

> Éste es el Sol que al mundo vivifica,
> quien lo conserva, rige y acrecienta,
> lo ampara, lo defiende y fortifica.

> . . . .

126 Chapter Four

> Si unos a otros se ayudan y obedecen,
> y en esta trabazón y engace humano
> los hombres con su mundo permanecen,
>
> el goloso interés les da la mano,
> refuerza el gusto y acrecienta el brío,
> y con el suyo hace todo llano
> . . . .
> Pues esta oculta fuerza, fuente viva
> de la vida política, y aliento
> que al más tibio y helado pecho aviva,
>
> entre otros bienes suyos dio el asiento
> a esta insigne ciudad en sierras de agua,
> y en su edifico abrió el primer cimiento.
>
> Y así cuanto el ingenio humano fragua,
> alcanza el arte y el deseo platica
> en ella y su laguna se desagua
> y la vuelve agradable, ilustre y rica.[21]

(. . . the distracting, deafening noise and clatter / the trade and that constant ferment / such that no one has a moment's peace. // Avarice seeps in on all sides and everywhere / for anything anyone says or does / is motivated by interest in one way or another. // This is the Sun that gives life to the world, / that preserves it, governs it and makes it grow, / that supports it, defends it and fortifies it. // . . . // If people help and obey each other, / and through this bond this human collective / establishes permanence for itself and its world, // greedy self-interest that gives it a helping hand, / it reinforces people's zest and redoubles their energy, / and smooths the way. // . . . // It is thus that this hidden force, the wellspring / of political life, and the breath / that animates the most lukewarm or icy breast, // among the gifts it confers, established the seat / of this great city in this watery wilderness, / and laid the first foundations for its construction. // And thus, everything human ingenuity can devise, / all arts and all desires conjoin there, / and they drain the lagoon, / and make it pleasant, illustrious, and prosperous.)

Codicia (greed) and *interés* (self-interest) establish foundations for the Spanish-American enterprise in a particular kind of original sin. People in the Americas and abroad recognized the unreconcilable conflict between Christianity and the extractive engine—what Balbuena calls the "máquina soberbia"—the Spanish set to work building in the Americas. Balbuena's allegories provide cover for the corrupt motivations of the enterprise by harmonizing them with a Christian doctrine in which all structures in this earthly world are tainted by sin. Furthermore, this normalized situation of corruption justifies the continuous political activity and the occasional outbreak of necessary, purging violence. Balbuena folds an authoritarian administrative structure into the elements he praises:

> Quitad a este gigante el señorío
> y las leyes que ha impuesto a los mortales,
> volveréis su concierto en desvarío.
>
> Caerse han las columnas principales
> sobre el mundo y su grandeza estriba,
> y en confusión serán todos iguales.[22]

(Free this giant from its master / and from the laws rule imposes on mortals, / and you will turn harmony to dissonance. // The principal columns / supporting its grandeur will tumble to earth, / and all will be leveled in the confusion.)

Concierto, although a divine gift, is implemented by means of authoritarian rule in a city descended from Thebes. In this way, these stanzas reiterate the eternal justification for empire: violent intervention in the "structures, sensibilities, and things"[23] that compose one people's world is a beneficial act. A conquering power carries out such projects motivated by the desire to order and contain humanity's worst appetites, channeling pagan, primitive energies to the service of productive civilization.

For Balbuena, and for a host of Spanish and *criollo* writers of the period, the myth of Amphion, with its associations to Mercury and Thebes, is uniquely suited to harmonize the event that is the creation of Spanish America. Thus, this is a chapter about Amphionic music. Moreover, it is a chapter about music of a specific kind: the music of ruination, the ongoing process that conquest and colonization set in motion in a "political project that lays waste to certain peoples and places, relations, and things."[24] The ruination in question is unleashed by the Requerimiento, an utterance that, once it is delivered, drags the existing world into the hellish pit Dante describes in canto 32 of the *Inferno*: "that dreadful hole toward which all other rocks point their weight."[25] Dante is relevant to the Spanish-American imperial formations on a number of levels. Spanish and *criollo* writers identified a hollowness in the cities and the cultures they were working to build up, and Dante featured prominently among

128 **Chapter Four**

the poetic resources they drew on as they worked to anchor those structures more securely. Terza rima, Dantean cantos, brought prestige and the binding, anchoring power of poetic language, well-devised and crafted, stacked in massy columns, to bear on the work of setting foundations for Spain's new polities. That Dante was ambivalent about earthly cities only enhanced his value as a resource for these writers. They incorporated his themes of avarice, corruption, and destruction into a teleology that foretold the redemptive power of Spanish Hapsburg violence. As a result, at the levels of both form and content, Dante's poetry is firmly incorporated into the foundations of the Spanish-American imperial formation.

Dante also furnishes a poetics for the music of ruination, however, and he attributes it to Amphion's lyre. As he embarks on creating the nightmarish scenes of civic and social breakdown in canto 32, Dante's speaker calls on Amphion's muses—here, the goddesses are not Horace's cheery *musa lyrae sollers*, but ladies who inspire rough noise and senselessness:

> S'io avessi le rime aspre e chiocce
> come si converrebbe al tristo buco
> sovra 'l qual pontina tutte l'altre rocce,
> io premerei di mio concetto il suco
> più pienamente; ma perch'io non l'abbo,
> non sanza tema a dicer mi conduco . . .
>
> Ma quelle donne aiutino il mio verso
> ch'aiutaro Anfione a chiuder Tebe,
> sì dal fatto il dir non sia diverso.

> (If I had harsh and clacking rhymes such as befit the dreadful hole toward which all other rocks point their weight, / I would press the juice from my concept more fully; but because I lack them, not without fear do I bring myself to speak . . . // But let those ladies aid my verse who helped Amphion enclose Thebes, so that the word may not be different from the fact.)[26]

This description of infernal music captures the world-ending hell of wars,[27] which not only crush buildings, destroy infrastructures, kill and maim people, and lay waste to environments, but attack the semantic fields in which metaphors and rhythms generate meaning, draining language (*verba*) of its poetry, substance, and resources (*res*). Sustained attacks on language, as a fundamental component of the imaginary envelopes that tether us to our worlds, are a consistent feature of the exercise of imperial power. In the second part of this chapter, I analyze the Amphionic music of Raúl Zurita's Dantean poetry. Like the *Inferno*, collections such as *Purgatorio* (1979), *Anteparaíso* (1982), and *La vida nueva* (1994), and poems such as "Canto a su amor desaparecido" (Song for his disappeared love; 1985) give lyric form to a catastrophic civic and social breakdown. Ruination and the continuous present that is the temporality of an imperial formation furnish a generative context through which to read further into Zurita's Dantean, Amphionic poetics.[28]

Amphion in the Yucatán

The *Cartas* of Cortés are Amphionic from the start. By design or simply because Amphion and the Amphionic are important structuring tropes within the sixteenth-century imperialist imaginary, the twin, unmovable piers that anchor Cortés's account are the ravaging of one great polis and the construction of another, which the Spanish raise on the old city's smoking ruins. Additional elements of the *Cartas* contribute to their Amphionic tenor as well. Cortés recounts his skillful speeches in encounters with leaders and populations, and he describes his thinking as he decides where to speak sweetly and where firmly; when to charm and when to threaten. Furthermore, he exhibits a keen awareness of the power of internecine strife, which he exploits as he makes his way through the peninsula. Regarding the Tlaxcalans and communities allied with Montezuma, he writes:

> Vista la discordia y desconformidad de los unos y de los otros, no hube poco placer, porque me pareció hacer mucho a mi propósito, y que podría tener manera de más aína sojuzgarlos . . . y con los unos y con los otros maneaba y a cada uno en secreto le agradecía el aviso que me daba, y le daba crédito de más amistad que al otro.[29]

> (Seeing the discord and the lack of agreement between them, I took no small pleasure, because it seemed to me to work to my ends, and that contained a way of subjecting them more quickly . . . and I gladhanded one and the other, and in secret, I thanked them for the warnings they gave me, and I told them that they were truer friends than the others.)

Amphion also furnishes Cortés with lyric devices that shape his rhetoric. Merrim calls attention to the anaphoristic structures of repetition that Cortés deploys as he describes markets and great cities, presented in recitations he structures with sentences that open with words such as "tenían" (they had), "hay" (there are), and "venden" (they sell).[30] The rhythm this pattern inscribes accomplishes two ends: it supports Cortés's larger claim that the civilizations encountered on the Yucatán are marvels

130   Chapter Four

of harmony and order (orden y concierto), and it contributes to the gathering momentum of what the *Cartas* present as destiny, in the form of God's will—the conquest of the Aztec empire and the undoing of their religion and their society. Cortés employs a number of devices to support this momentum. He punctuates his narrative of the journey toward Tenochtitlán with periodic accounts of visits from emissaries of Montezuma, who meet him on his way bearing requests that he not enter the city.[31] He also presents his replies: "Yo les respondí que la ida a su tierra no se podia excusar" (I replied that the journey to their land could not be avoided);[32] "Yo les respondí que si en mi mano fuera volverme que yo lo hiciese por hacer placer a Mutezuma; pero que he había venido en esta tierra por mandado de vuestra majestad" (I replied that if it were in my hands to turn back I would do so to please Montezuma; but that I had come to this land on orders from your majesty).[33] These exchanges take on a rhythmic character and a formulaic quality found in epic and ballad. As in those forms, repetition assists in accommodating readers to the *Cartas'* ethos, which is Amphionic. In this way, Cortés's narration naturalizes what comes next: Montezuma's imprisonment under house arrest; the toppling of the Aztec gods and the desecration of their holy sites; the quashing of desperate rebellions; the burning of homes; the destruction of the Aztec world. Notably, whereas the *Cartas* open with a case for settlement as a way of putting a stop to the destruction wrought by *rescate*, the conquest of the Yucatán unleashes destruction on an exponentially greater scale than what might be accomplished by individual raids.

The difference, as Cortés develops it, is divine inspiration. Even at its most brutal, Spanish murder, annihilation, and plunder take place under the sign of providence, and Cortés frequently presents himself as an intermediary. A striking example is his account of the destruction of Montezuma's aviaries, an act of violence whose excess Cortés openly acknowledges, and which he justifies by explaining that his purpose is to instruct:

> ... [V]iendo que estos de la ciudad estaban rebeldes y mostraban tanta determinación de morir o defenderse ... que daban ocasión y nos forzaban a que totalmente les destruyésemos. Y de esta postrera tenía más sentimiento y me pesaba el alma, y pensaba qué forma tenía para los atemorizar de manera que viniesen en conocimiento de su yerro y del daño que podían recibir de nosotros, y no hacía sino quemarles y derrocarles las torres de sus ídolos y sus casas. Y porque lo sintiesen más, este día hice poner fuego a estas casas grandes de la plaza, donde la otra vez que nos echaron de la ciudad los españoles y yo estábamos aposentados ... y otras que estaban junto a ellas, que aunque algo menores eran muy más frescas y gentiles, y tenía en ellas Mutezuma todos los linajes de aves que en estas partes

Amphion in the Americas   131

había; y aunque a mí me pesó mucho de ello, porque a ellos les pesaba mucho más, determiné de las quemar, de que los enemigos mostraron harto pesar y también los otros sus aliados de las ciudades de la laguna.[34]

(. . . [S]eeing that the inhabitants of the city were in revolt and showed such determination to die or defend themselves . . . they created the circumstances that would force us to destroy them completely. And I felt this last item greatly, and it weighed on my soul, and I pondered what forms of action I had at my disposal to frighten them in such a way that they would come into awareness of their errors and of the harm they might receive from us, something beyond just tearing down the great towers of their idols and burning their houses. And to increase their suffering, on that day I set fire to the great houses on the plaza, those where the Spanish soldiers and I were lodged the first time they routed us from the city . . . and to others next to them, which although somewhat smaller were quite cool and well-appointed, and in which Montezuma housed all the species of birds that are found in this area; and although the act weighed on me greatly, because it would weigh on them much more, I determined to burn them, at which our enemies showed great sorrow, as did their allies in the cities along the lagoon.)

In Cortés's telling, this scene of merciless destruction is engineered. It is a sign he devises to instruct the remaining inhabitants of Tenochtitlán that the Aztec world has reached its end of days. Such a message can only be communicated successfully by means of excruciating anguish, which Cortés inspires in all present with the gruesome spectacle of the incineration of the Aztecs' vibrant, tuneful patrimony. In keeping with his self-styled role as divine messenger, Cortés refers consistently to the goodwill he bears toward those whose communities, homes, and sacred sites he destroys, even in the final weeks of struggle. He is an empathic agent of God's will, effective because he has come to know these people, and thus how to terrorize them. But Cortés reports that he attended mass before carrying out the day's activities.

A subtext of the *Cartas*, then, is a detailed account of a perverse remaking of the Yucatán Peninsula, from a living place—an intelligible world and its inhabitants—into a nonsensical site in which existence is interrupted at whim by a deliberate, sociopathic violence. This dimension of the *Cartas* has been examined before on numerous occasions. What has not been brought to bear on Cortés's rhetoric is the myth of Amphion, but both the king and Thebes provide an important conceptual frame that serves the Spanish as they seek to harmonize their practices of systematic dispossession, enslavement, and massacre with a Christian world-

132   **Chapter Four**

view. A Christianized Thebes frames these actions as both fated and merciful. Moreover, the myth of Amphion smooths the way for an enthusiastic creation of a Spanish-American city that is more than a string of markets. Alongside these commercial centers, Europeans and *criollos* build up a culture that is animated not only by greed but also by a civilizational mission. However, the myth presents this new city and culture as constructed miraculously, by means of music and the will of Heaven. And in the Americas, the myth of Amphion contributes to the invisibility of the human toil that was required, both to construct the Spanish-American city and to maintain its new inhabitants. Yet at the end of the third letter, Cortés makes clear that self-sufficiency is simply unthinkable from the standpoint of the Spanish. He expresses his dismay at having to force the Aztecs, who in his view are nobler than the inhabitants of other regions of the Americas, to serve the needs of Spanish settlers. He would prefer to draw on populations from "the other islands," but none are available, and "cesando eso, los conquistadores y pobladores de estas partes no se podían sustentar" (if I cease this practice, the conquistadores and settlers of these parts will not be able to support themselves).[35]

This constellation of conditions—that conquest and settlement are intertwined so thoroughly with the generation of images composed for distant audiences; the necessity of justifying and harmonizing the destruction of worlds; and the equally fundamental necessity of rendering the inhabitants of those worlds as invisible sources of labor—illustrates Jacques Rancière's claim that politics is an aesthetic practice, a human appropriation of the power of world-making, in the form of the "distribution and redistribution of places and identities . . . [the] apportioning and reapportioning of spaces and times, of the visible and the invisible, and of noise and speech."[36] *Criollos* benefit from this system, but they are subjected and transformed by it as well. As José Antonio Mazzotti explains, the term *criollo* has a history before the conquest, but by the mid-1500s, it begins to refer predominantly to American-born people of Spanish descent. Furthermore, though ancestry plays a significant role in the designation *criollo*, the term also comes to refer to a cultural role and a relationship to power configured by the Spanish imperial formation, an example of empire's process of granting "deferred autonomy, meted out to particular populations incrementally."[37] Mazzotti identifies the *criollo* with "un sentimiento de pertenencia a la tierra y un afán de señorío" (a sense of belonging and an ambition to participate in the dominant ranks of society).[38] While such ambitions were frequently derailed and deferred, in keeping with the imperial logic of deferred and partial sovereignties, *criollo* writers examined in this section took it upon themselves to build a prestigious and learned city of letters, thereby anchoring their "Antarctic" world in a global social, political, and cultural imaginary. They employed various means to build this city, from assembling compendia of knowledges, poetry anthologies, and miscellanies; to creating festivals and poetry contests of the kinds discussed in chapter 3; to lobbying for recognition from peninsular Spanish authorities and cultural elites. Amphion lyric played a role in these efforts, as we have already begun to see through the "Epístola" of Amarílis. In the opening stanzas of the *Discurso en loor de la poesía* (1602), Clarinda, whom we met in the introduction to this book, summons her "southern" Muses to join familiar figures from the Renaissance humanist lyric tradition in the defense of poetry:

> La mano y el favor de la Cirene,
> a quien Apolo amó con amor tierno,
> y el agua consagrada de Hipocrene,
>
> y aquella lira con que del averno
> Orfeo libertó su dulce esposa,
> suspendiendo las furias del infierno,
>
> la célebre armonía milagrosa
> de aquel cuyo testudo pudo tanto
> que dio muralla a Tebas la famosa
> . . . .
> Aquí, ninfas del Sur, venid ligeras;
> pues que soy la primera que os implore
> dadme vuestro socorro las primeras;
>
> y vosotras, pimpleides, cuyo coro
> habita en Helicón, dad largo el paso
> y abrid en mi favor vuestro tesoro . . .[39]

(The hand and the favor of Cirene, / whom Apollo loved so tenderly, / and the sacred waters of Hippocrene, // and that lyre with which Orpheus freed / his sweet wife from the caves of Avernus, / suspending the furies of hell, // the celebrated miraculous harmonies / of he whose lyre was so powerful / that it gave walls to famous Thebes, // . . . // And come here, fleet nymphs of the South, / as I am the first to implore you / give me the first fruits of your aid; // and you, Pimpleides, whose chorus / dwells in Helicon, make the journey / and open your treasury for my benefit . . .)

The *Discurso en loor de la poesía* was published as the introduction to Diego Mexía de Fernangil's translation of selected lyrics from Ovid (the *Pri-*

134　Chapter Four

mera parte del Parnaso Antártico de obras amatorias [First part of the Antarctic Parnassus of the art of love], 1608). As a part of the volume, the poem contributed to the project of building up a culture of humanist letters and knowledge in the region. But the poem is also in its own right an example of Amphionic lyric directed specifically at the construction of the Spanish-American city. It is a massive composition of over eight hundred stanzas of terza rima, in which Clarinda draws ancient Greek and Roman poetic traditions, biblical tradition, the canons of Italian and peninsular Spanish poets, and the emerging poets of her own "southern" realm into a single, harmonious edifice. Clarinda calls to the Muses to help her accomplish her ends; however, Dante—and behind him, Amphion—provide both the structure (stacks of tercets) and the support for Clarinda's globalizing project. Dantean *canto* and terza rima confer humanist prestige on the *Discurso*; moreover, the lyric form once mediated between Hell, Purgatory, Earth, and Heaven. By setting her own poem in Dante's privileged form, Clarinda draws on the divine powers of music and the specifically Christian force of Dantean lyric as she creates a structure that gathers the Northern and Southern Hemispheres together into a harmonious whole.

Les Antiquitez de Thèbes

The most thoroughly developed Amphionic vision of the Spanish Americas, however, is *La grandeza mexicana*. A poem of roughly 650 stanzas, divided into nine chapters (*capítulos*) of varying length. Balbuena composes the poem in hendecasyllabic tercets of terza rima, although he uses quatrains to conclude each chapter.

La grandeza mexicana is simultaneously ordered and disordered. It is a massive heap of material: of language, and of language that points, moreover, to vast proliferations of things—of flora, fauna, goods, vehicles, persons, motivations, professions—all introduced in cascading lists. The lines that present these lists are barely intelligible, so burgeoning are they with nouns. Mexico is surrounded by

> . . . lejos y paisajes
> salidas, recreaciones y holguras,
> huertas, granjas, molinos y boscajes,
>
> alamedas, jardines, espesuras
> de varias plantas y de frutas bellas
> en flor, en cierne, en leche, ya maduras . . .[40]

(. . . vistas and landscapes / excursions, entertainments and delights, / orchards, farms, mills and glades, // groves, gardens, thickets / with a variety of plants and beautiful fruits / in flower, in bud, in their fullness, now ripe . . .)

It is peopled with

. . . hombres varios de varios pensamientos,
arrieros, oficiales, contratantes,
cachopines, soldados, mercaderes,
galanes, caballeros, pleiteantes;

clérigos, frailes, hombres y mujeres,
de diversa color y profesiones,
de vario estado y varios pareceres . . .[41]

(. . . various kinds of men with various thoughts, / muleteers, officials, tradesmen, / Spanish immigrants, soldiers, merchants, / gallants, knights, petitioners; // clerics, friars, men and women, / of diverse colors and professions, / of varying status and various appearances . . .)

They travel about in

[r]ecuas, carros, carretas, carretones,
de plata, oro, riquezas, bastimentos
salen, y entran a montones . . .[42]

([t]eams, carts, wagons, carriages, / laden with silver, gold, riches, supplies / exit and enter in great numbers . . .)

Emulating Amphion, however, Balbuena works to order the contents of the place he conjures, using lines, stanzas, and chapters devoted to specific topics: "De la famosa México el asiento" (Of where famed Mexico is situated); "Origen y grandeza de edificios" (On the origins and the grandeur of its buildings); "Caballos, calles, trato, cumplimento" (Horses, streets, manners, etiquette), et cetera. In this way, he shapes this teeming site of natural wonder and prodigious manufacture into a city.

Yet despite these measures, *copia* threatens language's semantic function. For example, the title of chapter 2, "Origen y grandeza de edificios," suggests that what follows will explain to readers curious about Mexico what kinds of buildings they will find there. But as Rodrigo Cacho Casal

136   **Chapter Four**

shows, the rich, varied, and highly technical vocabulary that Balbuena employs in these stanzas often fails to correspond to an actual structure.[43] Rather, the bishop appears to select and arrange words based on their musicality, and perhaps on the prestige of the source. Cacho Casal notes that much of the vocabulary in this section is drawn from Vitruvius; moreover, some of the terms are sufficiently recondite to stymie editors of the poem, who explain them with the simple designation, "an architectural term":[44]

> Suben las torres, cuya cumbre amaga
> a vencer de las nubes el altura
> y que la vista en ellas se deshaga.
>
> Las portadas cubiertas de escultura,
> obra sutil, riquísimo tesoro
> del coríntio primor y su ternura,
>
> los anchos frisios de relieves de oro
> istriados, triglifos y metopas,
> que en orden suben la obra y dan decoro . . .

(Its towers rise, whose peaks threaten / to conquer the clouds in their height / and which are lost from sight. // Their doors all over sculpted, / subtle work, a most valuable treasury / of Corinthian charm and tenderness, // the wide friezes with golden reliefs / engraved, triglyphs and metopes / ordered in such a way that they build up the work and furnish elegance . . .)

Later stanzas add to the delirium of objects:

> Jonio, coríntio, dórico compuesto,
> mosaico antiguo, áspero toscano
> y lo que falta aquí si más hay que esto.
>
> Oh ciudad bella, pueblo cortesano,
> primor del mundo, traza peregrina,
> grandeza ilustre, lustre soberano . . .

(Ionic, Corinthian, Doric, all composed, / ancient mosaic, Tuscan roughness / and anything else one might want, if more exists than all of this. // Oh beautiful city, gracious place, / ornament of the world, fleeting sign, / shining monument, sovereign beacon . . .)

Although it seems likely that Balbuena understood the technical definitions of the words he uses, they do not make sense in the context in which he uses them.[45] Cacho Casal refers to them as "Vitruvian collage."[46] Indeed, baroque art is intended to overwhelm viewers and readers, thereby instilling a sense of the glory, the mystery, and the power of the Christian God. Spanish Golden Age poetry carries out this task by working imagery, syntax, and music to achieve spectacular verbal effects, among them, the proliferation and excess that characterizes the burgeoning lines and stanzas of *La grandeza mexicana*.[47]

Baroque aesthetics and Counter-Reformation Spanish Christian doctrine do not entirely account for the design and execution of *La grandeza mexicana*, though. Balbuena's introductory remarks about Cortés, Amphion, and Thebes reveal his principal ambition, which was to create a lyric poem that would accomplish in language what Cortés accomplished with arms and stone. Of course, the "accomplishment" that Balbuena describes in his poem is tailored to the bishop's ends. The greatest feat of the conquest, in *La grandeza mexicana*, is a matter of containment and organization. Balbuena's lines and stanzas become poetic warehouses that store the products of proliferating abundance, the contents of the Mexican world. Lyric form is the material and the device by which to build these warehouses: great quantities of hendecasyllables, stacks of tercets.

The poem builds up, but Balbuena also seeks to lay foundations. Like Clarinda and fellow *criollo* writers, he recognizes the weak foundations of a Spanish-American city raised on terrain only recently occupied by Spain, and occupied, moreover, by means and with motivations that are morally and spiritually compromised. Balbuena addresses himself to this problem in two ways. He contributes materially to Spanish-American lyric presence by writing poems: *La grandeza mexicana*; a later pastoral, titled *Siglo de oro en las selvas de Erífile* (1608); as well as allegories, glosses, and sonnets that he contributes to festivals and poetry contests. He is also attentive to the significance of the worlding I discussed in chapter 1; that is, to the cultivation of a multifarious, textured discourse of belonging to a place or a site by creating physical and symbolic relationships with it. Casting Cortés as Amphion and Mexico as Thebes is this kind of gesture, as is using the myths of Cadmus, Thebes, and Amphion as the framework that gives meaning and sense to his decision to write a poem in celebration of a Mexican city. This work develops a mythography for Mexico that will anchor it more firmly in the Spanish imaginary.

Balbuena's Amphionic project makes resonant reading when we hold it next to Du Bellay's imperial poetics. Du Bellay addresses himself to the twin conundrums that lost Roman grandeur presents to an imperium-

138 Chapter Four

minded Renaissance humanist: Roman buildings do not mean what they once meant, and neither does Roman writing. In the *Antiquitez*, Du Bellay addresses this problem by transforming the debris left behind by ancient Roman civilization into "ruins" that serve as signs of imminent Valois imperium.[48] Allegorist Balbuena also presents Mexico as a sign. But the city is different. It is Thebes, not Rome. Thus the sign points to something different as well: the power of the Christian God, who has created Mexico as abundant, wondrous, and yet corrupt, and who appoints Spanish Hapsburg monarchs and their agents to redeem it, first through destruction, and then by means of orderly rebuilding and attentive supervision. Balbuena introduces the idea of signs again in the extended final chapter of *La grandeza mexicana*, which he titles "Todo en este discurso está cifrado" (Everything in this discourse is a cipher). This mythography takes the story of Thebes as its point of departure, as we have seen; and it incorporates Spanish power as one essential component of the Mexican world. Consistent with a city modeled on Thebes and not Rome, however, Balbuena's Mexico feeds on its inhabitants. In place of Du Bellay's abstractions and logic of sublimation, *La grandeza mexicana* incorporates the processes by which the Spanish imperial formation consumed human labor, the products of human effort, and, in the case of a large swath of the region's human inhabitants, human bodies, according to a perverse calculus that determined the relative value and expendability of human life.[49] Thus, on one hand, Balbuena portrays a Mexican city that burgeons with people. Early stanzas of *La grandeza mexicana* describe the many kinds of people who circulate through the city: "De varia traza y varios movimientos, / varias figuras, rostros y semblantes // . . . // diferentes en lenguas y naciones / . . . y aun a veces en leyes y opiniones" (Of various form and various gaits, / of varying figure, faces and appearances // . . . // different languages and nations / . . . and even at times laws and opinions).[50] The scintillating variety exhibited by the crowds accords with the baroque aesthetic appreciation for wondrous physiological differences, but it was also the case that Mexico was a hub of international trade. A subtext of these lines is thus economic profit from the commercial activity these people of different languages, nations, and customs carried out as they traveled through Mexico and on through the empire. The panoply also deflects attention from the fundamental source of Mexico's vibrancy, which are the populations of coerced and enslaved and people whose lives and well-being fall outside the purview of the cosmopolitan vision. *La grandeza mexicana* furnishes a glimpse of this life in the introduction to the poem, which is to say, in the poem proper's margins, where Balbuena describes Mexico's location as a remote western Indies:

Amphion in the Americas 139

[P]arece que la naturaleza, cansada de dilatarse en tierras tan fragosas y destempladas, no quiso hacer más mundo, sino que alzándose con aquel pedazo de suelo lo dejó ocioso y vacío de gente, dispuesto a solas las inclemencias del cielo y la jurisdicción de unas yermas y espantosas soledades, en cuyas desiertas costas y abrasados arenales a sus solas resurta y quiebre con melancólicas intercadencias la resaca y tumbos de mar, que sin oírse otro aliento y voz humana por aquellas sordas playas y carcomidas rocas suenas. O cuando mucho se ve coronar el peinado risco de un monte con la temerosa imagen y espantosa figura de algún indio salvaje, que en suelta y negra cabellera con presto arco y ligeras flechas, a quien él en velocidad excede, sale a caza de alguna fiera menos intratable y feroz que el ánimo que le sigue.[51]

([I]t seems as if nature, having tired of lingering so long in such harsh and pitiless lands, did not want to create any more world; rather, she raised up that piece of land and left it idle and empty of people, suited only to the bouts of weather and governed by barren, lonely reaches, on whose deserted coasts and burning sands resound the rise and fall of waves with a melancholy cadence; and no other breath or human voice sounds out through those deaf beaches and crumbling rocks. Or, ofttimes, as the fearsome image and frightening figure of some savage *indio*, who, his black hair loose, with his quick bow and those swift arrows whose velocity he himself outstrips, is seen to crown a bare mountain cliff, as he sets out to hunt some beast less wild and fierce than the soul who pursues it.)

Excluded from the cities that were imposed on them, Mexico's Indigenous inhabitants were rendered vulnerable not only to sin (as in the Christian allegory), but to the spectrum of exploitation and extractive practices that fueled the Spanish-American colonial enterprise. At the simplest level of Balbuena's allegory, the misnomer "*indio*" points to the error and sin that lie in wait to ensnare any unwary persons who might venture forth from the Christian city. Yet what for Balbuena and his intended readers is a picturesque detail points to the torturous moral and political logics by which Mexico's surviving Indigenous populations were forced into labor and service. Apologists for colonialism and slavery defended the practice on the grounds that it saved the souls of non-Christians. Through baptism and instruction in the Christian faith, Christian Europe's others would be spared future suffering in the tortures of hell. In the present, the label *indio* creates a category of invisible people in the Americas. Spanish and *criollo* subjects, residents of the imperial city, consumed their labor and their bodies as a matter of course in the polis that is the Spanish Americas.

140   Chapter Four

Theban Formations

Formally, at the level of content, and also through a network of intertextual allusions, Amphion and Dante play active roles in the colonial Spanish-American imaginary. Both within that imaginary and physically, via the writing that circulates in printed and manuscript form to justify and celebrate Spain's growing American cities, they contribute to an imperial formation that prioritizes economics over the well-being of human persons and communities, and issues "promissory notes" for sovereignty, autonomy, and grace to be enjoyed in the future.[52] In the present, the lot of the targets of the colonizing power's appetites is ruination, the ongoing grinding process of disrupting lives and laying waste to spaces and landscapes in the interest of greater needs on the part of the empire, nation, or state.[53]

Experiences of ruination are variously acute and subtle, active or dormant. Stoler writes, "Imperial effects occupy multiple historical tenses. They are at once products of the past imperfect that selectively permeate the present as they shape both the conditional subjunctive and uncertain futures."[54] The temporality of formation now carries this chapter from the conquest to the persistence of its structure in the regime imposed by the Pinochet government in Chile, in the 1970s and 1980s. Here, too, the poet Raúl Zurita uses Dante to give form and substance to conditions of radical, violent unworlding brought about by civil war. The *Divina commedia* and especially the *Inferno* furnish Zurita with poetic models for rendering hellscapes in language. Moreover, the language Zurita shapes is composed of *rime aspre e chiocce*, the "harsh and clacking rhymes" Amphion's muses inspire as the music that represents a world drained of *res* (meaning).

Zurita's poetry is shaped by the explosion of *codicia* and *interés* that takes place in the Americas from the middle of the twentieth century forward. In the countries and communities he represents in his lyrics, totalitarian regimes backed by sponsors abroad—notably, the United States—seize control and embark on massive social and political restructuring based on two principles: market economics and Catholic morality. One of Zurita's earlier poems, "Canto a su amor desaparecido" (1985), includes a section of stanzas that describe the remains of "the countries" (los países) of the Americas and the Caribbean in the wake of these interventions. The poem presents fragments of histories, peoples, materials, and products, stuffed into storage spaces in massive warehouses. Accompanying drawings show the shapes of these imagined buildings to be reminiscent of churches or cathedrals (see fig. 5, p. 156).

Trained as an engineer, Zurita was twenty-three in 1973 when the Chilean military deposed the country's elected president, Salvador Allende, and installed Augusto Pinochet as the new head of state. In support of the coup, the government engaged in two actions: it seized control of media and cultural institutions such as universities, museums, editorial houses, and the like, in order to effectively control the image and the narrative of Chile, both internally and abroad. In addition, it embarked on a program of raids, arrests, kidnappings, torture, and disappearances. This latter project was designed to help rid the regime of some of the groups it found most troublesome, and it terrorized many Chileans into silence and compliance. But it also supported the military's drive to remake Chile as a function of state power, in which every message and representation echoes or mirrors absolute, authoritarian control.

Not only is the truth what the regime says it is in an authoritarian polity, but both the violence and, in the case of the Chilean "disappearances," the refusal on the part of authorities to acknowledge violence or confirm the whereabouts of a detained person—whether they are alive or dead— have a particularly insidious effect on the social fabric. The phenomenon is described by numerous survivors of totalitarian regimes. When families and communities are deprived of the opportunity to mourn and bury their dead, this theft interrupts a fundamental trope for human existence, the idea of an arc of life that extends from birth to death. Instead of returning to the earth through burial or cremation, a beloved person persists, untethered from the ground, as the negative space of their absent form. With the accumulation of these absences, the mounting losses of parents, children, grandchildren, cousins, siblings, neighbors, classmates, the world—in the sense of the imaginary envelope of associations and memories that fosters an experience of dwelling and home—peels away from the existing terrain.[55] Critics of post-dictatorship culture have talked about this phenomenon as a crisis of "emplacement": the rupture of our imaginary relationships with the ground our bodies stand on disrupts our sense of ourselves over time and in space.[56] "Las espejeantes playas" (The sparkling beaches) captures the profound confusion that ensues from this forced rupture:

i. Las playas de Chile no fueron más que un apodo
   para las innombradas playas de Chile

ii. Chile entero no fue más que un apodo frente a las
    costas que entonces se llamaron playas innombradas
    de Chile

iii. Bautizados   hasta los sin nombres se hicieron allí
     un santoral sobre estas playas que recién entonces
     pudieron ser las innombradas costas de la patria

142　**Chapter Four**

En que Chile no fue el nombre de las playas de Chile sino sólo
unos apodos mojando esas riberas para que incluso los roqueríos
fueran el bautizo que les llamó playa a nuestros hijos . . .

> (i. The beaches of Chile were only a nickname
> for the unnamed beaches of Chile
>
> ii. All Chile was only a nickname before the
> coasts that were then called the unnamed
> beaches of Chile
>
> iii. Baptized　there even the nameless became a
> calendar of the saints above those beaches
> that could only then be the unnamed coasts
> of the country

In which Chile was not the name of the beaches of Chile but only
some nicknames washing those shores so that even the rookeries
could be the baptism that named our children beach.)[57]

Nothing affixes signifier to signified on these coasts. "Chile" is a nickname
(apodo), one iteration of countless possible names that might be tempo-
rarily affixed to a site before the movement of waves and wind and time
shake it loose. Zurita's stanzas present us with other things of value that
are also being tossed about by the churn as one world becomes aware that
it has been replaced by another. Baptism, in this poem, may indicate this
rebirth into awareness of a new symbolic order, which is merciless: human children and the rookeries where birds raise their young are similarly
unmoored from their traditional meanings. The reference to the *santoral*
(the calendar of the saints) in stanza iii thus suggests a cruel joke: visibly,
but just out of reach, Heaven redeems the extremes of pain and anguish
those human beings have suffered; and *res* is restored *verba* as they are collected into the community of saints, with their meaningful names and the
days set aside to celebrate their lives and trials. That restored relationship
is withheld from Chile in this poem.

The political conditions of totalitarianism pose obstacles to poetry. Regimes target individual poets, of course. Just as significant, however, they
produce conditions in which the integrity and power of the lyric voice itself is thrown into question. The charisma and malevolence of the dictator
contaminates the idea of powerful speech; hence any one person whose
voice holds sway over others is unreliable. Zurita navigates these challenges by mobilizing the Amphionic, which is both a guiding ethos and a
poetics in his work. His poetry is deeply engaged with the Chilean polis,

with Chilean social life, and with a larger collective of persons he refers to as "paisa." In this way, it draws inspiration from *musa lyrae sollers*, the Muse who inspires the poetry of daily life. It is also composed in rough, disjointed forms: fragments of dialogues, blocks of language, outlines, illogical syllogisms, and circular proofs. These jagged shapes and broken utterances are central to Zurita's lyric aesthetics. While they participate in the formal experiments of concrete poetry, Language poetry, and Latin American avant-garde and conceptual poetry, they also point to the conceptual influence of Dante's allusion to "rime aspre e chiocce" in canto 32 of the *Inferno*. Dante furnishes Zurita with a lyric discourse through which to bring Hell into the order of perceptibility.

In the introduction, I discussed how Amphion's lyre fashions the walls of Cocytus, the great frozen lake in the ninth circle of Hell. Dante invokes Amphion as the inspired composer of the harsh and clacking rhymes that reveal the horrors of this place, which holds the most egregious traitors from the Florentine civil war. Zurita refers to the *Divina commedia* throughout his work. This is true not only of the overtly Dantean volumes *Purgatorio* (1979), *Anteparaíso* (1982), and *La vida nueva* (1994), but also in "Canto a su amor desaparecido" (Song for his disappeared love; 1985), *INRI* (2003), and *Zurita* (2011), among other collections. Dante has personal associations for Zurita, who refers in interviews to having listened to his Italian grandmother recount stories from the *Divina commedia* when he was a child.[58] The shadowy, barren mountainous landscapes of the *Inferno*, peopled by the doomed and the suffering, and the temporality of searching and waiting in Purgatorio—which corresponds to the experience of time and daily life in a polity riven by disappearances—provide imagery for poems Zurita sets in the desert, in empty courtyards, in teeming "niches" and rooms where torture is carried out. But Dante also furnishes a model for how to create poetry in a situation where it is nearly impossible to speak meaningfully. Amphion's lyre, Dante tells us, is capable of generating songs in the impossible space where language is not different from the fact ("sì che dal fatto il dir non sia diverso").[59] This is the space into which Zurita sinks the piers of his lyric art: the narrow gap between the realities of Chilean life under the Pinochet regime and the way the regime uses language to maintain its grip on Chilean terrain.

Che dal fatto il dir non sia diverso

Dante invokes Amphion as he contemplates the challenge posed by Cocytus. The difficulty does not have to do with the landscape, but rather with the appalling sins of the region's inhabitants and how their violations will be punished in Hell. In the *Inferno*, a neighbor's betrayal of a

144 Chapter Four

neighbor—motivated by greed or a lust for power so strong that it leads people to maim, torture, and murder individuals and entire families—is the most grievous sin imaginable. Calling on Amphion's Muse, Dante figures it as predation. The most richly imagined scene in cantos 32 and 33 is the pilgrim's encounter with Count Ugolino, whom he encounters as he feasts miserably, disgusted, on the base of the skull of someone later identified as the Archbishop Ruggieri. Ugolino recounts that Ruggieri imprisoned him with his sons in a tower and paved over the door. Gradually, the father and sons starved to death. Ugolino describes the three weakening, then falling blind. The close of his account suggests that he may have fed on his sons' corpses, which is why he joins Ruggieri in Hell. He will gnaw on his adversary's nape for eternity. This is what Dante means when he describes a lyre that can join word to fact.

Zurita adopts Dante's Amphionic art in poems such as "Las cordilleras del Duce." Decidedly anti-lyrical in appearance and tone, and composed in the visually stark form of the proof—or perhaps the administrative memo embraced by bureaucratic political regimes—the poem sets out the logic by which the peaks of the Andes are not white:

> i. No son blancas las cordilleras del Duce
>
> ii. La nieve no alcanza a cubrir esas montañas del oeste
>
> Detenidas   frente a la cordillera de los Andes   aguardando como un cordón negro que esperara la subida final de todas ellas   allá en el oeste   solas   agrupándose tras la noche
>
> iii. Porque frente a los Andes se iban agrupando como la noche del oeste
>
> iv. Por eso la nieve no cubre las cordilleras del Duce Sus cumbres son la noche de las montañas
>
> Ciñéndose de negro frente a las nieves de Chile como si los nevados no fueran otra cosa que espinas hiriendo la noche y ellas pusieran entonces la corona sangrante de los Andes
>
> v. Por eso de sangre fue la nieve que coronó las cumbres andinas . . .
>
> (i. The Duce's cordilleras are not white
>
> ii. The snow cannot cover those mountains to the west

Halted   in front of the Andean cordillera   awaiting
their final ascent like a black cordon   there to the west
alone   forming up behind the night

> iii. Because they were forming up in front of the Andes
> like night to the west

> iv. That's why the snow does not cover the Duce's
> cordilleras.   His peaks are the mountains' night

Girding themselves with black in front of Chile's snows as if
the snow-covered peaks were nothing but thorns wounding the
night and then they donned the Andes' bloody crown

> v. That's why blood was the snow that crowned
> the Andean peaks . . .)[60]

The structuring conceit in this poem both is and is not a metaphor. The Duce is a poet: he transforms the cordillera from a mountain range—a feature of the natural landscape—to an allegory, a phenomenon that is decidedly not natural, and which furnishes visual proof of his power to ward off the snow itself. If he says his cordilleras will not be white, they will not be white. And while this fact will be proven true by one means or another—by an infantry that draws up along the mountainsides to darken them with their menacing shadows, or by airplanes that drop bloody bodies from the sky—the common denominator for the absence of snow is violence. And the efficient cause for this violence, its agent, is the Duce.

In the meantime, however, the speaker in the poem plays the secondary, minor role of designing and executing the form that makes the Duce's power perceptible. In this way, "Las cordilleras del Duce" is an example of *musa lyrae sollers*. The poem is minor in scope, compared to the awesome power wielded by the Duce, but it is important nevertheless in that it communicates important information about daily social life. The poem "El mar" is similarly shaped by the Pinochet regime, by its spectacular excesses of violence, and by the poet-speaker's self-appointed task: to render these conditions and the situation they produce comprehensible. But in this instance, Zurita employs more conventional lyric techniques. The poem is suggestive and whimsical in tone. At its opening, rippling anapests present the image of "strange showers of flesh" that rain from the sky:

Sorprenentes carnadas lleuven del cielo.
Sorprendentes carnadas sobre el mar. Abajo el

146 Chapter Four

océano, arriba las inusitadas nubes de un día
claro. Sorprendentes carnadas llueven sobre el
mar. Hubo un amor que llueve, hubo un día
claro que llueve ahora sobre el mar.

Son sombras, carnadas para peces. Llueve un día
claro, un amor que no alcanzó a decirse. El amor
ah sí el amor, llueven desde el cielo asombrosas
carnadas sobre la sombra de los peces en el mar.

(Strange flesh rains from the sky. Strange flesh
over the sea. Below the ocean, above the
unusual clouds on a cloudless day. Strange
flesh rains over the sea. There was a love that
rains, there was a cloudless day that now rains
over the sea.

All shadows, flesh for fish. It rains on a cloudless
day, a love that didn't get to be spoken. Love,
oh yes love, they rain from the sky astounding
flesh over the shadow of fish in the sea . . .)[61]

As in "Las cordilleras del Duce," "El mar" works its art in the interstices
between metaphor and lived reality. Factually, as we touched on, the Chilean military did drop the remains of tortured human bodies from the sky
into the ocean, so in this sense, the rain of flesh this poem speaks of is real.
But Zurita elaborates from that point; for example, by employing the word
carnada. The term derives from the Spanish word *carne*, or flesh, and it
also signifies "bait" in common parlance. In this way, *carnada* illustrates
the important work that Zurita's lyre performs by opening a space for linguistic play and creativity within the stark allegorical conditions of totalitarianism. Moreover, Zurita is a prolific writer who has published hundreds of poems, in media that extend from the printed word, to skywriting,
to lines bulldozed into the soil of the Atacama Desert, to his own face.[62]
So the efficacy of Zurita's lyric address to the dictatorship is in part a function of the Amphionic power of mass and volume. But Zurita is also a master of mercurial speech. We see this in "Las cordilleras del Duce" and
"El mar," as Zurita works the absurdities and the excesses of the regime
against themselves. These pieces demonstrate the possibilities he discovers in Amphionic lyric poetics. Another dimension of Zurita's Amphionic
technique contributes to the favorable reception his work receives by Chilean authorities. The "The Desert of Atacama" opens:

> i. Miremos entonces el Dierto de Atacama
>
> ii. Miremos nuestra soledad en el desierto
>
> Para que desolado frente a estas fachas el paisaje devenga
> una cruz extendida sobre Chile y la soledad de mi facha
> vea entonces el redimirse de las otras fachas: mi propia
> Redención en el Desierto
>
> > (i. Let's look then at the Desert of Atacama
> >
> > ii. Let's look at our loneliness in the desert
> >
> > So that desolate before these forms in the landscape becomes
> > a cross extended over Chile and the loneliness of my form
> > then sees the redemption of the other forms: my own
> > Redemption in the Desert)[63]

In the Santiago daily newspaper *El Mercurio* (ironically named, in the context of Amphion), the conservative critic who publishes under the name of Ignacio Valente praises Zurita for the profoundly Catholic themes he writes into his work.[64] Christian themes are indeed rife in Zurita's lyric, as we see above, as well as in "Las cordilleras del Duce." However, the Christian doctrine he writes into his work is not the hierarchical, patriarchal system that props up the South and Central American dictatorships. As is evident in the passage quoted above, Zurita's Christianity recognizes humanity as one flesh, a single mutable, malleable earthly form that is endlessly vulnerable to violence: to beatings, torture, fragmentation, and the shedding of blood. This shared flesh is the source of redemption, as people recognize their commonality here: "la soledad de mi facha / vea entonces el redimirse de las otras fachas" (the loneliness of my form / then sees the redemption of other forms). This mutual recognition, flesh to flesh, is what Zurita glosses as the meaning of Christianity's trope of Christ's infinite love.[65] The theme is ubiquitous across the body of Zurita's work. In "Canto a su amor desaparecido," he presents this love as the infinite and incommensurable experience of *paisa*.

Mio figlio, ov'è?

While cantos 32 and 33 furnish Zurita with an idea of the lyric poiesis that will bring Chilean and American suffering into legible forms, other sections of the *Inferno* that refer to Dante's neighbors and fellow Florentines inform his poetry as well. The opening of "Canto a su amor desapare-

148 **Chapter Four**

cido" is a direct allusion to *Inferno* 10.58–60, as Cavalcante de' Cavalcanti questions Dante's pilgrim: "'Se per questo cieco / carcere vai per altezza d'ingegno, / mio figlio, ov'è?" (If through this blind prison you / are going because of your high genius, where is my / son . . . ?)[66] The Cavalcanti were also caught up in the Florentine civil war. Cavalcante predeceases his son Guido and does not know what has become of him, but Dante's pilgrim knows that Guido is dead. It takes little adaptation to shape the statement to Chile in the 1970s. An unnamed interlocutor approaches Zurita to demand:

> Ahora Zurita—me largó—ya que de puro verso
> y desgarro pudiste entrar aquí, en nuestras
> pesadillas; ¿tú puedes decirme dónde está mi hijo?

> (So Zurita—he came at me—now that for all that verse
> and heartbreak you made it in here, into our
> nightmares: can you tell me where's my son?)[67]

Zurita follows the query with a dedication; the poem is for "paisa," the mothers of the Plaza de Mayo in Argentina, for the Agrupación de Familiares de los que no aparecen (Association of Family members of those who do not return) in Chile, and to "todos los tortura, palomos de amor, países chilenos y asesinos" (all those torture, doves of love, Chilean countries and assassins).[68]

The Mothers of the Plaza de Mayo was founded in 1977, as women came to stand in the square in front of the Casa Rosada, the seat of the Argentine government, demanding information about the whereabouts of their disappeared children. The Agrupación de los Familiares de los que no aparecen carry out similar protests in Chile. *Paisa* warrants explanation, as the word reaches to the animating core of Zurita's lyric, which is love. *Paisa* means "the people," in the political sense of a human collective. The love of *paisa* is solidarity. But it also encompasses people in their relationship to their home ground, what Zurita tends to refer to as *países*, or countries. *Paisa* insists upon habitation, the loving and imaginatively rich relationship to place. Thus, in the background of the dedication to "Canto a su amor desaparecido" is the resilient stubbornness of people who insist on living on the ground they call home. This stubbornness is a point of vicious contention in numerous regions and countries in which market economics, various state projects of modernization and reform, and ideals of social order and harmonious commercial production are pitted against people who are simply trying to live their lives.[69] The dedication to *paisa* therefore identifies "Canto a su amor desaparecido" as a song for the global collective of persons who have been subjected to the violent, extractive politics of the ordered city and its legacy, market economics.

Much of "Canto a su amor desaparecido" is set in *galpones*, which are sheds or, in another definition, warehouses. In either translation, they are associated with goods and storage. In this poem, they are also torture sites. The opening of the poem proper presents these themes together. As the lyric proceeds, their relationships are broken apart, processed, and rejoined in a way that suggests some degree of harmony for those who are forced to outlive those they love.

Canté, canté de amor, con la cara toda bañada canté de amor y los muchachos me sonrieron. Más fuerte canté, la pasión puse, el sueño, la lágrima. Canté la canción de los viejos galpones de concreto. Unos sobre otros decenas de nichos los llenaban. En cada uno hay un país, son como niños, están muertos. Todos yacen allí. Países negros, África y sudacas. Yo les canté así de amor la pena a los países. Miles de cruces llenaban hasta el fin el campo. Entera su enamorada canté así. Canté el amor:

> Fue el tormento, los golpes y en pedazos nos rompimos. Yo alcancé a oírte pero la luz se iba. Te busqué entre los destrozados, hablé contigo. Tus restos me miraron y yo te abracé. Todo acabó.

(I sang, I sang about love, with my face soaked I sang about love and the boys they smiled at me. I sang harder, with passion, the dream and tears. I sang the song about the old concrete warehouses. One on top of the other, dozens of niches filled them. In each there's a country, like children, they're dead. They all lay there, black countries, Africa and wetbacks. I sang like this to them about love and sorrow to the countries. Thousands of crosses filled the countryside. All her enamored woman this is how I sang. I sang love:

> It was agony, the beatings and we Broke into pieces. I managed to hear you but the light was fading. I searched for you among the ruined, I spoke with you. What was left of you saw me and I held you. It all ended.)[70]

150   Chapter Four

I have been emphasizing the Amphionic nature of Zurita's lyric, but Orpheus is at work here, too. The Amphionic is both a compositional style and an ethos, and it is oriented to politics and the collective. In keeping with this orientation, Zurita mobilizes Orphic song at the start of this poem, which issues an Orphic blast. Fueled, as Orpheus's are, by love, loss, and pain, the song portrays detention and the opening rounds of torture as a descent into the underworld, where bodies are broken into pieces and the light fades. The Orphic nature of the opening and subsequent stanzas is enhanced by the erotic energies that swirl around the speaker, both here and at other points in the poem. Of ambiguous gender, sometimes referred to with the feminine pronoun and sometimes with the masculine, the speaker indicates a past of rough trade: "—Fumo y pongo con los chicos. Sólo un poco del viejo pone y saca. / —Es bueno para ver colores." (—I smoke and hook up with the guys. Just some old fashioned hookup. / —It's good for seeing colors.)[71] They "fall in love" with their torturers: "—Pero son lindos. Aun así yo me reglo de verlos, mojo la cama y fumo. / —Yo me enamoro de ellos, me regio y me pinto entera." (—But they're lovely. With all that I go on the rag when I see them, wet my bed and smoke. / —I fall in love with them, do myself up and paint my whole face.)[72] And they are prey to the malevolent desire of others, such as guards who leer at the speaker's tight ass:

> —Cómo te llamas y qué haces me preguntaron.
> —Mira tiene un buen cul. Cómo te llamas buen bulo bastarda chica, me
> —preguntaron.
> —Pero mi amor ha quedado pegado en las rocas, el mar y las montañas.
> —Pero mi amor te digo, ha quedado adherido en las rocas, el mar y las
> —montañas.
> —Ellas no conocen los malditos galpones de concreto.

> (—What's your name and what do you do they asked me. / —Look, he's got a tight ass. What's your name tight ass bastard bitch, they / —said. / —But my love is still bound on the rocks, the sea and the mountains. / —But my love, I tell you, is still stuck on the rocks, the sea and the / —mountains. / —They don't know the goddamned concrete warehouses.)[73]

Eros and grief propel the song along its jagged tour through the hells of its locations—the warehouse, what seems like a courtyard, and a mass grave—as the speaker seeks to answer the father's question: "Where is my son?" In a further echo of Dante, however, the quest for the son—the beloved—initiates a process of conversion from the earthbound love of the couple to an all-encompassing love for *paisa*.

The first movements of "Canto a su amor desaparecido" are loosely held together by a human couple, two lovers who endure torture and mutilation, and who are eventually covered with quicklime and stones and left to die:

> Ay, amor, quebrados caímos y en la caída lloré mirándote. Fue golpe tras golpe, pero los últimos ya no eran necesarios. Apenas un poco nos arrastramos entre los cuerpos derrumbados para quedar juntos, para quedar uno al lado del otro. No es duro ni la soledad. Nada ha sucedido y mi sueño se levanta y cae como siempre. Como los días. Como la noche. Todo mi amor está aquí y se ha quedado:

—*Pegado a las rocas, al mar y a las montañas.*
—*Pegado, pegado a las rocas, al mar y a las montañas.*

(Oh, love, broken we fell and as I fell / I wept looking at you. It was blow / after blow, but the last ones weren't / necessary. We barely managed to drag ourselves among the fallen bodies / to stay together, to stay one next to / the other. Loneliness isn't hard, / nothing has happened and my / dream lifts up and falls like always. / Like days. Like the night. All my / love is here and here it stays: // —*Bound to the rocks the sea and the mountains.* / —*Bound, bound to the rocks the sea and the mountains.*)[74]

Ideal as the love is between the speaker and the beloved, here it dies with them. This is true, even as it does not end: ". . . El amor son las cosas que pa- / san. Nuestro amor muerto no pasa." (Love, these are things that come to / an end. Our dead love doesn't end.)[75] The paradox gestures simultaneously to the perfection of the couple's love and to the human flaw in that love. Shared between only two people, it is selfish, from the standpoint of the wider universe of people and things. Yet as the poem proceeds, Zurita begins to draw the suffering of individuals together with the theme of countries he introduced in the poem's opening. For example, after the couple's death, the speaker is again plunged into the chaotic scenes of violence in and around the warehouse, and he chants:

—Grandes glaciares vienen a llevarse ahora los restos de nuestro amor.
—Grandes glaciares vienen a tragarse los nichos de nuestro amor.

152 Chapter Four

—Las nicherías están una frente la otra.
—De lejos parecen bloques.
. . . .
—En cada nicho hay un país, están allí, son los países sudamericanos.
—Grandes glaciares vienen a recogerlos.
—blancos glaciares, sí, hermano, sobre los techos se acercan.
—Murió mi chica, murió me chico, desaparecieron todos.

Desiertos de amor.

(—Great glaciers come now to take away the remains of our love. / —Great glaciers come to swallow the niches of our love. / —The niches are one in front of the other. / —From far off they look like blocks. // . . . // —In each niche there's a country, they are there, they are the South American countries. / —Great glaciers come to collect them / —white glaciers, yes, brother, ceiling over they draw near. / —My girl died, my boy died, they all disappeared. / Deserts of love.)[76]

The theme of the countries continues to build through subsequent sections. As it does, the speaker finds himself joining in with a chorus of singers who give voice to collective lyrics—funeral lament, psalm, anthem:

Los países están muertos. Un Galpón
se llama Sudamérica y el otro América del norte.
Tormento me dio la vista, dije abrién-
dome. El responso cantamos.
. . . .
Nostalgia cantamos por los países y
por el país chileno.
Procesión fue y sentencia, cruzamos
los otros nichos y frente al del país
nuestro estalló el salmo.
Toda la pena.
Todo el psalmo cayó entonces sobre su
amor que no estaba.
De nostalgia cantó por ellos . . .
. . . .
La Internacional de los países muertos
creció subiendo y mi amor puse . . .[77]

(The countries are dead. One warehouse is called South America / and the other North. I saw torture I said, as I opened my- / self. We sang the prayer for the dead. // . . . // We sang our nostalgia for the countries, / for the Chilean country. / There was a trial and a sentence, we crossed the oth- / er niches and in front of our country's the psalm explod- / ed. All the shame. The entire psalm fell on your miss- / ing love. / The entire procession sang with nostalgia . . . // . . . // The Internationale of the dead countries grew larger, ascen- / ding, and I gave it my love.)[78]

Communal singing serves as a vehicle and an accompaniment for the speaker's passage in these stanzas from particular to universal, from personal love to the shared love for fellow beings, *paisa*. As the voices join together, individual losses—such as a father's loss of his son (in the poem's beginning) or a lover's loss of their beloved (in the story of the couple)— begin to pile up. And as they accumulate, it becomes clear that they are matters of pain and concern for entire countries, regions, and the Americas, South and North.

The movement between the particular and the universal, the universal and the particular, shapes the poem's final revelation. Having sung themselves into the recognition of *paisa*, the speaker begins to make sense of the endless agonies of suffering. "—Cantando, cantando a su amor desaparecido. / —Cantando, cantando a su amor desaparecido." (—Singing, singing for his disappeared love. / —Singing, singing to his disappeared love.) The poem speaker then stumbles upon a question:

—. . . es mi karma, ¿no?
—Todos los países míos natales se llaman del amor mío, es mi lindo y
—caído. Oh sí, oh sí.
—Todos están allí, en los nichos flotan.
—Todos los muchachos míos están destrozados, es mi karma, ¿no?
—Me empapo mucho y te quiero todo digo.

(—. . . this is karma, right? / —All the countries of my birth are named by my love, it is my lindo and / —my fallen. Oh yes, oh yes. / —They are all there, they're floating in the niches. / —All my boys are torn apart, this is my karma, right? / —I'm soaked and I love all of you I say.)[79]

What karma is this? Has the reader been offered a glimpse of it? The lines suggest two answers. The latter mention may refer to the speaker's past life of sex, smoking, and desire ("fumo, y pongo con los chicos"). But the first mention connects karma to the suffering countries, and this connection is confirmed in the stanza that follows the questions:

Del amor desaparecido también se
llaman los países. Emurallados ya-

154 Chapter Four

cen como nosotros.
Masacaron a los chicos y los países
se quedaron. Nosotros somos ellos,
tiré. Fue duro.

(Of disappeared love the countries / also call out. Walled up they lie / like us. They massacred the young / and the countries were left. We / are they, I cried out.)[80]

This stanza suggests a second interpretation: What has come home to exact its toll is the Spanish Thebes, the city raised by the forces of *codicia* and *interés*, a political form visited on the Americas by the conquest, and which has cycled through rise and fall over centuries with the same carnivorous appetite for human bodies, their labor, and the contents of their worlds. In the same grief-stricken, lovesick lament, the speaker describes a man, who might be himself, running from niche to niche, pit to pit, in two warehouses. The contents of *galpones* 12 and 13 consist of thirty niches, each represented by a blocklike stanza similar in appearance to blocks that have punctuated sections of disjointed dialogue at other points in the poem. The niches are piled three high, in two columns, for a total of six niches per page. Most "contain" a country and refer in hectic, fragmentary shorthand to massacres, outrages, civil strife, and wretchedness, either conditions found there presently or in the country's history; at times, both. As a representative example of these stanzas:

Nicho Paraguay. En Cuartel 13,
Debidamente señalizado. También
masacre entre los países, guerras del
Chaco, condominio y padecimien-
to. Yace ahora alambrado en nicho,
pasadizo y tumba. Dice aquí: des-
canso para el guaraní Marcos, y sonó
todo el Canto dice aquí, el nicho;
Canto de Paz de Paraguay, canto al
Helicóptero abatido, al país Ipacaray que mata con la caña. Todo esto
Acabado. El nicho dice día y sangró.
. . . .
Tumba Nicho Venezuela. Bolívar del
nicho dice. Lápidas, fosas del Tercer
Mundo, como una vez se los llamó
a los países. Nichos del país suda-

mericano, nuevo americano o todos los
países que al verdor sonrieron.
Adiós dicen. Todos juntos conforman
El Galpón especificado. Negro fue,
como las barras de las petroleras en
el mar. Es el Nicho Venezuela. Allí
solamente descansa un humano. Pe-
tróleo no hay ni tierra. Maldita noche.

(Niche of Paraguay. In Barrack 13, / duly noted. Also a massacre between /
those countries, the wars of Chaco, / joint lands and affliction. It lies now /
wired up in the niche, corridor and in / tomb. It says: Rest for the Guarani /
Marcos, and it sounded the whole / Song it says here, the niche; Song of /
Peace for Paraguay, song for the heli- / copter gunned down, for the country / Ipacaray that kills with reeds. All this / finished. The niche says day
and bled. // . . . // Tomb Niche Venezuela. Bolivar of the / niche it says.
Tablets, pits of the Third / World, like once that's what those coun- / tries
were called. Niches of the South / American country. New American or /
all those countries that to the green- / ness they smiled. Goodbye they say.
All / of them to the shape of the specified / Warehouse. Black, like the rods
of oil / companies in the sea. It is the Venezue- / lan Niche. There only one
human rests. / There is no oil nor land. Damn night.)[81]

Other stanzas contain the searcher's frantic, miserable responses to the
quantity and mass of brutality, death, betrayal, and waste stacked up eco-
nomically and precisely in the niches.

This section of the poem concludes with a pair of diagrams of the warehouses, visual representations of the conditions of their founding as colonial cities, and the reduction of a region and its world to a name and a list
of products (fig. 5).

The niches movement of "Canto a su amor desaparecido" returns us
to *Inferno*, canto 10, in which Dante's pilgrim wanders among tombs with
open lids.

El hombre tierra fue, vasija, párpado
de barro trémulo, forma de la arcilla,
fue cántaro caribe, piedra chibcha,
copa imperial o sílice araucana.
Tierno y sangriento fue, pero en la empuñadura
de su arma de cristal humedecido,
las iniciales de la tierra estaban /escritas.[82]

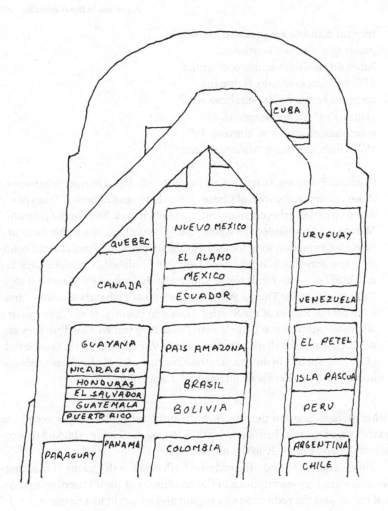

MAPA

Cuartel 13. Pasadizos y nicho, se lee ubicación por países según rayado y marca ay sí se dice, lloramos.

5. Raúl Zurita, "MAPA. Cuartel 13." From *Sky Below: Selected Poems*. English translation and introduction copyright 2016 by Anna Deeny Morales. Copyright © 2016 by Curbstone Books / Northwestern University Press. Published 2016. All rights reserved.

(Before the wig and the dress coat / there were rivers, arterial rivers: / there were cordilleras, jagged waves where / the condor and the snow seemed immutable: / there was dampness and dense growth, the thunder / as yet unnamed, the planetary pampas. // Man was dust, earthen base, an eyelid / of tremulous loam, the shape of clay—/ he was a Carib jug, Chibcha Stone, / imperial cup or Araucanian silica. / Tender and bloody was he, but on the grip / of his weapon the initials of the earth were / written.)

Where Neruda sets his vision in a romanticized, distant past, however, "Canto a su amor desaparecido" is from the first concerned with drawing Indigenous communities, pre-contact societies, and subalterns into its world in a manner that acknowledges the ongoing life and presence of this people within the larger community, *paisa*. In the opening stanza, the poetic speaker refers specifically to a song that folds "[p]aíses negros, África y sudacas" (black countries, Africa and wetbacks) into the community it memorializes. Whereas Neruda associates Indigenous communities with a distant Edenic past, "Canto a su amor desaparecido" builds them into the American present of 1985.

The differences between Neruda's and Zurita's stanzas represent the interruption and reordering of social life that takes place when neoliberal economics become the structuring paradigm for a country (*país*). Powerful voicing, the mastery of linguistic techniques, means something different in the 1980s than it did in the 1950s, when Neruda composed the *Canto general*. In the first half of the twentieth century, poetic creationism was a transgressive innovation; writers drew Indigenous cultures and their worlds into their poetry, thus making these cultures visible to modern national politics.[83] Poets served as political leaders to promote social justice (Neruda was elected to the Chilean senate in 1945). In "Canto a su amor desaparecido," and in Zurita's poetry generally, the relationship between power, language, and meaning is unstable, dangerous, even disastrous. Early in the poem, the speaker does not yet recognize that his world has been ripped away from him, and he attempts to speak to his tormentors:

—Yo dije—están locos, ellos dijeron—no lo creas.

(—I said, you're crazy, and they said—don't believe it.)[84]

The exchange echoes the Requerimiento. As was the case in the conquest, the utterance here does not initiate an exchange; rather, it is the execution of a trap set by a power that dominates and remakes the world. Such a power's targets are in position to be taught, violently, that the world

158 Chapter Four

has changed, and that they have no sense of its logic or how meaning is formed. In "Canto a su amor desaparecido," just after this stymied exchange, the torturers commence beating the speaker, their friends, and their parents with bayonets.[85] In these conditions, language belongs to the other, the master, and to entrust the kind of lyric work that both Neruda and Zurita seek to accomplish by conventional cultural practices is a risky bet. What Zurita can draw on is his long familiarity with Dante and his poetic sense for Amphion's lyre, which now furnish the resources that enable "Canto a su amor desaparecido" to both generate meaning and disclose the source of that meaning: not a person, but a people; not an economy, but *paisa*. The final two sections of the poem consist of one last interrogation, which the speaker may be conducting with himself:

¿Te acuerdas, chileno, del primer abandono cuando niño?

Sí, dice

¿Te acuerdas del segundo ya a los veinte y tantos?

Sí, dice

¿Sabes chileno y paloma que estamos muertos?

Sí, dice

¿Recuerdas entonces tu primer poema?

Sí, dice

(Do you remember, Chilean, as a child the first time you were abandoned? / Yes, he says / Do you remember the second time when you were already twenty-something? / Yes, he says / Do you know Chilean and dove were dead? / Yes, he says / Do you remember your first poem? / Yes, he says)[86]

"Sí"—yes. The poem bursts into careening singing, long assonances stretched out to resemble a hysterical utterance. Repetitions of the word *canta* deliver a sense of release:

dice sí sí dice sí sí siiiiiiiiiiiiiii oooooooo ho hoo hooo ho
ho hoo hoooo eeeeeee iiiiiii

. . . .

La noche canta, canta, canta, canta, canta
Ella canta, canta, canta, canta bajo la tierra

¡Aparece entonces!
Levántate nueva de entre los paisitos muertos
chilenos, karatecas, somozas y traidores,
levántate y lárgale de nuevo su vuelo y su canto
al que sólo por ti paisa vuela, canta y toma forma

Amphion in the Americas 159

devuélveselo a éste el más soñado y lloro
desaparecido el amor
palomo y malo

(he says yes yes says yes yes yes yiiiiiiiiiiiieeeeeeeeeeeeeeeeeeeeeeeeee / ee eeeeeoooooooooiiiiiiiiiiiiiiiiii / iiiiiiiiiiiiiiiooooooooiiiiiiiiiiiiieeeeeeeeeeeeeeeth-eeeeetheeeeeeeeee // . . . // The night sings, sings, sings, sings, sings / She sings, sings, sings, sings below the dirt // Show yourself then! / Get up then new among the little dead countries / Chileans, Karatecas, Somozas, and traitors, / get up and let loose again its flight and its song / that only soars for you paisa, sings and forms / return it to this its most dreamed and wept / disappeared of love / dove and evil)[87]

The poem ends on a new page, with word in italics: "*Sí, dice*" (Yes, he says).[88] The words convey the exhaustion after the paroxysm, as well as the radical renunciation of self. The confession has led the speaker to recognize the simultaneity and the contiguity of his experience—first betrayal, second betrayal, death, first poem—with the experience of all things. With this recognition, the speaker also becomes complicit in abuse and the state's egregious failure to love. The "Sí" at the end of the poem acknowledges both facts, and with this acknowledgment, the speaker is freed of the final obstacle to reconciliation: identity, the idea that there is a difference between the dove and evil, or the sense that "todos los tortura" (all those torture), the line in the poem's dedication, requires explanation, a clearer description of whether the line means "all those who are tortured" or "all those who torture." "Países chilenos y asesinos" (Chilean countries and assassins), from the same line in the dedication, are the same thing. When the speaker comes to inhabit that recognition, peace descends. It is as if Cavalcante sinks back into his tomb and the lid is miraculously closed.[89]

Amphionic Postscript

Amphion has the final word here. His music sets ruination and regeneration on a constant continuum. For Amphion, the destruction of one world is not the devastation of all worlds. In the context of the predations of the Pinochet regime, he steers us to consider the ongoing poetic project carried out by poets of the Mapuche nation,[90] whose lyrics reinscribe the territory of the Southern Cone to assert the living presence, even in conditions of ongoing duress, of a world their people have inhabited continuously since before the Spanish conquest.[91] This work comes into view for Western readers in the late 1980s, through collections published in

160 Chapter Four

Spanish by writers such as Elicura Chihuailaf Nahuelpán (b. 1952) and Leonel Lienlaf (b. 1969). The recent volume *Poetry of the Earth: Mapuche Trilingual Anthology* (2014) advances the project by making a wide selection
of Mapuche poems available to Hispanic and Anglophone readers. This
diverse body of poetry includes lyrics that carry on the work of remapping
and resignifying the valleys, forests, mountains, rivers, and skies that sur-
round them; for example, in "Liangafnag wechukey yómpewe ñi waychüf
püle/El amanecer ocurre tras los cristales/Dawn Behind the Windows," in
which Maribel Mora Curriao defamiliarizes domestic space by structuring
it from the perspective of a native bird, *Sturnella loyca*:

> From the top of the foliage
> a solitary loica looks at me
> and takes pity.
> On me! so protected
> by these four walls.[92]

Or poems such as "Üyechi pülom mew ta pewman/Sueños en el valle/
Dreams in the Valley," which communicates both the anguish of being
forcibly separated from one's land and the power and resonance of that
land and its spirits, whose world continues to proceed along its courses,
despite the incursions of Western civilization.[93] Other writers included
in the volume engage intentionally with monuments of Western culture:
both cities and poems, drawing forms and poetic lines composed in one
culture into new significance as they are incorporated into a different
world. For example, in "Pulotre 1916," Bernardo Colipán draws a line from
T. S. Eliot's "The Wasteland," repurposing it to ends that serve his community. The poem is motivated by an oral account of a murder that took
place during a smallpox epidemic in 1916. The poet-speaker describes a
vision of the event:

> And I was only fifteen
> when I saw life run like a dog
> thrown on the ashes.
> So I told my brother:
> *I will show you fear*
> *in a handful of dust. (Eliot)*
> Stay calm.
> Death is an accident, nothing else matters.[94]

Amphion's lyre is playing here. Colipán takes up two poems central to
the high modern Anglophone tradition ("Pulotre 1916" invokes W. B.

Yeats's "Easter, 1916") and builds them into a new framework of meaning, thereby reanimating the work's resonances. The poem shows us that 1916 was a momentous year for countless reasons, in countless lives lived in countless worlds, and that fear and dust are powerful symbols across the breadth and variety of the human species. Both the anthology and the wider body of scholarship and dialogue that grows up around Mapuche poetry make this collection a powerful engine of cultural production that works across and through simultaneous, living worlds, Western and Indigenous.

Amphion Dancing [CODA]

Here is Amphion today (fig. 6). He is massive, a bronze sculpture weighing tons, and he is dancing. He presides over a semicircular patio on the campus of the Central University of Venezuela, in Caracas. Created by the French artist Henri Laurens (1885–1954), *L'Amphion* was commissioned by architect Carlos Raúl Villanueva, who wrote Laurens, a well-known artist and illustrator of his day, with an invitation to contribute something "tremendous" to his new project, animated by the optimistic spirit of

6. Henri Laurens, *Amphion* (1953). Photograph: GermanX (Wikimedia Commons CCA-SA 4.0 International).

164 **Coda**

mid-twentieth-century modernity. Villanueva planned a university whose campus would be not the usual quadrangle, but a fully formed city, a *ciudad universitaria* modeled on the one built by Mario Pani and Enrique del Moral in Mexico.[1]

Laurens sent him *Amphion*. Magnificent, simultaneously humanoid and inhuman, *Amphion* has been in place for over seventy years now, serenely dancing to his own mercurial rhythms, regardless of social upheaval and civic calm. He is traversed by the lyre, represented here by striations that run through his core and support his back. Two slender bars form a circle, as if he embraces the air. Attenuated segments at the ends look like fingers he might use to pluck strings. One long piece of bronze looks like a leg and curves behind Amphion, bent, as if to catch his weight and send him surging upward again. Both a striking feature of the courtyard and indifferent to it, Amphion has no face, no gaze. Just energy and action, masses and forces in balance and tension.

Acknowledgments

This project began as an inkling that Amphion hides in plain sight. I am grateful to the community of colleagues and friends who helped me gather the evidence: Raquél Barragán Aroche for prompting me to look at *La grandeza mexicana*; Karen Jackson Ford for steering me to "Lapis Lazuli"; Felice Gambini and Lorena Uribe Bracho for reminding me of Alciato's *foedera*; Michael Stern for sending me Carolyn Forché's "Museum of Stones"; and Sonia Velázquez for introducing me to *Rome's Wreck*. Thanks are also due to two brilliant Dantisti, Warren Ginsberg and F. Regina Psaki, who each communicated firmly, though kindly, that Puttenham's and Sidney's Amphion is not the Amphion of Dante.

I am grateful to Alan Thomas, Randy Petilos, and the staff at the University of Chicago Press, and to Nan Da and Anahid Nersessian, series editors for Thinking Literature, for recognizing this book when it was in preliminary form, and for trusting me to see the project through. Deepest thanks as well to the two anonymous readers for the Press who gave thorough, generous attention to the manuscript and offered expert advice. I hope to have done their observations justice. Erin DeWitt performed keen-eyed editing of the manuscript. I am grateful for her expert work and for her patience. Any remaining missteps or errors in this book are my own.

The collective membership of the Society for Renaissance and Baroque Hispanic Poetry offered crucial feedback and support as I worked these ideas out. Discussion at the 2018 American Comparative Literature Association seminar, "Towards a Global Theory of the Lyric," coordinated by Marisa Galvez and Andrew Hui, was instrumental in helping me shape this project. SOCE—a collective of readers, thinkers, and friends who will take on pages and chapters at a moment's notice to offer wise counsel—is composed of Amanda Doxtater, Karen Emmerich, Lanie Millar, Fabienne Moore, Marc Schacter, and Casey Shoop. The long list of additional friends, students, and colleagues who furnished assistance and support along the way includes Michael Allan, Emilie L. Bergmann, Rodrigo Cacho Casal, Anthony J. Cascardi, A. E. B. Coldiron, Eva Coulon, Robert L. Davis, Ann T. Delehanty, Geri Doran, Alana Dunn, Drue Edney, Cecilia Enjuto Rangel, Andrea Frisch, Yuruhary Gallardo García, Lynn Glaser, Roland Greene, Sarah Grew, Miguel Antonio Guevara, Sophie Middlebrook Hayward, Nathalie Hester, Ellie Klopp, Ignacio López Alemany, Maria Losada Friend, Elmira Louie, Kyle Malashewski, Michelle McKinley, Ahmad Nadalizadeh, Ricardo Padrón, Amanda E. Powell, Amanda W. Powell, Chad Reeves, Elizabeth Terry Roisen, Brett Rushforth, Senna Steward, Cynthia Stockwell, Tze-Yin Teo, Cornesha Tweede, Felipe Valencia, Alejandro Vallega, David Wacks, Ryan Walker, Jessica Wolfe, and Elizabeth Wright. Friends, your thoughtfulness added depth and variety to this project, which was in many ways a community endeavor.

Ken Calhoon has been a sterling colleague and a true friend over our years together at the University of Oregon. As department head, he held various forces at bay while I wrote the book I wanted to write. Thanks are also due to Karen Jackson Ford and Harry Wonham, who in their capacities as Associate Deans for the Humanities were generous readers of early chapter drafts. The College of Arts and Sciences awarded me a term of leave in support of this project. The extraordinary staff of the University of Oregon libraries, both in Eugene and at the Learning Commons in Portland, went above and beyond to help me track down hard-to-find volumes and materials. Your professionalism, goodwill, and ingenuity is always on display, all the more so during the pandemic. Thank you. Grateful acknowledgment is also due to the staff of the Sala Cervantes in the Biblioteca Nacional de España, as is a note of respectful recognition of the work of Javier Docampo Capilla (1962–2020), who served as director of manuscripts and rare books at the BNE until his life was cut short by COVID-19.

Chris Haverty is the sine qua non, every moment of every day. Thank you, CMH, and thanks as well to the Ivonhouse gang for the world we build and share.

Some of my favorite parts of this book emerged over the course of long conversations with my father, Jonathan Middlebrook. He recognized Amphion right away, and he kept me going when the mercurial demigod had me at wit's end. Thank you for your unflagging support, Pop, as well as for your wise, practical, nuts-and-bolts help. This book is dedicated to you.

Notes

Preface

1. Throughout this book, I talk about Amphion as Horace shapes him. For this reason, I refer to Mercury, the god's Roman name. I refer to "Hermes" here because I am recounting the Greek myth.

Introduction

1. Cornejo Polar, *Discurso en loor de la poesía*, 148; my translation.

2. "Antarctica" was a term for South America. Antonio Cornejo Polar, Clarinda's most thorough editor, discovered no information beyond a footnote in Marcelino Menéndez y Pelayo's *Historia de la Poesía II* pointing back to Clarinda's reference. See Cornejo Polar, *Discurso en loor de la poesía*, 59. On Clarinda's identity, see Del Barco, "El anonimato como performance textual."

3. Bettina Reitz-Joosse examines the history of Amphion's association with charming stones and building up structures. It appears that he starts to do both things in Latin writing, while in ancient Greek poetry he sometimes charms, sometimes builds, and occasionally does both. See Reitz-Joosse, *Building in Words*, 173–98.

4. Virginia Jackson discusses the "stipulative functions" of lyric forms before critics reshaped the concepts of poetry and lyric in the nineteenth century: "Songs, riddles, epigrams, sonnets, epitaphs, *blasons*, lieder, elegies, marches, dialogues, conceits, ballads, epistles, hymns, odes, eclogues, and monodramas considered lyric in the Western tradition before the early nineteenth century were not lyric in the same sense as the poetry we think of as lyric." See Jackson, "Who Reads Poetry?," 183, as well as the expanded discussion of the "lyricization" of poetry she presents, with Yopie Prins, in *The Lyric Theory Reader*, 1–8.

5. In chapter 4, I discuss the case of Bernardo de Balbuena (ca. 1562–1627), who makes Cortés a Christian Amphion.

6. See Fuchs, "Another Turn for Transnationalism." On lyric and social and political remaking, see Greene, *Unrequited Conquests*; Hampton, *Literature and Nation in the Sixteenth Century*, esp. 1–33; and Helgerson, *Forms of Nationhood*. See also Torres, *Love Poetry in the Spanish Golden Age*.

168 Notes to Pages 3–7

7. See Vega and Esteve, *Idea de la lírica, en el renacimiento (entre Italia y España)*, 1–42.

8. For an overview of the history of the lyric genre, see Jackson and Prins, *The Lyric Theory Reader*, 1–8.

9. Horace, *Satires and Epistles*, trans. Davie, 116. "Siluestris homines sacer interpresque deorum / caedibus et uictu foedo deterruit Orpheus . . . dictus et Amphion, Thebanae conditor urbis, / saxa mouere sono testudinis et prece / blanda / ducere quo uellet" (Horace, *Epistles*, 71).

10. Gail Kern Paster discusses the conflicting views that premodern and early modern writers from Augustine to Renaissance humanists held regarding the concept of the city. One strain of thought considered the founding of cities to be a pious act: poets such as Orpheus instructed people to adopt civilized practices and create laws; Aeneas obeyed the will of the gods when he founded Rome. Another tradition established the origins of the city in fratricide; this was the influential line of argument maintained, for example, by Saint Augustine in *The City of God*. This idea took shape in the writings of both ancient Christians and pagans, who understood the city to be a divine concept, first, and a material construction, second. See Paster, *The Idea of the City in the Age of Shakespeare*, 9–32.

11. Orpheus enjoys a wide-ranging career in poetics because the myth is flexible and highly adaptable. The variety of sources for the Orpheus myth and the range of ways writers made use of it can create confusion. I limit discussion here to the aspects of Orpheus that inform the *Ars Poetica* and the concept of *musa lyrae sollers*. On versions of the myth in early modern Spain, see Armas, *Ovid in the Age of Cervantes*, esp. ix–xix, 203–27. See also Llopis, *El mito de Orfeo en la literatura barroca española*. On Orpheus in the Anglophone tradition, see DuBrow, *The Challenges of Orpheus*, 18–26. On Orpheus and the Renaissance, see Warden, *Orpheus*, as well as Mann, *The Trials of Orpheus*.

12. Bourdieu, *Outline of a Theory of Practice*, 86.

13. Grossman with Halliday, *The Sighted Singer*, 283. Grossman's wider discussion of the politics of blank verse is illuminating in this respect (279–84).

14. Puttenham, *The Art of English Poesy*, 93.

15. Puttenham, 94.

16. For example, in the *Défense et illustration de la langue française* (The defense and enrichment of the French language), Joachim du Bellay celebrates the French everyone speaks, but his arguments make it amply clear that he is in fact positing a language that no one speaks yet, beyond the small circle of humanists who called themselves La Pléiade. See Du Bellay, *"The Regrets," with "The Antiquities of Rome," Three Latin Elegies, "The Defense and Enrichment of the French Language,"* ed. and trans. Helgerson, esp. 318–40.

17. Puttenham, *The Art of English Poesy*, 97, 98.

18. As Susan Stewart observes, "Telling as telling slant makes lyric capable of evoking not only meaning but also the conditions under which meaning is formed" (Stewart, *Poetry and the Fate of the Senses*, 82).

19. Puttenham, *The Art of English Poesy*, 95.

20. Puttenham, 96. Puttenham's lines on Orpheus present him as teaching lessons,

Notes to Pages 7–10   169

". . . assembl[ing] . . . the wild beasts to come in herds to harken to his music and by that means ma[kes] . . . them tame, implying thereby, how by his discreet and wholesome lessons uttered in harmony and with melodious instruments, he brought the rude and savage people to a more orderly life . . ." (96). We might say that Amphion's art is a function of its form, whereas Orpheus creates meaningful content.

21. Puttenham, 96.

22. Andrea Alciato, *Emblematum liber* (Augsburg: Heinrich Steiner, 1534), available at Alciato at Glasgow, https://www.emblems.arts.gla.ac.uk/alciato/books.php?id=A34a. I am grateful to Dr. Lorena Uribe Bracho for calling the emblem to my attention.

23. As we will see in chapter 3, writers sometimes confused Orpheus with Amphion; however, most writers recognized the distinct lyric powers and functions of their different arts.

24. On stones as a long-standing thought partner with human beings in the domain of earthly life, see Cohen, *Stone*.

25. Mutlu Konuk Blasing reads Plato's ban on poetry in *The Republic* in terms of animation. The "real threat" poetry poses to the republic, she observes, "is not mimesis but a language use that mobilizes emotions, the variability and inconstancy of which pose a further problem. . . . While 'reason' would standardize a citizenry of coherent, self-determining subjects in charge of the 'city' within their souls, the 'other principle' is subject to variations, both within and among individuals. Poetry plays to the volatile part of our 'nature' and thus has the power to create 'bad' cities: it can move the 'promiscuous crowd' at 'public festivals,' for it is a 'sort of rhetoric which is addressed to a crowd of men, women, and children, freemen and slaves'" (Blasing, *Lyric Poetry*, 1).

26. See Stewart, *Poetry and the Fate of the Senses*, 2. For both Stewart and Grossman, the purpose of poetry is "the keeping of the image of the person in the world" (Grossman, *Sighted Singer*, 6). Stewart describes poetry as "an anthropomorphic project; the poet undertakes the task of recognition in time—the unending tragic Orphic task of drawing the figure of the other—the figure of the beloved who reciprocally can recognize one's own figure—out of the darkness" (2). When pressed to explain what he means by "the keeping of the image of persons as present in the world," Grossman explains that poetry accomplishes this work in two ways: "One is the function of poetry that is exemplified by the very fact that we are discoursing together, that we have something to talk about as between us, something that brings to mind the question of persons and the conserving of their value across time. Secondly, we have observed that the most ancient cases of poetry seem situated on the business of preserving images of persons" (7). Stewart asserts that "poetry is a force against effacement—not merely for individuals but for communities through time as well" (2). Neither Grossman nor Stewart discusses Amphion, although each seem to point at various junctures to the lyric functions that I associate with Amphion in this book.

27. Aurora Egido recounts Dámaso Alonso's energetic dismissal of contest lyrics, whose poets "are all the middling writers, the followers, the obscurantists, those who have nothing to say and no one to listen to their verses" (Egido, "Poesía de justas y academias," 119–20). I provide the Spanish-language version of the quotation and discuss it further in chapter 3.

170   **Notes to Pages 10–17**

28. Izenberg, *Being Numerous*, 1–2. On relationships between poetry and social and cultural life, see also Ramanzani, *Poetry and Its Others*.

29. Hirsch, *How to Read a Poem*, 2; Vendler, *The Art of Shakespeare's Sonnets*, 1–2. See also the influential ideas of Jonathan Culler on the "internal monologue," expanded and developed most recently in *Theory of Lyric*.

30. Alice Oswald defines poetic energeia as "bright, unbearable reality . . . the word used when gods come to earth not in disguise but as themselves" (Oswald, *Memorial*, 1). *Memorial* is a good example of Amphionic renewal. While the great passions that destroy worlds are often the stuff of epic—as in the case of *The Iliad*—the work of recovering those worlds and the communities they contain is best accomplished by lyric devices. To recover the energeia of *The Iliad*, Oswald writes, it was necessary to dispense with seven-eighths of the poem, "as you might lift the roof off a church in order to remember what you're worshipping" (1). What she preserves are lyric devices: antiphonal song and similes.

31. Stoler, McGranahan, and Perdue, *Imperial Formations*, 8–9.

32. Yeats, "Lapis Lazuli." On Yeats and Amphion, see Izenberg, *Being Numerous*, 43.

33. On lyric and rhythm, see Glaser and Culler, *Critical Rhythm*. The introductory essays by the book's two editors are especially useful as readings of rhythm and prosody, even as they are shaped by a concept of lyric defined in terms of the self. See Glaser, "Introduction," 1–17; and Culler, "Why Rhythm?," 21–38.

34. Stoler, McGranahan, and Perdue, *Imperial Formations*, 8.

35. "'Modernity' is a complex narrative whose point of origination was Europe; a narrative that builds Western civilization by celebrating its achievements while hiding at the same time its darker side, 'coloniality.' Coloniality, in other words, is constitutive of modernity—there is no modernity without coloniality" (Mignolo, *The Darker Side of Western Modernity*, 2–3).

36. See Stoler, "Imperial Debris."

37. See Stoler, and below, chapter 2, 65, 88.

38. As poetry is lyricized in the eighteenth and nineteenth centuries, Mercury becomes associated less with poetry than he is with periodicals. On the role that poetry published in newspapers played in establishing Hispanic identity in the United States, see Gruesz, *Ambassadors of Culture*.

39. A particularly elaborate representation of the connection appears in the 1614 *Viaje del Parnaso* (Journey to Parnassus), in which Miguel de Cervantes figures imperial Spain as a galleon whose parts are made not of wood, hemp, metal, and canvas, but rather of a wide variety of Spanish and Italian verse forms. The ship is captained by Mercury. I discuss this allegory more closely in chapter 3. On Mercury in the Renaissance, see Armas, "Bajo el signo de Mercurio" and *Cervantes's Architectures*.

40. On Amphion and Zethus in Euripides and Plato, see Nightingale, "Plato's *Gorgias* and Euripides' *Antiope*."

41. Reitz-Joosse, *Building in Words*, 173–98.

42. "sic tempora verti / cernimus atque illas adsumere robora gentes, / concidere has; sic magna fuit censuque virisque perque decem potuit tantum dare sanguinis an-

Notes to Pages 17–22 171

nos, / nunc humilis veteres tantummodo Troia ruinas / et pro divitiis tumulos ostendit avorum. / Clara fuit Sparte, magnae viguere Mycenae, / nec non et Cecropis, nec non Amphionis arces. / Vile solum Sparte est, altae cecidere Mycenae, / Oedipodioniae quid sunt, nisi nomina, Thebae?" (Ovid, *Metamorphoses*, XV.420–28). See "P. OVIDI NASONIS METAMORPHOSEON LIBER QVINTVS DECIMVS," The Latin Library, https://www.thelatinlibrary.com/ovid/ovid.met15.shtml.

43. "In nova fert animus mutatas dicere formas / corpora; di, coeptis (nam vos mutastis et illas) / adspirate meis primaque ab origine mundi / ad mea perpetuum deducite tempora carmen!"

44. Dante, *Inferno*, trans. Durling, 274–75.

45. Dante, canto 32.1–12, 498–99.

46. Dante, canto 32.73–79, 502–3.

47. In fact, Horace instructs readers to either teach or delight (aut . . . aut). The original meaning shifted over time.

48. "Grais ingenium, Grais dedit ore rotundo / Musa loqui, praeter laudem nullius auaris." Horace, *Epistles: Book II and Epistle to the Pisones ("Ars Poetica")*, ed. Rudd, 69. Unless otherwise noted, English translations of the *Ars Poetica* are by John Davie: Horace, *Satires and Epistles*, trans. Davie. The lines quoted above appear on 114.

49. A Roman coin.

50. Horace, *Satires and Epistles*, trans. Davie, 114. "Romani pueri longis rationibus assem / discunt in partis centum diducere. 'Dicat / filius Albini: si de quincunce remota est / uncia, quid superat? . . . Poteras dixisse.'—'Triens.'—'Eu! / Rem poteris seruare tuam. Redit uncia, quid fit?' / 'Semis.' An, haec animos aerugo et cura peculi / cum semel imbuerit, speramus carmina fingi / posse linenda cedro et leui seruanda cupresso?" (Horace, *Epistles*, 69).

51. Niall Rudd discusses the challenges Horace faced in satisfying Augustus's demands that the poet write him an ode. See Horace, *Epistles*, ed. Rudd, 1–12. See also Miller, *Propertius at Baiae*.

52. Horace, *Satires and Epistles*, trans. Davie, 107. "Sumite materiam uestris, qui scribitis, aequam / uiribus et uersate diu quid ferre recusent, / quid ualeant umeri" (Horace, *Epistles*, 59).

53. Horace, *Satires and Epistles*, trans. Davie, 116. "Siluestris homines sacer interpresque deorum / caedibus et uictu foedo deterruit Orpheus, / dictus ob hoc lenire / tigris rabidosque leones; / dictus et Amphion, Thebanae conditor urbis, / saxa mouere sono testudinis et prece / blanda / ducere quo uellet. Fuit haec sapientia quondam, / publica priuatis secernere, sacra profanis, / concubitu prohibere uago, dare iura maritis, / oppida moliri, leges incidere ligno. / Sic honor et nomen diuinis uatibus atque / carminibus uenit. Post hos insignis Homerus / Tyrtaeusque mares animos in Martia bella / uersibus exacuit, dictae per carmina sortes, / et uitae monstrata uia est et gratia regum Pieriis temptata modis ludusque repertus / et longorum operum finis: ne forte pudori / sit tibi Musa lyrae sollers et cantor Apollo" (Horace, *Epistles*, 71–72).

54. ". . . causa viae est coniunx, in quam calcata venenum / vipera diffudit crescentesque abstulit annos. / posse pati volui nec me temptasse negabo: / vicit Amor. supera deus hic bene notus in ora est; / an sit et hic, dubito: sed et hic tamen auguror esse, /

172 **Notes to Pages 22–29**

famaque si veteris non est mentita rapinae, / vos quoque iunxit Amor. per ego haec loca plena timoris, / per Chaos hoc ingens vastique silentia regni, / Eurydices, oro, properata retexite fata. / omnia debemur vobis, paulumque morati / serius aut citius sedem properamus ad unam. / tendimus huc omnes, haec est domus ultima, vosque / humani generis longissima regna tenetis. / haec quoque, cum iustos matura peregerit annos, / iuris erit vestri: pro munere poscimus usum; / quodsi fata negant veniam pro coniuge, certum est / nolle redire mihi: leto gaudete duorum" (10.23–39) (Ovid, *Metamorphoses: The New, Annotated Edition*, trans. Humphries, ed. Reed, 235).

55. The ancient Greeks associate the work of the lyre with a number of archaic singers: Orpheus (the lawgiver); Amphion (who built walls); Musaeus (who discovered harmony and measure); Linus (who invented funeral laments); Sappho and, at times, Homer (both associated with hymns). For an account of the ancient singers, see Schmidt, *The First Poets*.

56. Maria José Vega and Cesc Esteve point out that Horace's remarks on lyric occupy quite a small space in a long poem. Vega and Esteve, *Idea de la lírica*, 20.

57. The poems are collected in a trilingual anthology that makes them available to Hispanic and Anglophone readers.

Chapter One

1. Horace, *Satires and Epistles*, trans. Davie, 116. "Siluestris homines sacer interpresque deorum / caedibus et uictu foedo deterruit Orpheus, / dictus ob hoc lenire / tigris rabidosque leones; / dictus et Amphion, Thebanae conditor urbis, / saxa mouere sono testudinis et prece / blanda ducere quo uellet" (Horace, *Epistles*, 71).

2. Jackson, "Who Reads Poetry?," 183.

3. See introduction, 21, 171n53.

4. Zapata, *El arte poetica de Horatio*, n.p.; my translation.

5. Zapata, 4–5; my translation.

6. Pelletier, *L'Art Poétique*, 8–9; my translation.

7. On cheerfulness, see Hampton, *Cheerfulness*. I discuss the topic further in chapter 3.

8. See figures 1 and 3, 4, 14.

9. Sidney, *The Defence of Poesy*. Verse "charm" was a powerful idea in sixteenth-century verse culture, as we will see again, later in this chapter, with respect to Hernando de Acuña and Jerónimo de Urrea.

10. Beechy, *The Poetics of Old English*, 4.

11. Shakespeare, Sonnet 18.

12. Amphion is often associated with orators, especially in the French tradition. But the power of Amphionic oratory derives from the lyre, not from Amphion's own voice.

13. Horace, *Ars Poetica*. I am not arguing here that Amphionic poetry cannot be revived. We will see plenty of examples of poems in this book that slide in and out of meaning and relevance, over time. My point here is that Amphionic poetry does not respond to the reading practices we usually bring to lyric. At the very least, to read

Notes to Pages 29-32   173

this poetry, it is necessary to get curious about its context and to prepare to suspend judgment about metered and verse. See below in this chapter, on the "dismal four-teener."

14. Alonso de Cervantes, whose dates are unknown, is not related to Miguel de Cervantes, who was born in 1547, forty-six years after 1501, the date of Alonso's prologue to his gloss of the *Coplas*. I will refer to Alonso de Cervantes as "Alonso" in this discussion, to avoid confusion. For an overview of what is known of Alonso de Cervantes's life, see Marino, *Jorge Manrique's "Coplas por la muerte de su padre,"* 37–41.

15. ". . . ya puesto por espacio de tiempo de cuatro años: con tan penoso y pobre destierro: en este para mi tan estraño reino de Portugal" (. . . stuck here for going on four years, in such painful and poverty-stricken exile, in this, to me strange, kingdom of Portugal). Alonso de Cervantes, "Prólogo de la glosa hecha y compuesta por el Licenciado Alonso de Cervantes sobre las coplas de don Jorge Manrique que hizo sobre la Muerte de su padre: dirigida al muy illustre y muy magnifico senor el Señor don Álvaro de Zuniga, Duque de Bejar: Marqués de Gibraleón: Conde de Bañares: Justicia mayor de Castilla: Señor de las villas de Burgillos y Capilla" (1501), in Pérez y Gómez, ed., *El ayre de la almena*, ii. I have modernized the spelling. All translations to this volume are my own, prepared in consultation with Elmira Louie.

16. Alonso de Cervantes, "Prólogo," ii.

17. They continue to, to the present day. This is especially the case with stanza 3, reproduced below. The *Coplas por la muerte de su padre* was composed by Jorge Manrique (1440–1479) around the time of the death of his father, Santiago Rodrigo Manrique, in 1476. In forty stanzas of *pie quebrado* verse (stanzas of octosyllables marked by the regular insertion of a tetrasyllabic line; thus, a "broken foot," or *pie quebrado*), the *Coplas* reflects on death and on the exemplary life of Don Rodrigo, who embodied the ideas of aristocratic Castilian masculinity. The *Coplas* enjoyed great popularity and wide circulation in sixteenth-century Spain. It remains a touchstone in Spanish culture, although not uncontroversially. One of the structuring principles of the *Coplas'* cosmos is a militant Christian ethnopolitics, and the poem is virulently anti-Muslim. On the history and reception of the *Coplas por la muerte de su padre*, see Marino, *Jorge Manrique's "Coplas por la muerte de su padre."*

18. Beltrán, *Coplas que hizo Jorge Manrique a muerte de su padre*; my translation, prepared in consultation with Elmira Louie. In the case of this poem, in particular, the task is difficult, given the rich link between the *pie quebrado* verse form and the Spanish language. Infelicities in the English above illustrate my point about the cultural specificity of verse "charm," which I discuss below.

19. Alonso de Cervantes, "Prólogo," iiii. All translations to this volume are my own, prepared in consultation with Elmira Louie.

20. Glossing is a blanket term used to describe a variety of interpretive and explicative practices. Spanish poetry also contains a lyric form called the *glosa*, which further complicates the situation.

21. For example, in Sidney: "The Greeks called him 'a poet,' which name has, as the most excellent, gone through other languages. It comes of this word *poiein*, which is 'to make'; wherein I know not whether by luck or wisdom we Englishmen have met with the Greeks in calling him 'a maker.'"

174 **Notes to Pages 32–36**

22. Marino discusses the fashion for glossing the *Coplas*, which extended through the sixteenth and well into the seventeenth century. The primary use was for funeral laments for the nobility; however, a number of sixteenth-century glossers worked with the poem to build worlds for themselves, in the manner Alonso did. See especially the glosses of Rodrigo de Valdepeñas, who discovered his vocation while glossing the *Coplas* and eventually joined the Carthusian order. Later in life, he shared his glosses with his father, as the two contemplated his father's imminent death. See Marino, *Jorge Manrique's "Coplas por la muerte de su padre,"* 41–43.

23. "la glosa hecha y compuesta por el Licenciado Alonso de Cervantes" (Alonso de Cervantes, "Prólogo," ii).

24. Poetic glosses are reliably based on a seed or "tutor" text, which a writer reflects and expands on. Thus, glossing always entails play with tensions between obedience and inventiveness. Glosses also generate copious amounts of material, as they are invariably far longer than the fragments they build on. See Velasco, *Microliteraturas*.

25. Alonso de Cervantes, "Prólogo," iii.

26. *On Literary Worlds*, 24–25.

27. I am adapting these terms from Jean Luc Nancy's discussion of "world," "inhabitant," and "sojourner" in *The Creation of the World*; see 31–55, esp. 42.

28. Alonso de Cervantes, "Prólogo," iii.

29. Marino, *Jorge Manrique's "Coplas por la muerte de su padre,"* 41.

30. Alonso de Cervantes is not the only writer to discuss the power of glossing the *Coplas*. In introductory remarks to his glosses, Rodrigo de Valdepeñas (1505–1560) describes a lifelong engagement with Manrique's poem: he prepared glosses of twenty-two stanzas as a youth attending the university at Alcalá de Henares, as he discovered his vocation; years later, having entered the Carthusian order, he completed the work. Valdepeñas recounts that when his father was in need of consolation ("que a la sazón tenía harta necesidad de consuelo"), he sent him a fragment of his gloss. His superior at the monastery requested the work, and Valdepeñas showed it to him (and it is his superior who had the collected glosses printed). As in the case of Alonso de Cervantes, glossing the *Coplas* draws Valdepeñas into social and political identities. The glosses and Valdepeñas's prologue are included in the same volume that contains Alonso's glosses: Pérez y Gómez, ed., *El ayre de la almena*, vol. 5. Marino discusses them in *Jorge Manrique's "Coplas por la muerte de su padre,"* 41–43.

31. Ramachandran, *The Worldmakers*, 8.

32. Greene, *Five Words*, 152.

33. On the Orphic lyric self, see Greene's discussion of the "global I" and Renaissance lyric, in *Five Words*, 148–56. On the Petrarchan self, see the classic studies by Mazzotta, *The Worlds of Petrarch*; Roche, *Petrarch and the English Sonnet Sequences*; and Freccero, "The Fig Tree and the Laurel." On Petrarch and gender, see Vickers, "Diana Described."

34. Mimi Yiu notes that Jonson marked the passage on Orpheus and Amphion in his copy of Horace's *Ars Poetica*. See Yiu, "Sounding the Space between Men," 80. On Jonson and Amphion, see also Paster, "Ben Jonson and the Uses of Architecture," 306–20.

35. Jonson, "To Penshurst," lines 1–8.

Notes to Pages 36–45 175

36. In Ovid's *Metamorphoses*, book 15: "Troy was great in her riches and people; / for ten long years she was able to / spend the blood of so many / sons in her cause." On this passage see above, introduction, 16–17.

37. Garcilaso de la Vega, *Poesía Castellana*, 270. All translations to this volume are my own, prepared in consultation with Elmira Louie.

38. Carroll B. Johnson reads the poem in terms of Orpheus and Renaissance belatedness, concluding that though Garcilaso "may not calm the seas and incline the trees . . . [his song] has competed creditably with Ovid's." See Johnson, "Personal Involvement and Poetic Tradition in the Spanish Renaissance."

39. On the significance of Garcilaso's choice of mood and verb tense in the Ode, see Cascardi, *Ideologies of History in the Spanish Golden Age*, 247–85.

40. Garcilaso de la Vega, *Poesía Castellana*, 270.

41. Garcilaso de la Vega, 271.

42. The princess Anaxarete mocks impoverished Iphis, a shepherd who seeks to woo her. Iphis hangs himself, and Venus turns Anaxarete to stone (book 14.698–771).

43. Garcilaso de la Vega, *Poesía Castellana*, 272.

44. Although the context of the Ode differs in significant ways from the contexts that Maria Lugones examines in "Heterosexualism and the Colonial/Modern Gender System," the thinking in that essay is fundamental to the analysis and criticism of gender as a discourse of Western modernity. Jacques Rancière's characterization of a human appropriation of the power of world-making, in the form of the "distribution and redistribution of places and identities . . . [the] apportioning and reapportioning of spaces and times, of the visible and the invisible, and of noise and speech," also seems relevant here, particularly given the highly self-conscious artifice of world-making as Garcilaso performs it in this poem. See Rancière, *Aesthetics and Its Discontents*, 24. On gender and sixteenth- and seventeenth-century lyric poetry, see Valencia, *The Melancholy Void*.

45. Acuña invokes the "bad poet's" "traducción furiosa," or "frenzied translation." The phrase points to Orlando Furioso, which Urrea translated from Italian into Castilian in 1549. I will return to this point.

46. Acuña, "A un buen caballero." n.p. Translations to this work are my own, prepared in consultation with Elmira Louie.

47. The investigation was ordered by Philip II and was carried out by the Order of the Knights of Santiago, one of Spain's most powerful and aristocratic fraternities. The king's decision to call upon the Order and impose secrecy on the process probably had to do with his respect for the Urrea family, which was highly placed in the Aragonese aristocracy, and for Urrea, personally, as a captain and a well-regarded member of the imperial retinue. See Geneste, *Le capitaine-poète aragonais Jerónimo de Urrea*.

48. Ovid, *Metamorphoses*, trans. Raeburn, 386. Raeburn is more consistent with the Latin than Humphries. Book 10, lines 83–85: "ille etiam Thracum populis fuit auctor amorem / in teneros transferre mares citraque iuventam / aetatis breve ver et primos carpere flores." I am grateful to Marc Schachter for helping me think through Acuña's subtexts here.

49. See Martin, *An Erotic Philology of Golden Age Spain*, 43–56.

176 **Notes to Pages 45-51**

50. See Fuchs, *Passing for Spain*; and Fra-Molinero, "Ser mulato en España y América." On seventeenth-century discourses that shaped Black masculinity, see also Wright, *Juan Latino*.

51. I discuss Cortés's letters and the conquest more fully in chapter 4.

52. Johnson, *Cultural Hierarchy in Sixteenth-Century Europe*, 161–96. Johnson's discussion of the wider culture of exclusion during the period is also relevant to my discussions here (135–60).

53. ". . . aquí le perdonáramos al señor capitán que no le hubiera traído a España y hecho castellano; que le quitó mucho de su natural valor, y lo mismo harán todos aquellos que los libros de verso quisieren volver en otra lengua." Cervantes, *Don Quijote I*, ed. Allen, 153. (. . . here, we might have excused the captain for not having brought him to Spain and made him a Castilian; for he robbed him of much of his natural valor, and all those who seek to turn books of verse into another language will do the same.) Cervantes, *Don Quixote*, trans. Grossman, 48.

54. See Sutch and Prescott, "Translation as Transformation," esp. 284–86.

55. Urrea, *Discurso de la vida humana y aventuras del caballero determinado traduzido de frances por Don Jerónimo de Urrea*.

56. Acuña, *El cavallero determinado*, front matter, n.p.; my translation.

57. My reading here is congruent with theirs, as my concern has less to do with the idea of original translation than it does with what is enabled and precluded by decisions about pattern and rhythm.

58. "In the autumn of both / My life and of the year, / On the spur of the moment / I went outside my house / By myself, alone except for Thought, / Who stayed with me that day / And made me recall / My earliest youth." Marche, *Le Chevalier délibéré* (*The Resolute Knight*), ed. Carroll, trans. Carroll and Wilson.

59. "In the final season / of the year and of my life / a sudden event / caused me to depart / my home and my country. / As I made this journey alone / my thought awoke / to ponder forgotten memory / of my history and the time / of my childhood." My translation.

60. The Spanish synalepha (*sinalefa*) plays an important role here: as in Anglophone poetry, the device combines syllables ending in a vowel with the following syllable if that syllable begins with a vowel. So line 9, for example, would read, "re-no-van-del-tiem-poy-cuen-to."

61. "*Nación*," like "nation," has a number of meanings during this period. However, in this context, Acuña uses the term in the sense of the *patria*, or homeland.

62. Acuña, *El cavallero determinado*, front matter, n.p.; my translation.

63. Urrea, *Discurso de la vida*, front matter, n.p.; my translation.

64. Grossman with Halliday, *Sighted Singer*, 224.

65. "In the final season of the month and of the year, / and of the flower of my youth, / a strange incident took me from my house. / Because of something that happened all of a sudden / I left my homeland, and my contented state, / to embark on a disagreeable quest / traveling along lonely paths." My translation.

Notes to Pages 52–57 177

66. In the "Reprensión contra los poetas españoles que escriben en verso italiano" (Reproof to Spanish poets who write in Italian verse): "Bien se pueden castigar / a cuenta de anabaptistas, / pues por ley particular / se tornan a bautizar / y se llaman petrarquistas." (It is suitable that they be punished / on charges they are anabaptists, / for by laws of their own making / they rebaptize themselves / and call themselves Petrarchans.) My translation.

67. Boscán, *Obra completa*, 116; my translation.

68. In the "Reprensión." On the significance of the *nueva poesía* and its relationship to Spanish politics, see Middlebrook, *Imperial Lyric*.

69. Boscán, *Obra completa*, 116; my translation.

70. Alemany, "El sonsoneto y la práctica poética cortesana del siglo XVI."

71. Urrea, "Discurso de la vida," front matter, n.p.; my translation.

72. See Anne R. Sweeney's concise and striking portrait of the period, *Snow in Arcadia*, esp. 1–37.

73. Grossman's pronouncement on blank verse (unrhymed iambic pentameter) is representative of this view: "Blank Verse . . . is the order speech takes when it gives the picture of the well-formed social person." Grossman, *Sighted Singer*, 282. See also Greenblatt, *Renaissance Self-Fashioning*. On Tottel and the regularization of meter, see Thompson, *The Founding of English Metre*, 1–36.

74. See Quitslund, "'Without Pity Heare Their Dying Groanes'"; and Valdivia, "Mere Meter."

75. Sutch and Prescott, "Translation as Transformation," 289.

76. Thompson, *The Founding of English Metre*, 35–36.

77. Martínez Valdivia, "Mere Meter." With reference to the theories and methods of the New Lyric studies, Martínez Valdivia argues that the relative invisibility of Sternhold and Hopkins as an influence on English lyric arises from "a blinkered focus on a purely literary poetic heritage routed through *Tottel's Miscellany*," one of whose outcomes is that "the history of the sound of post-medieval English poetry has relied on divorcing it from its origins in musical church practices." She continues: "The historical mistelling that severs metrical verse psalmody from poetry writ large has two dimensions. . . . First, a critical emphasis on the category of the *literary*—the scholarly validation of and insistence on distinguishing between supposedly high and low, elite and common, literary and popular poetry—created generic divisions that were not in fact operational during the formative century and subsequent years of post-medieval English verse. . . . The second angle of mistelling is that critics have distanced the study of poetry from religion." See Martínez Valdivia, "Mere Meter," 556–58.

78. *Ars Poetica*.

79. On poulter's measure, see Greene, *The Princeton Encyclopedia of Poetry and Poetics*, 1100.

80. Bateman, *Trauailed Pilgrime*, 2. I have lightly modernized the spelling.

81. On the significance of the woodcuts to *Le Chevalier délibéré*, Acuña's *Cavallero determinado*, and Bateman's work with the poem in the *Trauailed Pilgrime*, see Prescott,

178   Notes to Pages 57–60

"Chivalric Restoration." Sutch and Prescott present a thorough analysis of Bateman's refashioning of the poem in "Translation as Transformation," 290–308, esp. 291–92.

82. Contrast Bateman's note to his readers with the boasts in Cordero's sonnet, for example: "Though the matter (gentle Reader) contained in this my simple treatise, be not altogether fruitless, but that many things therein might very well be amended . . . favorably consider the good will of the writer, and then if anything chance contrary to thy mind, show forth thy friendly commendations, with such ordered corrections, as may not only encourage the Author, but also get to thyself in like effect like commendation or praise" (Bateman, *Trauailed Pilgrime*, 5).

83. Bateman, 10.

84. Bateman, 10. Bateman rhymes at the hemistich, thus producing the sound of common meter: IN *Hyems* force, both trée and herbe (A) doth vade as rest of life, (B) / On sudden then to me appeard (A) the state of worldly strife: (B) / As I thus going all alone (C) (one) did to me appeare, (D) / Awake, quoth he, from pensive mone, (C) of me have thou no feare. (D)

85. In the preface to a volume of collected essays, Daniel-Henri Pageaux draws a connection between Amphion and literary criticism, "an art that lacks neither power nor originality as critics construct, reconstruct, reconstitute the disparate materials furnished by reading, analysis, and the privileged contact critics enjoy with the work that is called the critical experience. Because it is in this experience that, between the already of the work and the not yet of the criticism, the words, the images rise up and order themselves, and allow us to glimpse how the trajectory of the work of criticism can join and recover the poetic project." (". . . ne manquerait ni de puissance ni d'originalité celle de symboliser le travail, critique qui construit, reconstruit, reconstitute las matériaux épars qu'ont fournis les lectures, l'analyse, et ce contact privilégié avec l'oeuvre que se nomme expérience critique. Car c'est elle qui, entre le déjà-là de l'oeuvre et le pas encore du discours critique, fait se lever et s'ordonner les mots, les images, et permet d'entrevoir comment le trajet du travail critique peut et doit rejoiner, retrouver le projet poétique.") Pageaux, *La lyre d'Amphion*, 7.

86. Vázquez, "Poesía morisca."

87. On the complexity of sixteenth-century Spanish policies on Moriscos, see Cavanaugh, "Litigating for Liberty." On Moriscos, see García-Arenal and Wiegers, *The Expulsion of the Moriscos from Spain*. On the effects of the 1567 edict (premática), see Irigoyen, *Moors Dressed as Moors*.

88. Barbara Fuchs points out that "Morisco . . . could refer both to light- and dark-skinned people, to Muslims in Spain as well as in North Africa, and even, occasionally, to Turks or sub-Saharan peoples" (Fuchs, "The Spanish Race," 88). Christina Lee argues that the othering and eventual expulsion of this group arose from a widespread "anxiety of sameness," observing that "while conspicuous religious and socio-cultural difference was certainly perturbing and unsettling, in some ways it was not as threatening to the dominant Spanish identity as the potential discovery of the arbitrariness that separated them from the undesirables of society—and therefore the recognition of fundamental sameness" (Lee, *The Anxiety of Sameness in Early Modern Spain*, 4; see also "Moriscos and the Reassurance of Difference," 153–84).

Notes to Pages 60–63   179

89. This is my characterization of the cultural and social functions that Vázquez analyzes. However, he remarks on a passage in which the Morisco poet Ibrahim Taybilí (Juan Pérez) (ca. 1580–ca. 1650) navigates the Spanish poetic topos of the muses—figures who are problematic to a Muslim writer—who understands references to divinities other than Allah as idolatry. Vázquez notes that in the dedication of his 1628 *Contradictión de los catorçe artículos de la fe Cristiana, missa y sacrifiçios, con otras pruebas y argumentos contra la falsa trinidad* (Contradiction of the fourteen articles of the Christian faith, mass, and sacrifices, with other evidence and arguments against the false trinity), Taybilí demonstrates his thorough understanding of the convention, his sense that it is appropriate to his poem, and the necessity such a reference produces for careful explication. This, Taybilí writes, ". . . y si fue costumbre de los sabios de la antigüedad guardada con no menos piedad y Relijión que superstiçion y banidad después de edificar templos, consagrar aras, ençender fuegos y quemar yncendios a la mentirossa deydad de las fabulossa muças . . ." See Vázquez, "Poesía morisca," 231. On Islamic presence in Spanish literature, see López-Baralt, *Islam in Spanish Literature*.

90. Quoted in Vázquez, "Poesía morisca," 227; my translation. I have modernized the spelling slightly.

91. In *Don Quijote, Part II*, the Morisco character Ricote also presents a convoluted defense of the expulsion. See *Don Quijote, Part II*, ed. Allen, chap. 54. I discuss the episode in chapter 3.

92. Quoted in Vázquez, "Poesía morisca," 224; my translation. I have modernized the spelling slightly.

93. In addition to Jones, see Finley, *Amplifications of Black Sound from Colonial Mexico*.

94. See Jones, "Cosmetic Ontologies, Cosmetic Subversions," and "Sor Juana's Black Atlantic."

95. See Jones's illuminating reading of the space the Song of Songs opens up for Black presence in Spanish culture, in "Cosmetic Ontologies, Cosmetic Subversions," 41–49; and "Sor Juana's Black Atlantic," 279–80.

96. Jones points out that his reading practices build from early, pathbreaking work by scholars including Baltasar Fra-Molinero (in Spanish studies) and Kim F. Hall (in British studies), and from the methodologies developed by critics and scholars working in the areas of Black studies and African and Africana studies. His readings of Spanish lyrics participate in wider discussions of early modern racialization that include illuminating close readings of drama, for example, Ndiaye, *Scripts of Blackness*; and Brown, *Shakespeare's White Others*.

97. See Jones, "Cosmetic Ontologies, Cosmetic Subversions," 29–30.

98. See Jones, 39–41.

Chapter Two

1. Boileau, *L'Art poétique*; my translation.

2. See introduction, 7.

180 **Notes to Pages 64–67**

3. See chapter 1, 38, 51.

4. John Freccero draws the comparision between the Petrarchan sequence and modern technology in his classic essay "The Fig Tree and the Laurel: Petrarch's Poetics": "The extraordinary innovation in the *Canzoniere* is . . . to be found in what the verses leave unsaid, in the blank spaces separating these lyric 'fragments,' as they were called, from each other. The persona created by the serial juxtaposition of dimensionless lyric moments is as illusory as the animation of a film strip, the product of the reader's imagination as of the poet's craft; yet, the resulting portrait of an eternally weeping love remains Petrarch's most distinguished poetic achievement. Because it is a composite of lyric instants, the portrait has no temporality" (34). Roland Greene further develops the idea of Petrarchan lyric technology in *Post-Petrarchism*, where he proposes that the lyric sequence is a "highly adaptable technology" that writers use to devise "specific solutions to local cultural and aesthetic problems" (1).

5. Speaking directly to this caprice, Sor Juana Inés de la Cruz (1649–1691) writes, "En Petrarca hallé una copia / de una Laura, o de una duende, / pues dicen que ser no tuvo / más del que en sus versos tiene" (In Petrarch I found a copy / of a Laura, or of an imp, / for they say that she had no life / beyond what she has in his verses). *Obras Completas de Sor Juana Inés de la Cruz,* ed. Mendez Plancarte, 124. On Petrarchan self-creation and the objectification of women, see Vickers, "Diana Described."

6. On the rise of civil conflict in France in the lead-up to the French Wars of Religion, see Davis, "The Rites of Violence."

7. Stoler, "Imperial Debris," 194.

8. Stoler suggests that we substitute "imperial formations" for the term "empire," "to register the ongoing quality of processes of decimation, displacement, and reclamation. Imperial formations are relations of force. They harbor political forms that endure beyond the formal exclusions that legislate against equal opportunity, commensurate dignities, and equal rights. In working with the concept of imperial formation rather than empire, the emphasis shifts from fixed forms of sovereignty and its denials, to gradated forms of sovereignty and what has long marked the technologies of imperial rule—sliding and contested scales of differential rights" (Stoler, "Imperial Debris," 193).

9. Richard Helgerson, ed. and trans., *Joachim du Bellay: "The Regrets," with "The Antiquities of Rome," Three Latin Elegies, "The Defense and Enrichment of the French Language": A Bilingual Edition* (University Park: Penn State University Press, 2006), 252–53. Quotations and translations from this volume are reprinted with permission of the University of Pennsylvania Press.

10. Helgerson, 274–75.

11. Helgerson, 264–65.

12. Helgerson, 252–53.

13. Helgerson, 26–32.

14. Helgerson, 328–329. The parenthesis on "François" refers to the recent death of François I, who embarked on the project of political, linguistic, and cultural reform in the interest of establishing a sovereign and centralized France. On *monarchie* and the

Notes to Pages 67-73 181

French imitation of Roman power, see Helgerson, 1-2. See also Hampton, *Literature and Nation*, 150-94; and Kennedy, *The Site of Petrarchism*, 77-93.

15. On rhetoric, language, and early ideas of French identity in the wake of the centralizing efforts of François I, see Hampton, *Literature and Nation*, 1-28, especially 20-27.

16. Helgerson, *Joachim du Bellay*, 246-47.

17. Helgerson, 254-55.

18. Helgerson, 248-49.

19. Helgerson, 248-49.

20. Ovid, *Metamorphoses*, 614. In Latin, the lines read: "sic tempora verti / cernimus atque illas adsumere robora gentes, / concidere has; sic magna fuit censuque virisque perque decem potuit tantum dare sanguinis annos, / nunc humilis veteres tantummodo Troia ruinas / et pro divitiis tumulos ostendit avorum. / Clara fuit Sparte, magnae viguere Mycenae, / nec non et Cecropis, nec non Amphionis arces. / Vile solum Sparte est, altae cecidere Mycenae, / Oedipodioniae quid sunt, nisi nomina, Thebae?" ("P. OVIDI NASONIS METAMORPHOSEON LIBER QVINTVS DECIMVS," The Latin Library, 420-35).

21. Ovid, *Metamorphoses*, 614. "Dardaniam fama est consurgere Romam, / Appenninigenae quae proxima Thybridis undis / mole / sub ingenti rerum fundamina ponit: haec igitur formam crescendo mutat et olim / inmensi caput orbis erit!" ("P. OVIDI NASONIS METAMORPHOSEON LIBER QVINTVS DECIMVS," The Latin Library, 420-35).

22. Hassan Melehy explains the logic: "The absence of the 'original' Rome in which these writings were produced is not simply lamented in the *Antiquitez*; rather their current lack of groundedness allows them to be taken up and reworked by the French Renaissance poet, who thereby produces the space in which a properly French poetry will take place. That is, the *Antiquitez* are not primarily an expression of lamenting nostalgia, but instead a production of a poetry in the present and for the future" (Melehy, "Du Bellay's Time in Rome," 1). See also Bizer, *Les lettres romains de Du Bellay*; and Bellenger, ed., *Du Bellay et ses sonnets romains*.

23. Helgerson, *Joachim du Bellay*, 272-73.

24. Helgerson, 274.

25. Helgerson, 268.

26. Helgerson, 262-63.

27. Helgerson, 266-67.

28. Helgerson, 264-65.

29. See Melehy, "Du Bellay's Time in Rome."

30. Helgerson, *Joachim du Bellay*, 278-79.

31. Domestic imperium faltered. Overseas, French expansion was less an exercise of crown-directed imperialism than a commercial affair in the sixteenth and seventeenth centuries. Contact and early colonial activity in Africa and the Americas is carried out

182 **Notes to Pages 74–79**

by merchants over whom French rulers maintain unstable control. Hodson and Rush-forth, *Discovering Empire*, chap. 2.

32. Quevedo, "A Roma, sepultada en sus ruinas"; my translation.

33. On Quevedo and Du Bellay, see Cacho Casal, "The Memory of Ruins."

34. Spenser, *Complaints*. I have modernized the spelling lightly.

35. For example, influential compilations such as Hernando del Castillo's *Cancionero general*, in Spain, which went through multiple editions throughout the sixteenth century, and the Portuguese *Cancionero de García de Resende* (1516), which provided the basis for an early modern canon of Portuguese lyric.

36. A. E. B. Coldiron discusses Spenser's translation as substituting "genius" in the "imperial sense" for an earlier meaning that had to do with the concept of "genius loci, the governing spirit that presided at the birth of the *Antiquitez*." See Coldiron, "How Spenser Excavates Du Bellay's 'Antiquitez,'" 42. On Spenser as the English Orpheus, see Cheney and Armas, *European Literary Careers*. See also Nelson, "Ovidian Fame."

37. Spenser, *Complaints*. On Spenser and the "national Orpheus," see Cheney and Armas, *European Literary Careers*.

38. British aggrandizement also informs local translational choices; for example, when Spenser translates line 3 of Sonnet 22, "De ce peuple qui tient les bords de la Tamize," as "With Thames inhabitants of noble fame."

39. Sonnets 18 and 25 allude most directly to the powers of Amphion, and the extent to which Longfellow might have identified with the myth is unclear.

40. The organization and scope of *Poems and Places* is characteristic both of Long-fellow and of the nineteenth-century worldview he shared with intellectual elites in the United States and the parts of Europe we now tend to conceive of in terms of the "global North." The series devotes four volumes to England, one to Ireland, another three to Scotland, Iceland, Norway, and Sweden, grouped together; France and Savoy are grouped in a two-volume pair; full volumes are dedicated to Italy, Russia, and Germany; other entries include two volumes on Spain, Portugal, Belgium, and Holland (the European portions of the Spanish Hapsburg empire), Asia, Oceania; five volumes for America, followed by one for Americas, one volume for Africa, etc.

41. Joyce, *Rome's Wreck*. Quotations from this volume are reprinted with permission of Cusp Books.

42. In *Incomparable Poetry*, Robert Kiely describes Ireland's colonial and postcolonial economic trajectory succinctly. The Celtic Tiger, as he summarizes the phenomenon, "refers to the economy of the Republic of Ireland for the decade or so spanning the mid-1990s to the mid-2000s. In the early 1990s, Ireland was a relatively poor country by Western European standards, with high poverty, unemployment, emigration, inflation, and low economic growth. It had failed to separate church and state and the resulting policing of morality in Ireland sharply differentiated it from many liberal European countries. With the advent of the Celtic Tiger, this changed by degrees as Ireland underwent a period of relatively rapid economic growth fueled by FDI slowly causing corresponding changes in Irish culture. Former Taoiseach Garret FitzGerald says that Ireland's ability to 'catch up' with its EU partners during the Celtic Tiger years 'owed everything to a happy timing coincidence between the period of peak demand by for-

Notes to Pages 79–85 183

eign industry for Irish labour in Ireland and a parallel peak in the availability of Irish labour'" (21–22).

43. As an example of Joyce's postmodernism, consider *Rome's Wreck* alongside the opening lines of John Ashbery's "Daffy Duck in Hollywood," with its irreverent tone, its compressed temporality, and its allusions to late medieval and early Renaissance poetry: "Something strange is creeping across me. / La Celestina has only to warble the first few bars / Of 'I Thought about You' or something mellow from / *Amadigi di Gaula* for everything—a mint-condition can / Of Rumford's Baking Powder, a celluloid earring, Speedy / Gonzales, the latest from Helen Topping Miller's fertile / Escritoire, a sheaf of suggestive pix on greige, deckle-edged / Stock—to come clattering through the rainbow trellis" (31).

44. Helgerson, *Du Bellay*, 264–65.

45. See introduction. In Euripides's play *Antiope* and in Plato's *Gorgias*, Hermes/Mercury resolves a dispute between Amphion and his twin brother, Zethus, with the prophecy that in future generations, Amphion's lyre will be credited with building walls for Thebes, not Zethus's physical strength.

46. Joyce, *Rome's Wreck*, Sonnet VII.

47. See Reed, "Idea Eater," 3. See also Dworkin and Goldsmith, *Against Expression*, xvii–liv.

48. Kiely continues: "Is it the nationality of the individual investor, or is it the company as legal entity? Is it currency, or is it the nationality of the labor force whose expropriated labor power the money represents? In the Ireland of the Celtic Tiger and still now, dependence on foreign firms means that there is a high divergence between Gross Domestic Product (GDP) and Gross National Product (GNP) (also called Gross National Income, or GNI . . .). Economists highlighted over-reliance on FDI [foreign direct investment] repeatedly as a major structural weakness in the Irish economic model" (Kiely, *Incomparable Poetry*, 19). FDI is an economic procedure by which an investor resident in one economy establishes a lasting interest in businesses located in another economy. These investments usually bring with them a significant amount of social influence. In this way, the FDI lends itself to comparison with the beloved as the structuring center of Petrarchan lyric. See Kiely, 19–20, in comparison to the classic essays by Freccero, "The Fig Tree and the Laurel"; and Vickers, "Diana Described."

49. David Lloyd sets Joyce's poetry in the contexts of mannerist and baroque art. See Lloyd, *Counterpoetics and Modernity*, 162–85. See especially his discussion of mannerism as a recurrent style that emerges in the context of the "destabilization of the relation between the individual and traditional institutions" (163).

50. Actually, Du Bellay and Spenser coincide with Joyce in this respect. All three versions of Sonnet 4 deploy an anti-Petrarchan catalog, which Du Bellay initiates when he presents his initial "chef," "estomac," "ventre," "main," "pied." But both Du Bellay and Spenser mask misogynist violence that subtends their sonnets with vocabularies of imperial grandeur, with erudite witticisms, and with stanzas that point to Petrarch, who authorizes the gender dynamics.

51. Kiely, *Incomparable Poetry*, discusses the impact of the economic explosion and crisis on gender relations and on women.

184 Notes to Pages 88-90

52. Helgerson, *Du Bellay*, 252–53.

53. Helgerson, 256–57.

54. Helgerson, 270–71. Like many mid-sixteenth-century French writers (e.g., Agrippa D'Aubigné), Du Bellay was certainly moved by the bloodletting that French Protestants and Catholics, "brothers" in Frenchness and also in the Christian faith, were carrying out against each other during the period.

55. Helgerson, 274–75.

56. Compare with *Antiquitez*, Sonnet 6, quoted above, and with Spenser's *Complaints*:

> Such as the Berecynthian Goddess bright
> In her swift chariot with high turrets crowned,
> Proud that so many Gods she brought to light;
> Such was this City in her good days found:
> This city, more than the great Phrygian mother
> Renowned for fruit of famous progeny,
> Whose greatness by the greatness of none other,
> But by herself her equal match could see:
> Rome only might to Rome comparèd be,
> And only Rome could make great Rome to tremble:
> So did the Gods by heavenly doom decree,
> That other deathly power should not resemble
> Her that did match the whole earth's puissaunce,
> And did her courage to the heavens advance.

57. Compare with Du Bellay, Sonnet 2, quoted above, and Spenser's *Complaints*:

> Great Babylon her haughty walls will praise,
> And sharpèd steeples high shot up in air;
> Greece will the old Ephesian buildings blaze;
> And Nylus' nurslings their Pyramids fair . . .

58. Dimock, "A Theory of Resonance," 1061.

59. Greene is one of few twentieth-century literary critics to notice Amphion, although his discussion is limited by the reigning concept of lyric at the time. In his discussion of the *Antiquitez*, Greene recognizes Amphion's significance as a structuring trope that "reveal[s] . . . Du Bellay as one of the great architects of the French sonnet," a writer who creates a sequence in which "political, architectural and poetic activity is all parallel." His analysis concludes in the vein of poetic agon that dominates mid- and late twentieth-century criticism, however. Poems such as Sonnet 1 and Sonnet 25 demonstrate to Greene that Du Bellay "cannot yet claim the authority . . . that Virgil claimed. . . . Compared to Virgil, he seems unsupported and isolated. He can only hope to be effective by the sympathetic magic of verbal imitation." Du Bellay's subtext of Amphion and Orpheus suggests that to access the "sympathetic magic of verbal imitation" was both *precisely* the point and no small achievement in this sequence. Building

Notes to Pages 91–94   185

on Greene's important reading, I argue here that unlocking the energies that animate the *translatio* of the polis, Du Bellay demonstrates his skills with Amphion's lyre. See Greene, *The Light in Troy*, 222–23.

60. Don Mee Choi writes lucidly about translation's ability to engage and unravel experiences of US imperialism, in particular. See Choi, *Translation Is a Mode = Translation Is an Anti-Neocolonial Mode*.

61. Of particular interest to the contexts and topics pursued in this book are recent translations of Homer by Emily Wilson (*The Iliad*, *The Odyssey*), as well as Anne Carson's ongoing engagement with Greek works, and Stephanie McCarter's translation of *Metamorphoses*, all of which direct a deliberately female gaze at tradition; in *Memorial*, an "excavation" of Homer's *Iliad*, Alice Oswald describes as being shaped by her desire to recover the sacredness of human community that she identifies as the center of the poem. This work can be traced back much further, of course; for example, to Derek Walcott's *Omeros*.

Chapter Three

1. Cervantes, *Viaje del Parnaso*, ed. Fernández García, 51. All translations to this volume are my own, prepared in consultation with Elmira Louie.

2. The pun in Spanish is between *crujía*, the term for this kind of rail, and a colloquial phrase for a patch of bad luck or loss: "Hecha ser la crujía se me muestra / de una luenga y tristísima elegía, / que no en cantar, sino en llorar es diestra. / Por esta entiendo yo que se diria / lo que suele decirse a un desdichado, / cuando lo pasa mal, pasó crujía." (It seemed to me that the rail [crujía] was formed / of a long and very sad elegy, / which it is appropriate to weep, not sing / and for this reason I understand why it is said / of one who has suffered misfortune / that when he suffers, he suffers *crujía*.) The description of the ship appears in Cervantes, *Viaje del Parnaso*, ed. Fernández García, 51–54.

3. "La racamenta, que es siempre parlera, / toda la componían redondillas, / con que ellas se mostraba más ligera." (The tack, which is always chatty, / was made all of *redondillas*, / which made it lighter.) Cervantes, 53.

4. Cervantes, 51.

5. On the terraqueous globe, see Padrón, *The Spacious Word*, 1–8.

6. ". . . la heróica hazaña / donde con alta de soldados gloria, / y con propio valor y airado pecho / tuve, aunque humilde, parte en la victoria." (. . . that heroic feat / in which, among the number of glorious soldiers, / and with the necessary valor and a raging breast / I played a humble part in securing victory.) Cervantes, 47.

7. "Entre los arrojados, se oyó un ciego, / que murmurando entre las ondas iba / de Apolo con un 'peste y reniego.' // . . . // Otro, que al parecer iba mohíno, / con ser un zapatero de obra prima, / dijo dos mil, no un solo desatino. / Trabaja un tundidor, suda y se anima / por verse a la ribera conducido, / que más la vida que la honra estima." (Among those thrown overboard / a blind man was heard as he tossed in the waves / muttering of Apollo, "plague and rancor" // . . . // Another, who looked downcast, / as he was a first-class shoemaker [the pun is with making feet, in shoes and in verse], / said two thousand, and not just one bit of nonsense.) Cervantes, 77.

186 Notes to Pages 95–101

8. Cervantes, 75–76.

9. Cervantes, 127.

10. See, for example, chapter 1 of Rabelais's *Pantagruel*.

11. On Renaissance *copia*, see Cave, *The Cornucopian Text*, 18–34.

12. Cervantes's view of Parnassian poets is not entirely negative. The *Parnaso* acknowledges writers such as Lope de Vega, Fernando de Herrera, and Luis Barahona de Soto, whom he admires and describes as contributing in meaningful ways to Spanish culture.

13. See Middlebrook, "Cervantes's Orphic Mode."

14. Cascardi, *Cervantes, Literature, and the Discourse of Politics*, 7.

15. Francisco Márquez Villanueva analyzes Don Diego's attire as exotic, burlesque finery modeled on the jester's motley. The outfit alerts readers to the paradoxes and contrasts that form the structuring framework for the episode. Márquez Villanueva reads these paradoxes as a prompt to readers to interpret the scene in the manner of Erasmian folly. See Márquez Villanueva, *Personajes y temas del Quijote*, 147–227. Erasmus is clearly an influence in a section of the novel so preoccupied with *copia*. In the context of the expulsion of the Moriscos that informs *Don Quixote, Part II* throughout, I suggest that we understand the *verde gabán* to be a reference to Islam (green is the color of Islam).

16. English-language quotations from *Don Quixote* are drawn from Cervantes, *Don Quixote*, trans. Grossman, 552. Subsequent citations refer to this text.

17. Cervantes, *Don Quixote*, trans. Grossman, 567–68. "Halló don Quijote ser la casa de don Diego ancha como de aldea, las armas, empero, de piedra tosca, encima de la puerta de la calle." Spanish citations from *Don Quixote* are drawn from Cervantes, *Don Quijote I*, ed. Allen; and Cervantes, *Don Quijote II*, ed. Allen. This quotation appears in *Don Quijote II*, 184.

18. I am drawing forward the ways in which the Miranda family conforms to Renaissance humanist ideals of moderation and self-restraint. Another way to read the episode is as an account of a people under threat. Moriscos were a targeted population throughout the sixteenth and seventeenth centuries, as I discuss in chapter 1. Don Diego's self-description as an ardent worshipper of the Virgin Mary, in chapter 16; the silence that reigns in the Miranda household, which Don Quixote marvels at a dinner in chapter 18; and the meticulous self-sufficiency of the household might reflect the family's fear of attack, as takes place with Ricote. See 38–41. For a concise overview of the historically overlooked category of assimilated Spanish Moriscos, see Fuchs, *Exotic Nation*, 127–28.

19. Cervantes, *Don Quijote II*, ed. Allen, 168.

20. Cervantes, *Don Quixote*, trans. Grossman, 555.

21. Cervantes, 599–600.

22. Cervantes, *Don Quijote II*, ed. Allen, 170–71.

23. Cervantes, *Don Quixote*, trans. Grossman, 557.

24. Cervantes, *Don Quijote II*, ed. Allen, 184.

Notes to Pages 101–104 187

25. Cervantes, *Don Quixote*, trans. Grossman, 567.

26. See chapter 1.

27. "¡O dulces prendas por mi mal halladas / dulces y alegres cuando Dios quería...!"

28. "El señor Don Diego de Miranda, padre de vuesa merced, me ha dado noticia de la rara habilidad y sutil ingenio que vuestra merced tiene, y, sobre todo, que es vuesa merced un gran poeta." Cervantes, *Don Quijote II*, ed. Allen, 186.

29. Cervantes, *Don Quijote II*, ed. Allen, 186–87.

30. Cervantes, *Don Quixote*, trans. Grossman, 171.

31. The Amphionic logic that underwrites the early modern poetry contest explains a detail that has often puzzled scholars of these events. Many writers apparently did not seek the glories of personal recognition. Famed writers such as Guillén de Castro, Hernando de Acuña, Lope de Vega, and Luis de Góngora contributed poems anonymously or wrote poems for other entrants to submit under their own names (Egido, "Poesía de justas y academias"). Inmaculada Osuna Rodríguez speculates why this might be the case: perhaps a writer belonged to a select group that would already know his or her name; or perhaps, in contests with a religious motivation, anonymous or pseudonymous participation attested to a participant's selfless devotion to the saint, parish, house, religious order, or festival being celebrated. It also seems likely that poets sought social and political favor, and perhaps compensation, for work submitted on behalf of others. But during the years of political and social remaking in Spain, France, England, and the Americas, it was possible to enjoy a successful poetic career without achieving individual Orphic fame (Osuna Rodríguez, "Literary Academies and Poetic Tournaments," 154). On gender and *anonimato* in Spanish and Spanish-American texts, see Del Barco, "El anonimato como performance textual," 101–17. On Orphic fame, see Nelson, "Ovidian Fame."

32. On poetry contests, see Egido, "Poesía de justas y academias"; and Osuna Rodríguez, "Literary Academies and Poetic Tournaments." See Chang-Rodríguez, *"Aquí ninfas del sur, venid ligeras,"* 23, on the significance of poetry contests and festivals to Spanish-American culture. See also Heaton et al., "Poetic Contests."

33. The contest in question was celebrated in Valencia in 1614. See Mas i Usó, *Justas valencianas barrocas*, 216.

34. For example, see Guillaume Berthon on the significance of the poetry contest held during the Congrès de Nice, convened to unite the great Christian princes of the Mediterranean, Charles V and François I, in common cause against the Ottomans. Berthon, "L'année poetique et politique 1538," 359–73.

35. "... la casi inabarcable montaña de relaciones publicadas y los muchos manuscritos existentes en las bibliotecas nacionales y extranjeras. La empresa puede resultar desmoralizadora, pues no es la calidad literaria la que impera entre tantos centones de versos. Ya lo señaló Dámaso Alonso: 'Se canta allí con temas impuestos (y a veces muy extravagantes) ... y a ellas concurren todas las medianías, todos los seguidores, los oscurecidos, los que no tienen nada que decir, ni auditorio para sus versos.'" (... the nearly unscalable mountain of published proceedings and the many manuscripts that exist in national libraries and abroad. The enterprise can be demoralizing, as literary quality does not reign supreme in these many hundreds of verses. Dámaso Alonso said

188 **Notes to Page 105**

it well: "They sing on set themes handed to them (and sometimes these themes are quite extravagant) . . . and the competitors are all middling writers, the followers, the obscurantists, those who have nothing to say and no one to listen to their verse.") Egido, "Poesía de justas y academias," 119–20.

36. Cervantes lampoons Don Lorenzo's contest lyrics and Don Quixote's responses to it. Don Lorenzo recites stanzas such as the following, based on a Salamanca-generated prompt on the theme of Pyramus and Thisbe:

> El muro rompe la doncella hermosa
> que de Píramo abrió el gallardo pecho;
> parte el Amor de Chipre y va derecho
> a ver la quiebra estrecha y prodigiosa . . .
> (*Don Quijote II*, 189)

And Don Lorenzo recites lines from his gloss-in-progress:

> Si mi fue tornase a es,
> sin esperar más será,
> O viniese el tiempo ya
> De lo que será después . . .
> (*Don Quijote II*, 191–92)

(The wall is breached by the beauteous maid / who pierced the gallant bosom of Pyramus; / Love flies from Cyprus, faster than an arrow, / to see the rift, so prodigious and so narrow . . .) Cervantes, *Don Quixote*, trans. Grossman, 572.

He further presents a gloss on the lines "If my *was* would be an is, / not waiting for a *will* be, / or if at last the time would come / when later is now and here . . ." Don Quixote responds enthusiastically: "¡Bendito sea Dios—dijo don Quijote habiendo oído el soneto a don Lorenzo—, que entre los infinitos poetas consumidos que hay he visto un consumado poeta, como lo es vuesa merced, señor mío, que así me lo da a entender el artificio deste soneto!" Allen, *Don Quijote II*, 192. ("Praise be to God! . . . Among the infinite number of consumptive poets, Señor, I have seen a consummate poet, which is what your grace is, and what the artfulness of this sonnet leads me to believe!"; Cervantes, *Don Quixote*, trans. Grossman, 574.) Cervantes is making two jokes here: Don Quixote delivers his praise of Don Lorenzo in the same hyperbolic, ornate language that Cervantes pokes fun at with his examples of Don Lorenzo's poetry. Moreover, Don Quixote's judgment is not especially reliable. It is, after all, issued by the man whose life was transformed by phrases such as "The reason for the unreason to which my reason turns so weakens my reason that with reason I complain of thy beauty" (20). ("La razón de la sinrazón que a mi razón se hace, de tal manera mi razón enflaquece, que con razón me quejo de la vuestra fermosura"; Cervantes *Don Quijote I*, 8.)

37. Aurélie Delattre and Adeline Lionetto introduce the idea of enthusiasm as they frame the social power of *poésie de circonstance*: more important than fixing a given event in history, creators of this poetry sought to engender forms of enthusiasm and consensus ("la vision que les auteurs tendent à y doner de l'Histoire, ou . . . leur désir non pas de transmettre des informations que de faire naître une forme d'entousiasme et

Notes to Pages 106-115 189

un consensus"). Delattre and Lionetto, *La Muse de l'ephemère*, 8. "Enthusiasm" captures perfectly the spirit of animated goodwill and productivity that Amphion represents in his happiest aspects.

38. Mas i Usó, *Justas valencianas barrocas*, 51. All translations from the volume are my own.

39. Hampton, *Cheerfulness*, 13.

40. See Williams, *Keywords*, 54-55. See also J. Hillis Miller's discussion of Williams in *Communities in Fiction*, 1-7.

41. Izenberg, *Being Numerous*, 141-42.

42. Izenberg, 2. In his discussion of Language poetry, Izenberg draws a distinction between his understanding of poetic projects such as *Tjanting*, by US poet Ron Silliman, or *Leningrad*, carried out by a collective composed of US Language poets and members of the Russian "Poetic Function" circle of poets in 1989, and what writers in the group might say about their work themselves. Izenberg, 139; on *Tjanting*, see 140-41; on *Leningrad*, see 143-54.

43. Izenberg, 2-4.

44. On Amphion and Zethus, see introduction, 15-16.

45. Izenberg, *Being Numerous*, 141.

46. Izenberg, 142; his italics.

47. For example, if we set early modern lyric and the late twentieth-century movements that Izenberg discusses on a through line of coloniality, the imperial formation that structures Western modernity is organized to systemically devalue human personhood in the interest of feeding the state. On imperial formation, see introduction and chapter 4.

48. Páez de Valenzuela, *Relación breve*. The pages of this volume are not consistently numbered, so I refer to the book as a whole. All translations from this volume are my own, prepared in consultation with Elmira Louie.

49. On the significance of Saint Teresa's beatification to coalescing ideas of Spanish national identity, see Rowe, *Saint and Nation*.

50. Páez de Valenzuela, *Relación breve*.

51. Thomás, *Certamen Poético*.

52. Thomás, *Certamen Poético*. The pages of the volume are inconsistently numbered, so I refer to the volume as a whole. All translations are my own, prepared in consultation with Elmira Louie.

53. Thomás, *Certamen Poético*.

54. The front matter consists of a dedication, an approval by an officer of the Inquisition, and letters of praise and endorsement for the book.

55. Thomás, *Certamen Poético*.

56. Thomás, *Certamen Poético*.

57. See Williams, "Community," in *Keywords*, 54-55.

58. On Amphion and Zethus above, see introduction, 15-16.

190   **Notes to Pages 116–120**

59. Catalá de Valeriola, *Justas poéticas hechas a devoción de Don Bernardo Catalán de Valeriola*.

60. Catalá de Valeriola, *Justas poéticas hechas*; my translation, prepared in consultation with Elmira Louie.

61. "con una zaranda que allí halla, / no sé si antigua o si de nuevo hecha, / zarandó mil poetas de gramalla" (and with a fishing net he found there, / I do not know if it was old or new, / he scooped off a thousand poets in gramalla); Fernández García explains that *gramalla* is an outfit often worn by public administrators. Fernández García, ed., *Viaje del Parnaso*, 77.

62. See Cascardi, *Cervantes, Literature, and the Discourse of Politics*.

63. Cascardi writes that *Don Quixote, Part II* engages the complexity of relationships between communities, be they religious, anchored in regional identity, or otherwise imagined and lived: "Rather than offer a polarized set of view that would pit the politics of the nascent secular nation-state against the politics of religious and race—which quite clearly ran together at many points—Cervantes asks a more fundamental set of questions: what is it that people imagine as finding them together and, by contrast, what is it that drives the apart? Why does it seem necessary to push some groups out in order for others to form strong bonds?" (Cascardi, *Cervantes, Literature, and the Discourse of Politics*, 179–80).

64. That is, reading *copia* involves a shift in emphasis, "from 'poems' as objects of occasions for experience to 'poetry' as an occasion for reestablishing or revealing the most basic unit of social life and for securing the most fundamental object of moral regard," the person (Izenberg, *Being Numerous*, 1–2).

Chapter Four

1. World-obliterating violence precedes construction in the myth of Amphion, which begins with the rape of Antiope and includes Amphion's and Zethus's vengeance against Lycus and Dirce, before Amphion builds walls for Thebes. See above, preface, xiii–xiv. Even before Zeus attacks Antiope, however, the land Thebes is raised on is riven by destructive violence. Cadmus, the city's first founder, wanders to Boeotia in search of his abducted sister, Europa. His kingdom is populated by fratricidal men who are born from the teeth of a dragon sacred to Mars, the god of war.

2. The Treaty of Tordesillas, signed in 1494, divided all existing lands beyond Europe, known and unknown, between the Spanish and the Portuguese empires. Pope Alexander VI participated in the negotiations and approved the division. Only Spain and Portugal signed the treaty, of course; and other European powers later embarked on projects of colonization and trade in these lands. The Requerimiento was formalized in 1510 and was read out to people in advance of Spanish conquest. It informed them of the authority of the pope over the entire world and presented Spain and its monarchs as the pope's agents, announcing that henceforth the people addressed were vassals to the Spanish king.

3. Ángel Rama points out that, technically, Pedro Arías Dávila was the first Spanish conquistador to found cities, in his 1513 expedition along the Central American isth-

Notes to Pages 120–122   191

mus. See Rama, *La ciudad letrada*. Translations of Rama are drawn from Chasteen, *Angel Rama*. At times I lightly adapt the translation to closer approximate Rama's wording.

4. Cortés, *Cartas de relación*, 7. The first letter is written by the municipal council of Veracruz, not by Cortés himself, although he clearly consulted closely on it. The letter is addressed to *vuestras majestades*, or "your majesties," plural, apparently because Cortés and his company did not know that Charles's mother, Queen Juana of Castile, had been marginalized from power. Subsequent letters are addressed to Charles V only. Translations of the *Cartas de relación* are my own, prepared in consultation with Cortés, *Letters from Mexico*, trans. Pagden.

5. Cortés, *Cartas de relación*, 18–19.

6. Glantz, "Ciudad y escritura," 165–74. "No es exagerado ni gratuito afirmar que la Conquista de México se hace explícita en el instante mismo en que Cortés funda, el 22 de abril de 1519, la Villa Rica de la Vera Cruz en un lugar cercano al actual puerto, llamado originariamente Chalchicuecan. Los regidores y alcaldes que firman la llamada 'Primera Carta de Relación' o 'Carta de Cabildo' explican que, por convenir al servicio de 'vuestras majestades,' Cortés se ha dejado 'con vencer' y ha aceptado el requerimiento de sus hombres que le exigen trocar el signo de la expedición, desconocer el nombramiento otorgado por Velázquez y pretender que está directamente al servicio del Rey: 'Y luego comenzó con gran diligencia a poblar y a fundar una villa, a la cual puso por nombre la Rica Villa de la Vera Cruz y nombrónos a los que la presente suscribimos, por alcaldes y regidores de la dicha villa, y en nombre de vuestras reales altezas recibió de nosotros el juramento y solemnidad que en tal caso se acostumbra y suele hacer.'" (It is no exaggeration, nor is it gratuitous, to affirm that the conquest of Mexico becomes explicit in the same instant that Cortés founds, on April 22, 1519, la Villa Rica de Vera Cruz at a site near the then port, originally called Chalchihuecan. The magistrates and mayors who sign the so-called "First Letter of Relation," or the "Letter from the Council," explain that, in order to better serve "your majesties," Cortés has allowed himself "to be defeated" and has accepted the petition of his men that demands that he change the aim of the mission, break with the title conferred by Velázquez, and undertake to serve the king directly: "And then he began with great diligence to populate and found a town, to which he gave the name Veracruz, and he named those of us who have signed this letter as mayors and magistrates of said town, and in the name of your royal majesties he received of us the oath and ceremony that are accustomed to be performed in such situations.") Glantz, 165–66.

7. Jorge Cañizares-Esguerra points out that the English Pilgrims who established the colony of New Plymouth in 1620 would use nearly identical arguments for colonization as those Cortés employed. See Cañizares-Esguerra, "The 'Iberian' Justifications of Territorial Possession by Pilgrims and Puritans in the Colonization of America," in *Entangled Empires*, 167–69.

8. Cortés, *Cartas de relación*, 41.

9. Cortés, 63–64.

10. Johnson, *Cultural Hierarchy in Sixteenth-Century Europe*, 34–56, 97–134.

11. Merrim, *Spectacular City*, 57.

192 **Notes to Pages 122–123**

12. Merrim takes the concept of the scriptural economy from Michel de Certeau. See Merrim, 57. Her ideas also seem shaped by Foucault's discussion of conducted societies in *Security, Territory, Population.*

13. Rama is drawing on the ideas Foucault develops in *Security, Territory, Population.* On "city of letters," see Rama, *La ciudad letrada.* See also Moraña, *Ángel Rama y los estudios latinoamericanos.* Merrim draws a distinction between the process of the ordered city Rama describes in his discussion of Cortés and the conquest, and the "baroque city" that emerges in seventeenth-century vice realms. See Merrim, *Spectacular City,* 50. On the relationship of writing to the rise to dominance of the Spanish-American Creole (*criollo*) caste, see Mazzotti, *Agencias criollas.*

14. Rama, *La ciudad letrada,* 2–3.

15. This spatialized image of the Americas that the Spanish elaborate differs from how writers figure other sites of encounter, conflict, commerce, and colonialism, for example, in Africa. During roughly the same period in which Cortés's *Cartas* circulate, inspiring the astonishment, wonder, horror, and greed of Europeans, Garcilaso de la Vega composes his well-known Sonnet 33, "A Boscán desde la Goleta" (To Boscán, from the Goleta), whose opening celebrates the Spanish victory over Barbarossa's forces in Tunis:

> Boscán, las armas y el furor de Marte,
> que con su propia fuerza el africano
> suelo regando, hacen que el romano
> imperio reverdezca en esta parte,
> han reducido a la memoria el arte
> y el antiguo valor italiano,
> por cuya fuerza y valerosa mano
> África se aterró de parte a parte.
> Aquí donde el romano encendimiento,
> donde el fuego y la llama licenciosa
> sólo el nombre dejaron a Cartago,
> vuelve y revuelve Amor mi pensamiento,
> hiere y enciende el alma temerosa,
> y en llanto y en ceniza me deshago.

(Boscán, the arms and the fury of Mars, / which, irrigating the African ground with its own force, cause the Roman empire / to flourish once again in this place, / have relegated to memory that art / and that ancient Italian valor, / by whose strength and worthy hand / Africa was rent, from one end to the other. / Here, where the Roman conflagration, / where the fire and the licentious flame / left only the name of Carthage, / my thoughts turn and return to Love, / my fearful soul grieves and burns, / and in weeping and ashes I am undone.) Garcilaso de la Vega, *Poesía castellana,* 202; my translation.

Like the Spanish-American texts we have examined thus far, this poem mobilizes the trope of a triumphant Spain that flowers (reverdezca: to become green again) over a former civilization it has "reduced to memory" (reducida a la memoria). But in Son-

Notes to Pages 123–129   193

net 33, it is not the city of Tunis, a physical place and a territory—a space—with its flora, fauna, inhabitants (and markets) that are at stake; rather, space and place are abstract in a poem oriented by Hapsburg imperium: the idea of Spain as the new Rome and Charles V as both the modern Caesar and the interiorized, subjective self, the distracted and suffering lover. As a Petrarchan poem, Sonnet 33 figures worlds and their contents as functions of the self; in this case, Garcilaso's worried lover, who delimits the poem's scope. But Sonnet 33 is nonetheless instructive as a comparator that sets the *Cartas* in relief; the contrast points to the specificity of the imaginary that Spanish writers elaborate around Spanish war and violence in the Americas. Imperium looks different here, as do the stakes of battle, which are rooted in the material world and its valuable contents, not in the rivalries for the imperial Roman mantle that poets engage in on European ground. Although Spain and Portugal trade with African ports and embark on chattel slavery, it is the American continent that writers and rulers figure as a fertile site for occupation, reformation, and extraction. The difference is particularly evident when Cortés compares African cities with the cities of the Yucatán, in terms that indicate the Spanish appreciation for the sophistication of some African societies (see Cortés, *Cartas de relación*, 41). On Garcilaso's Sonnet 33, see Helgerson, *A Sonnet from Carthage*.

16. Chang-Rodríguez, *"Aquí ninfas del sur, venid ligeras,"* 240; my translation, prepared in consultation with Elmira Louie.

17. Amarílis does not invoke Amphion in this stanza, but refers to him later on, as she advises the lyric's addressee, the Spanish poet Lope de Vega, to turn his Amphionic talents to the service of Heaven by writing religious poetry. "Pues, peregrino mío, / vuelve a tu natural, póngate brío / no las murallas que ha hecho tu canto / en Tébas engañosas, / mas las eternas, que te importan tanto." (My pilgrim, / return to your true nature, dedicate your energies / not to the Theban walls your song has built, / but to the eternal ones, / that are most important to you.) Chang-Rodríguez, 239.

18. Balbuena, *Grandeza mexicana*, 145. All translations to this volume are my own, prepared in consultation with Elmira Louie.

19. See Ovid, *Metamorphoses*, book 4.

20. Balbuena, *Grandeza mexicana*, 145.

21. Balbuena, 171–73.

22. Balbuena, 173.

23. Stoler, "Imperial Debris," 194.

24. Stoler, 196.

25. "Il triste buco / sovra 'l qual pontan tutte l'altre rocce"; Dante, *Inferno*, canto 32.2–3, trans. Durling, 498. See my discussion of canto 32 in the introduction, 17–19, and below.

26. Dante, *Inferno*, canto 32.1–12, trans. Durling, 498–99.

27. Canto 32 of the *Inferno* refers to the Florentine civil wars. See above, introduction, 17–19.

28. "Unlike empires . . . [imperial formations] are states of becoming, not fixed things. Not least, they are states of deferral that mete out promissory notes that are not

194 Notes to Pages 129–140

exceptions to their operation but constitutive of them: imperial guardianship, trustee-
ships, delayed autonomy, temporary intervention, conditional tutelage, military take-
over in the name of humanitarian works, violent intervention in the name of human
rights and security measures in the name of peace." Stoler, "Imperial Debris," 193. In
the Spanish-American case, we can add Christian salvation.

29. Cortés, *Cartas de relación*, 42.

30. Merrim, *Spectacular City*, 56.

31. See Cortés, *Cartas de relación*, 42, 46, 48.

32. Cortés, 46.

33. Cortés, 48.

34. Cortés, 140.

35. Cortés, 171.

36. Rancière, *Aesthetics and Its Discontents*, 24.

37. Stoler, McGranahan, and Perdue, *Imperial Formations*, 8.

38. See Mazzotti, *Agencias criollas*, 8–16. The line quoted appears on 11.

39. Chang-Rodríguez, *Clarinda y Amarílis*, 85–87. On Clarinda and the *Discurso*, see
Cornejo Polar, *Discurso en loor de la poesía*.

40. Balbuena, *Grandeza mexicana*, 168. All translations to this volume are my own,
prepared in consultation with Elmira Louie.

41. Balbuena, 170.

42. Balbuena, 169.

43. This is the case in this particular passage. Cacho Casal also demonstrates that
Balbuena's description of the great cathedral is in fact accurate. See Cacho Casal, "Dialectic Spaces," 149–51.

44. See Balbuena, *Grandeza mexicana*, 175–81.

45. Cacho Casal, "Dialectic Spaces," 149.

46. Cacho Casal, 152–53.

47. On *La grandeza mexicana* and baroque style, see Merrim, *Spectacular City*, 91–
127; see also Cacho Casal, "Balbuena's *Grandeza mexicana* and the American Georgic."

48. See chapter 2, 73.

49. On the convoluted logic by which the Catholic Church, monarchies, and mer-
chant traders determined the categories of *extra ecclesiam* and *herrschaftlos* (sovereign-
less persons) in the early modern period, see Bennett, "Sons of Adam."

50. Balbuena, *La grandeza mexicana*, 170.

51. Balbuena, 161.

52. "Imperial formations thrive on deferred autonomy, meted out to particular populations incrementally, promised to those in whose lives they intervene. They create
new subjects that must be relocated to be productive and exploitable, dispossessed to
be modern, disciplined to be independent, converted to be human, stripped of old cultural bearings to be citizens, coerced to be free." Stoler, McGranahan, and Perdue, *Imperial Formations*, 8.

Notes to Pages 140-148 195

53. Pablo Neruda's "La United Fruit Co." concludes with the vision of a body rolling on the sea floor: "un cuerpo rueda, una cosa / sin nombre, un número caído, / un racimo de fruta muerta / derramada en el pudridero" (a body rolls down, a nameless / thing, a fallen number, / a bunch of lifeless fruit / dumped in the rubbish heap). Neruda, *Canto general: Edición de Enrico Mario Santi*, 346; translation by Schmitt, 179. These lines are jarring, not only for the precise and graphic portrayal of devalued human life, but also, perhaps, because of the romanticizing tone and stance of the lyric speaker in the poem. The lines run the risk of reproducing imperial violence, as the figure of the Indigenous body is not brought to the reader's attention as something of the greatest conceivable value (the human person), but to help the lyric speaker make a point. On the complexity of Neruda's stance and legacies, see Franco, *The Decline and Fall of the Lettered City*.

54. Stoler, "Imperial Debris," 195.

55. A frequent trope in Zurita's work is adhesion; for example, the fragments of Chilean personhood that are "stuck" (pegado) to the rocks, the sea, and the mountains: "pegado a las rocas el mar y las montañas," in "Canto a su amor desaparecido." See Zurita, *Sky Below*, trans. Deeny Morales, 100-101.

56. On emplacement, see Andermann, "Expanded Fields." On the disruption of self, see Rowe, "Raúl Zurita."

57. Zurita, *Anteparadise*, trans. Schmitt, 18-19.

58. Zurita offers the anecdote regularly; however, among numerous interviews that discuss his process, the conversation with Benoît Santini is especially informative. Zurita and Santini, "En Zurita, van a aparecer las ruinas, pedazos de poemas antiguos."

59. Dante, *Inferno*, 498-99.

60. Zurita, *Anteparadise*, trans. Schmitt, 70-71.

61. Zurita, *Sky Below*, trans. Deeny Morales, 170-71.

62. For a brief overview of Zurita's career to date, see Zurita, *Sky Below*, trans. Deeny Morales, ix-xix. See also Zurita and Santini, "En Zurita, van a aparecer las ruinas, pedazos de poemas antiguos."

63. Zurita, *Sky Below*, trans. Deeny Morales, 28-29.

64. See Ignacio Valente, "Zurita entre los Grandes," *El Mercurio*, October 24, 1982, Archivo de Referencias Críticas, http://www.bibliotecanacionaldigital.gob.cl/bnd/628/w3-article-566395.html.

65. Deeny Morales associates this theme in Zurita's work with Emmanuel Levinas's idea of the face (see *Sky Below*, xii-xiv); and in fact, "facha," in Spanish, means face, not form. But Deeny Morales points out that the face that *facha* connotes is richer than the English word might suggest. This is why she uses "form" in her translation. Although Deeny Morales does not say so, it seems likely that "countenance," which is in some ways a useful substitute, is more erudite and formal than is suitable to what Zurita points to in these poems.

66. Dante, *Inferno*, 156-57.

67. Zurita, *Sky Below*, trans. Deeny Morales, 94-95. I have adapted Deeny Morales's translation slightly to better capture the resemblance between Dante's lines and those

196 **Notes to Pages 148–159**

of Zurita. Although both Deeny Morales and Borzutzky use justified margins in their reproductions of this and further fragments in the poem, they make different choices about lineation. In this passage, Deeny Morales ends the first line with the full word *verso*, for example, whereas Borzutzky cuts the word in half to end the line with *ver-*. In the first fragment of the canto, proper, Deeny Morales breaks the first line at *los*, but Borzutzky breaks it at *pasión*, and so on. It seems likely that Zurita agreed to modification of the individual lines of the poem but stipulated the block shape.

68. Zurita, *Sky Below*, 96–97. Deeny Morales translates "todos los tortura" as "all those torture." Zurita's language is deliberately ambiguous here.

69. See Letelier, "Economic Freedom's Awful Toll."

70. Zurita, *Sky Below*, trans. Deeny Morales, 98–99.

71. Zurita, 102–3.

72. Zurita, 106–7.

73. Zurita, 102–3.

74. Zurita, 100–101.

75. Zurita, 104–5.

76. Zurita, 106–9.

77. Zurita, 108.

78. Zurita, *Song for His Disappeared Love*, trans. Borzutzky, 12. I use Borzutzky here both for his translation of *estalló* as "exploded" and for his reading of "procesión . . . y sentencia" as "trial and sentence." Deeny Morales translates the former as "broke out" and the latter as "procession and judgment." See Zurita, *Sky Below*, trans. Deeny Morales, 109.

79. Zurita, *Sky Below*, trans. Deeny Morales, 108–11.

80. Zurita, 110–11.

81. Zurita, 116–19.

82. Neruda, *Canto general*, 105–6; translation by Schmitt, *Canto General*, 11. Neruda's romanticism in these stanzas can be jarring to readers today. Jean Franco's thoughtful reflections on Neruda and his legacy consider how social class, cultural elitism, and race inform his writing on Indigenous Americans. Franco, *The Decline and Fall of the Lettered City*.

83. Osvaldo de la Torre demonstrates the importance of Gabriela Mistral's poetry to this ongoing process. See Torre, "On Loss and Not Losing It."

84. Zurita, *Sky Below*, trans. Deeny Morales, 102–3.

85. "—De un bayonetazo me cercenaron el hombre y sentí mi brazo al caer al / —pasto. / —Y luego con él golpearon a mis amigos. / —Siguieron y siguieron pero cuando les empezaron a dar a mis padres / —corrí al urinario a vomiter." (—From one bayonet blow they clipped my shoulder and I felt my arm as I fell / —to the grass. / —Then with it they beat my friends. / —They went on and on, but when they began to strike my parents / —I ran to the urinal to throw up.) Zurita, 102–3.

86. Zurita, 126–27.

87. Zurita, 126–27.

88. Zurita, 128–29.

89. All the tombs are open in canto 10 of the *Inferno*, perhaps because the inhabitants of that region are heretics. My point is that Zurita's speaker has been converted from selfish love to *paisa*. Having recognized divine love, he might, if he were in Dante, be allowed a coffin with a closed lid.

90. In the introduction to *Poetry of the Earth: Mapuche Trilingual Anthology*, Jaime Luis Huenún Villa refers to Mapuche poetry. James Park discusses the distinct regional identities and affiliations of the diverse group of writers who engage in the project of bringing an othered community, in all its variation and specificity, into (Western) discourse. See Park, "Ethnogenesis or Neoindigenous Intelligentsia," 15–18. On "durabilities of duress," see Stoler, "Imperial Debris," 192.

91. The Mapuche (also known as the Araucanian-Mapuche people) successfully resisted conquest by the Spanish. They were brought under Chilean state domination in the late nineteenth century. See Huenún Villa, *Poetry of the Earth*, xii–xiv. On the relationships of the Mapuche people to Western political geography, see Park, "Ethnogenesis or Neoindigenous Intelligentsia," as well as García Barrera, Carrasco Muñoz, and Contreras Hauser, *Crítica situada*. See also Cooke, "Orpheus in the New World."

92. Huenún Villa, *Poetry of the Earth*, 55. All poetry in the volume is produced in the Mapuche language, Spanish, and English.

93. For example, in the poems "Üyechi pülom mew ta pewman/Sueños en el valle/ Dreams in the Valley" and "Tañi ñuke ülkantulelal/Canto a mi madre/Song for My Mother," by Maribel Mora Curriao, collected in Huenún Villa, *Poetry of the Earth*, 41–49.

94. Huenún Villa explains that Huilliche oral histories recount the murder of an old couple, who were burned alive when it was discovered they had contracted smallpox. The story is recorded in cultural memory, held by the community's elders (and now, in this poem). See Huenún Villa, *Poetry of the Earth*, 8–10.

Coda

1. On Laurens's brief collaboration with Villanueva, see Labedski, "His Most Famous Sculpture (L'Amphion), Henri Laurens." The modern art that Villanueva commissioned for the campus has been a topic of discussion recently, as financial and political crises in Venezuela interfere with their maintenance. See Vegas, "This World Heritage Site Is in Ruins, and That's Not by Accident." Having said that, when I mentioned Amphion to a group of students who completed their undergraduate work on the Caracas campus, they spoke of him warmly, as one might speak of a school mascot. They told me new graduates take selfies with him—along with other major works of modern art by Villanueva built into the campus—before leaving the campus to make their way out into the world.

Bibliography

Acuña, Hernando de. "A un buen caballero y mal poeta: La lira de Garcilaso contrahecha." *Varias poesías / compuestas por don Hernando de Acuña*. Alicante: Biblioteca Virtual Miguel de Cervantes, 2022.

Acuña, Hernando de. *El cavallero determinado, traduzido de la lengua Francesa en Castellana, por Don Hernando de Acuña, y dirigido al Emperador Don Carlos Quinto Máximo, Rey de España nuestro Señor*. Biblioteca Nacional de España, MS. 1475.

Alciato, Andrea. *Emblematum liber*. Augsburg: Heinrich Steiner, 1534. Available at Alciato at Glasgow. https://www.emblems.arts.gla.ac.uk/alciato/books.php?id=A34a.

Alemany, Ignacio López. "El sonsoneto y la práctica poética cortesana del siglo XVI." *Revista de Estudios Hispánicos* 50, no. 3 (2016): 583–603.

Andermann, Jens. "Expanded Fields: Postdictatorship and the Landscape." *Journal of Latin American Cultural Studies* 21, no. 2 (2012): 165–87.

Armas, Frederick de. "Bajo el signo de Mercurio: Viajes, mitos y latrocinios en *La gitanilla*." *Hispania Felix* 4 (2013): 58–75.

Armas, Frederick de. *Cervantes's Architectures: The Dangers of Outside*. Toronto: University of Toronto Press, 2022.

Armas, Frederick de, ed. *Ovid in the Age of Cervantes*. Toronto: University of Toronto Press, 2010.

Ashbery, John. "Daffy Duck in Hollywood." In *Houseboat Days: Poems*. New York: Viking Press, 1977.

Aubert, Guillaume. "The Blood of France: Race and Purity of Blood in the French Atlantic World." *William and Mary Quarterly* 61, no. 3 (July 2004): 439–78.

Austin, John. *How to Do Things with Words*. Cambridge, MA: Harvard University Press, 1962.

Bacich, Damian. "Negotiating Renaissance Harmony: The First Spanish Translation of Leone Hebreo's *Dialoghi D'amore*." *Comitatus: A Journal of Medieval and Renaissance Studies* 36 (2005): 114–41.

Balbuena, Bernardo de. *La grandeza mexicana*. Edited by Asima F. X. Saad Maura. Madrid: Cátedra, 2011.

Bibliography

Barletta, Vincent. "Lusofonia and Eternal Empire: Notes from the Sixteenth Century." *Portuguese Literary and Cultural Studies* 25 (2013): 96–116.

Barletta, Vincent. *Rhythm: Form and Dispossession*. Chicago: University of Chicago Press, 2021.

Bateman, Stephen. *The Trauailed Pilgrime*. Edited by Katie Gezi. Scotts Valley, CA: Create Space Independent Publishing Platform, 2016.

Beechy, Tiffany. *The Poetics of Old English*. Farnham, UK: Ashgate, 2010.

Bellenger, Yvonne, ed. *Du Bellay et ses sonnets romains: Études sur "Les Regrets" et "Les Antiquitéz de Rome."* Geneva: Slatkine, 1994.

Beltrán, Vicente. *Coplas que hizo Jorge Manrique a muerte de su padre: Edición crítica.* Barcelona: PPU, 1991.

Bennett, Herman. "Sons of Adam: Text, Context, and the Early Modern Subject." *Representations* 92, no. 1 (2005): 16–41.

Berthon, Guillaume. "L'année poetique et politique 1538." In *La muse de l'ephemère*, edited by Aurélie Delatte and Adeline Lionetto, 359–73. Paris: Classiques Garnier, 2014.

Bizer, Marc. *Les lettres romaines de Du Bellay: "Les Regrets" et la tradition epistolaire.* Montréal: Les Presses de la Université de Montréal, 2001.

Blasing, Mutlu Konuk. *Lyric Poetry: The Pain and the Pleasure of Words*. Princeton, NJ: Princeton University Press, 2007.

Boileau, Nicolas. *L'Art poétique*. 1674.

Boscán, Juan. *Obra completa*. Edited by Carlos Clavería. Madrid: Cátedra, 1999.

Bourdieu, Pierre. *Outline of a Theory of Practice*. Cambridge: Cambridge University Press, 1977.

Brown, David Sterling. *Shakespeare's White Others*. Cambridge: Cambridge University Press, 2023.

Cacho Casal, Rodrigo. "Balbuena's *Grandeza mexicana* and the American Georgic." *Colonial Latin American Review* 24, no. 2 (April 2015): 190–214.

Cacho Casal, Rodrigo. "Dialectic Spaces: Poetry and Architecture in Balbuena's *Grandeza mexicana*." In *Artifice and Invention in the Spanish Golden Age*, edited by Stephen Boyd and Terrence O'Reilly, 148–60. London: Routledge, 2014.

Cacho Casal, Rodrigo. "The Memory of Ruins: Quevedo's Silva to Roma Antigua y Moderna." *Renaissance Quarterly* 62, no. 4 (Winter 2009): 1167–203.

Cañizares-Esguerra, Jorge. *Entangled Empires: The Anglo-Iberian Atlantic, 1500–1830.* Philadelphia: University of Pennsylvania Press, 2018.

Carvallo, Luis Alfonso de. *Cisne de Apolo* [The swan of Apollo]. Kassel: Reichenberger, 1602.

Cascardi, Anthony J. *Cervantes, Literature, and the Discourse of Politics*. Toronto: University of Toronto Press, 2011.

Cascardi, Anthony J. *Ideologies of History in the Spanish Golden Age*. University Park: Pennsylvania State University Press, 1997.

Catalá de Valeriola, Don Bernardo. *Justas poéticas hechas a devoción de Don Bernardo Catalán de Valeriola*. Valencia: Casa de Juan Chrysostomo Garriz, 1602.

Cavanaugh, Stephanie M. "Litigating for Liberty: Enslaved Morisco Children in Sixteenth-Century Valladolid." *Renaissance Quarterly* 70 (2017): 1282–87.

Cave, Terence. *The Cornucopian Text: Problems of Writing in the French Renaissance*. Oxford: Oxford University Press, 1979.

Cervantes, Miguel de. *Don Quijote de la Mancha I*. Edited by John Jay Allen. Madrid: Cátedra, 2011.

Cervantes, Miguel de. *Don Quijote de la Mancha II*. Edited by John Jay Allen. Madrid: Cátedra, 2016.

Cervantes, Miguel de. *Don Quixote: A New Translation by Edith Grossman*. New York: HarperCollins, 2003.

Cervantes, Miguel de. *Viaje del Parnaso y otras poesías*. Edited by Laura Fernández García. Barcelona: Penguin Clásicos, 2007.

Chamard, Henri. *Histoire de la Pléiade*. Paris: Didier, 1963.

Chang-Rodríguez, Raquel. *"Aquí ninfas del sur, venid ligeras": Voces poéticas virreinales*. Madrid: Iberoamericana, 2008.

Chang-Rodríguez, Raquel, ed. *Clarinda y Amarílis: Discurso en loor de la poesía; Epístola a Belardo*. Estudio preliminar, edición anotada, y bibliografía de Raquel Chang-Rodríguez. Lima: Pontifica Universidad Católica de Peru, 2007.

Chasteen, John Charles. *Angel Rama: The Lettered City*. Durham, NC: Duke University Press, 1996.

Cheney, Patrick, and Frederick de Armas, eds. *European Literary Careers: From Antiquity to the Renaissance*. Toronto: Toronto University Press, 2002.

Chiong-Rivero, Horacio. "Between Scylla and Charybdis: The Paradoxical Poetics of Empire and the Empire of Poetics in Cervantes' *Viaje al Parnaso*." *Cervantes* 28, no. 2 (2008): 57–87.

Choi, Don Mee. *Translation Is a Mode = Translation Is an Anti-Neocolonial Mode*. Brooklyn: Ugly Duckling Presse, 2020.

Claviez, Thomas, ed. *The Common Growl: Toward a Poetics of Precarious Community*. New York: Fordham University Press, 2016.

Cohen, Jeffrey Jerome. *Stone: An Ecology of the Inhuman*. Minneapolis: Minnesota State University Press, 2015.

Coldiron, A. E. B. "Cultural Amphibians." *Yearbook of Comparative and General Literature* 51 (2003–2004): 43–58.

Coldiron, A. E. B. "How Spenser Excavates Du Bellay's 'Antiquitez'; or, The Role of the Poet, Lyric Historiography, and the English Sonnet." *Journal of English and Germanic Philology* 101, no. 1 (January 2002): 41–67.

Cooke, Stuart. "Against Place (The Lyrebird Shows the Way)." In *New Directions in Contemporary Australian Poetry*, edited by Dan Disney and Matthew Hall, 119–31. Cham, Switzerland: Palgrave Macmillan, 2021.

Cornejo Polar, Antonio. *Discurso en loor de la poesía: Studio y edición*. Berkeley, CA: Centro de Estudios Literarios "Antonio Cornejo Polar," Latinoamericana Editores, 2000.

Cortés, Hernán. *Cartas de relación*. Nota preliminar de Manuel Alcalá. Mexico City: Editorial Porrúa, 1992.

Cortés, Hernán. *Letters from Mexico*. Translated by Anthony Pagden. New Haven, CT: Yale University Press, 1971.

Covarrubias Orozco, Sebastian de. *Tesoro de la lengua castellana o española*. Barcelona: Alta Fulla, 1987.

Culler, Jonathan. *Theory of the Lyric*. Cambridge, MA: Harvard University Press, 2015.

202 Bibliography

Dante Alighieri. *The Divine Comedy of Dante Alighieri.* Vol. 1: *Inferno.* Edited and translated by Robert M. Durling. Notes and introduction by Ronald L. Martinez. Oxford: Oxford University Press, 1996.

Davis, Natalie Zemon. "The Rites of Violence: Religious Riot in Sixteenth-Century France." *Past and Present* 59 (May 1973): 51–91.

Delattre, Aurélie, and Adeline Lionetto. *La Muse de l'éphemère: Formes de la poésie de circonstance de l'Antiquité à la Renaissance.* Paris: Classiques Garnier, 2014.

Del Barco, Valeria. "El anonimato como performance textual: 'Clarinda' y Amarilis reconsideradas." *Calíope* 22, no. 2 (2017): 101–17.

Dimock, Wai Chee. "A Theory of Resonance." *PMLA* 12, no. 5 (1997): 1060–71.

Du Bellay, Joachim. *"The Regrets," with "The Antiquities of Rome," Three Latin Elegies, and "The Defense and Enrichment of the French Language."* A Bilingual Edition. Edited and translated by Richard Helgerson. University Park: Penn State University Press, 2006.

DuBrow, Heather. *The Challenges of Orpheus: Lyric Poetry and Early Modern England.* Baltimore: Johns Hopkins University Press, 2007.

Dworkin, Craig, and Kenny Goldsmith, eds. *Against Expression: An Anthology of Conceptual Writing.* Evanston, IL: Northwestern University Press, 2011.

Duval, Edwin. *The Design of Rabelais's "Tiers Livre de Pantagruel."* Geneva: Librarie Droz, 1997.

Egido, Aurora. "Poesía de justas y academias." In *Fronteras de la poesía en el barroco.* Barcelona: Editorial Crítica, 1990.

Emerson, Ralph Waldo. *Emerson: Essays and Lectures: Nature: Addresses and Lectures/ Essays: First and Second Series/Representative Men/English Traits/The Conduct of Life.* New York: Library of America, 1983.

Emmerich, Karen. *Literary Translation and the Making of Originals.* New York: Bloomsbury, 2017.

Espaillat, Rhina. "Francisco de Quevedo: Love That Endures Beyond Death." *Literary Matters* 10, no. 2. https://www.literarymatters.org/10-2-francisco-de-quevedo -love-that-endures-beyond-death/.

Ferguson, Frances. "Now It's Personal: D. A. Miller and Too-Close Reading." *Critical Inquiry* 41, no. 3 (Spring 2015): 521–40.

Finley, Sarah. *Amplifications of Black Sound from Colonial Mexico: Vocality and Beyond.* Nashville: Vanderbilt University Press, 2024.

Foucault, Michel. *Security, Territory, Population: Lectures at the Collège de France, 1977– 1978.* Edited by Michael Senellart. Translated by Graham Burchell. New York: Palgrave MacMillan, 2009.

Fra-Molinero, Baltasar. "Ser mulato en España y América: Discursos legales y otros discursos literarios." In *Negros, mulatos, zambaigos: Derroteros africanos en los mundos ibéricos,* edited by Berta Ares Queija and Alessandro Stella, 123–47. Seville: Escuela de Estudios Hispano-americanos de la Universidad de Sevilla, 2000.

Franco, Jean. *The Decline and Fall of the Lettered City: Latin America in the Cold War.* Cambridge, MA: Harvard University Press, 2002.

Freccero, John. "The Fig Tree and the Laurel: Petrarch's Poetics." *Diacritics* 5, no. 1 (1975): 34–40.

Fuchs, Barbara. "Another Turn for Transnationalism: Empire, Nation, and Imperium in Early Modern Studies." *PMLA* 130, no. 2 (March 2015): 412–18.

Bibliography 203

Fuchs, Barbara. *Exotic Nation: Maurophilia and the Construction of Early Modern Spain.* Philadelphia: University of Pennsylvania Press, 2011.

Fuchs, Barbara. *Mimesis and Empire: The New World, Islam, and European Identities.* Cambridge: Cambridge University Press, 2009.

Fuchs, Barbara. *Passing for Spain: Cervantes and the Fictions of Identity.* Champaign: University of Illinois Press, 2003.

Fuchs, Barbara. "The Spanish Race." In *Rereading the Black Legend: The Discourses of Religious and Racial Difference in the Renaissance Empires,* edited by Margaret Greer, Walter Mignolo, and Maureen Quilligan, 88–98. Chicago: University of Chicago Press, 2006.

García-Arenal, Mercedes, and Gerard Wiegers, eds. *The Expulsion of the Moriscos from Spain: A Mediterranean Diaspora.* Amsterdam: Brill, 2015.

García Barrera, Mabel, Hugo Carrasco Muñoz, and Verónica Contreras Hauser, eds. *Critica situada: El estado actual del arte y la poesía Mapuche.* Chile: Universidad de la Frontera, 2005.

Garcilaso de la Vega. "Ode ad florem Gnidi." In *Poesía castellana,* edited by Julián Jiménez Heffernan and E. Ignacio García Aguilar, 270–73. Madrid: Akal, 2017.

Geneste, Pierre. *Le capitaine-poète aragonais Jerónimo de Urrea: Sa vie et son oeuvre ou chevalerie et renaissance dans l'Espagne du XVI siècle.* Paris: Ediciones Hispano-americanas, 1978.

Glantz, Margo. "Ciudad y escritura: La Ciudad de México en las 'cartas de relación.'" *Hispamérica* 19, nos. 56/57 (August–December 1990): 165–74.

Glaser, Ben, and Jonathan Culler, eds. *Critical Rhythm: The Poetics of a Literary Life Form.* New York: Fordham University Press, 2019.

Góngora, Luis de. *Sonetos Completos.* Madrid: Clásicos Castalia, 1969.

Greenblatt, Stephen. *Renaissance Self-Fashioning: From More to Shakespeare.* Chicago: University of Chicago Press, 1980.

Greene, Roland. *Five Words: Critical Semantics in the Age of Shakespeare and Cervantes.* Chicago: University of Chicago Press, 2013.

Greene, Roland. *Post-Petrarchism: Origins and Innovations of the Lyric Sequence.* Princeton, NJ: Princeton University Press, 1991.

Greene, Roland. *Unrequited Conquests: Love and Empire in the Colonial Americas.* Chicago: University of Chicago Press, 1999.

Greene, Roland, ed. *The Princeton Encyclopedia of Poetry and Poetics.* Princeton, NJ: Princeton University Press, 2012.

Greene, Thomas M. *The Light in Troy.* New Haven, CT: Yale University Press, 1982.

Greer, Margaret, Walter Mignolo, and Maureen Quilligan, eds. *Rereading the Black Legend: The Discourses of Religious and Racial Difference in the Renaissance Empires.* Chicago: University of Chicago Press, 2006.

Grossman, Allen, with Mark Halliday. *The Sighted Singer: Two Works on Poetry for Readers and Writers.* Baltimore: Johns Hopkins University Press, 1992.

Gruesz, Kirsten Silva. *Ambassadors of Culture: The Transamerican Origins of Latino Writing* Princeton, NJ: Princeton University Press, 2002.

Hampton, Timothy L. *Cheerfulness: A Literary and Cultural History.* Brooklyn: Zone Books, 2022.

Hampton, Timothy L. *Literature and Nation in the Sixteenth Century: Writing Renaissance France.* Ithaca, NY: Cornell University Press, 2001.

204 Bibliography

Hayot, Eric. *On Literary Worlds*. Oxford: Oxford University Press, 2012.

Heaton, Wade, Walter Ward Parks, Earl Miner, and Marisa Galvez. "Poetic Contests." In *The Princeton Encyclopedia of Poetry and Poetics*, edited by Roland Greene, Stephen Cushman, Clare Cavanagh, Jahan Ramazani, and Paul Rouzer, 1054–56. Princeton, NJ: Princeton University Press, 2015.

Helgerson, Richard. *Forms of Nationhood: The Elizabethan Writing of England*. Chicago: University of Chicago Press, 1992.

Helgerson, Richard. *A Sonnet from Carthage: Garcilaso de la Vega and the New Poetry of Sixteenth-Century Europe*. Philadelphia: University of Pennsylvania Press, 2007.

Herbert, George. *The Complete Poetry*. Translated by Victoria Moul. Edited by John Drury. London: Penguin Classics, 2015.

Hirsch, Edward. *How to Read a Poem: And Fall in Love with Poetry*. Boston: Houghton Mifflin, 1999.

Hodson, Christopher, and Brett Rushforth. *Discovering Empire: France and the Atlantic World from the Crusades to the Age of Revolutions*. New York: Oxford University Press, forthcoming.

Homer. *The Odyssey*. Translated by Emily Wilson. New York: W. W. Norton, 2017.

Homer. *The Iliad*. Translated by Emily Wilson. New York: W. W. Norton, 2023.

Horace. *Ars Poetica*. Translated by C. Smart and E. H. Blakeney. Poetry Foundation. https://www.poetryfoundation.org/articles/69381/ars-poetica.

Horace. *Epistles: Book II and Epistle to the Pisones ("Ars Poetica")*. Edited by Niall Rudd. Cambridge: Cambridge University Press, 1989.

Horace. *Satires and Epistles*. Translated by John Davie. Oxford: Oxford University Press, 2011.

Huenún Villa, Jaime Luís, ed. *Poetry of the Earth: Mapuche Trilingual Anthology*. Carindale, Australia: Interactive Press, 2014.

Irigoyen, Javier. *Moors Dressed as Moors: Clothing, Social Distinction, and Ethnicity in Early Modern Iberia*. Toronto: University of Toronto Press, 2017.

Izenberg, Oren. *Being Numerous: Poetry and the Ground of Social Life*. Princeton, NJ: Princeton University Press, 2011.

Jackson, Virginia. *Dickinson's Misery: A Theory of Lyric Reading*. Princeton, NJ: Princeton University Press, 2009.

Jackson, Virginia. "Who Reads Poetry?" *PMLA* 123, no. 1 (January 2008): 181–87.

Jackson, Virginia, and Yopie Prins, eds. *The Lyric Theory Reader*. Baltimore: Johns Hopkins University Press, 2014.

Johnson, Barbara. "Anthropomorphism in Lyric and Law." *Yale Journal of Law and the Humanities* 10, no. 2 (1998): 549–74.

Johnson, Carina. *Cultural Hierarchy in Sixteenth-Century Europe: The Ottomans and the Mexicans*. Cambridge: Cambridge University Press, 2014.

Johnson, Carroll B. "Personal Involvement and Poetic Tradition in the Spanish Renaissance: Some Thoughts on Reading Garcilaso." *Romanic Review* 80, no. 2 (1989): 288–304.

Jones, Ann Rosalind. *The Currency of Eros: Women's Love Lyric in Europe (1540–1620)*. Bloomington: Indiana University Press, 1990.

Jones, Nicholas R. "Cosmetic Ontologies, Cosmetic Subversions: Articulating Black

Beauty and Black Humanity in Luís de Góngora's 'En la fiesta del Santísimo Sacramento.'" *Journal for Early Modern Cultural Studies* 14, no. 1 (2015): 26–54.

Jones, Nicholas R. "Sor Juana's Black Atlantic: Colonial Blackness and the Poetic Subversions of *Habla de negros*." *Hispanic Review* 86, no. 3 (2018): 265–85.

Jones, Nicholas R. *Staging "Habla de Negros": Radical Performances of the African Diaspora in Early Modern Spain*. University Park: Penn State University Press, 2019.

Jonson, Ben. "To Penshurst." Poetry Foundation. https://www.poetryfoundation .org/poems/50674/to-penshurst.

Joyce, Trevor. *Rome's Wreck: Translated from the English of Edmund Spenser's "Ruines of Rome."* Los Angeles: Cusp Books, 2014.

Kennedy, William. *The Site of Petrarchism: Early Modern National Sentiment in Italy, France, and England*. Baltimore: Johns Hopkins University Press, 2003.

Kiely, Robert. *Incomparable Poetry: An Essay on the Financial Crisis of 2007–2008 and Irish Literature*. Santa Barbara, CA: Punctum Books, 2020.

Labedski, Annette. "His Most Famous Sculpture (L'Amphion), Henri Laurens." Canteramelia. https://canteramelia.wordpress.com/2012/02/09/his-most-famous -sculpture-lamphion-henri-laurens/.

Langer, Ullrich. *Perfect Friendship: Studies in Moral Philosophy from Bocaccio to Corneille*. Geneva: Librarie Droz, 1994.

Lee, Christina H. *The Anxiety of Sameness in Early Modern Spain*. Manchester: Manchester University Press, 2015.

Letelier, Orlando. "Economic Freedom's Awful Toll: The 'Chicago Boys' in Chile." *Review of Radical Political Economics* 8, no. 3 (1976): 44–52.

Llopis, Ane Gamechogoicoechea. *El mito de Orfeo en la literatura barroca española*. Valladolid: Universidad de Valladolid, 2011.

Lloyd, David. *Counterpoetics of Modernity: On Irish Poetry and Modernism*. Edinburgh: Edinburgh University Press, 2022.

López-Baralt, Luce. *Islam in Spanish Literature: From the Middle Ages to the Present*. Translated by Andrew Hurley. Leiden: Brill, 1992.

Lugones, Maria. "Heterosexualism and the Colonial/Modern Gender System." *Hypatia* 22, no. 1 (2007): 186–209.

Mann, Jenny C. *The Trials of Orpheus: Poetry, Science, and the Early Modern Sublime*. Princeton, NJ: Princeton University Press, 2021.

Manrique, Jorge. *Coplas por la muerte de su padre: Poesía competa*. Introducción, Notas, Ejercicios, y Glosarios por Ana Navarro Pascual, 145–67. Barcelona: Editorial Humanitas, 1961.

Marche, Olivier de la. *Le Chevalier délibéré (The Resolute Knight)*. Edited by Carleton W. Carroll. Translated by Carleton W. Carroll and Lois Hawley Wilson. Tempe: Arizona Center for Medieval and Renaissance Studies, 1999.

Marino, Nancy F. *Jorge Manrique's "Coplas por la muerte de su padre": A History of the Poem and Its Reception*. Woodbridge, UK: Tamesis, 2011.

Márquez Villanueva, Francisco. *Personajes y temas del Quijote*. Barcelona: Bellaterra Ediciones, 2011.

Martin, Adrienne Lasker. *An Erotic Philology of Golden Age Spain*. Nashville: Vanderbilt University Press, 2008.

Bibliography

Martínez Valdivia, Lucía. "Mere Meter: A Revised History of English Poetry." *ELH* 86, no. 3 (Fall 2019): 555–85.

Mas i Usó, Pasqual. *Justas, academias y convocatorias literarias en la Valencia barroca (1591–1705): Teoría y práctica de una convención.* Alicante: Biblioteca Virtual Miguel de Cervantes, 2004.

Mas i Usó, Pasqual. *Justas valencianas barrocas.* Valencia: Generalitat Valenciana, 2009.

Mazzotta, Giuseppe. *The Worlds of Petrarch.* Durham, NC: Duke University Press, 1993.

Mazzotti, José Antonio. *Agencias criollas: La ambigüedad "colonial" en las letras hispanoamericanas.* Pittsburgh: Instituto Internacional de Literatura Iberoamericana, 2000.

Melehy, Hassan. "Du Bellay's Time in Rome: *The Antiquitez.*" *French Forum* 22, no. 2 (2001): 1–22.

Melehy, Hassan. "Spenser and Du Bellay: Translation, Imitation, Ruin." *Comparative Literature Studies* 40, no. 4 (2003): 415–38.

Mendez Plancarte, Alfonso, ed. *Obras Completas de Sor Juana Inés de la Cruz. I. Lírica Personal.* Mexico: Fonda de Cultura Económica, 1951.

Merrim, Stephanie. *The Spectacular City, Mexico, and Colonial Hispanic Literary Culture.* Austin: University of Texas Press, 2010.

Middlebrook, Leah. *Imperial Lyric: New Poetry and New Subjects in Early Modern Spain.* University Park: Pennsylvania State University Press, 2009.

Middlebrook, Leah. "Poetry and the *Persiles*: Cervantes' Orphic Mode." In *"Si ya por atrevido no sale con las manos en la cabeza": El legado poético del "Persiles" cuatrocientos años después,* edited by Mercedes Alcalá Galán, Antonio Cortijo Ocaña, and Francisco Layna Ranz. *eHumanista/Cervantes* (University of California, Santa Barbara) 5 (2016): 370–86.

Mignolo, Walter. *The Darker Side of the Renaissance: Literacy, Territoriality, and Colonization.* Ann Arbor: University of Michigan Press, 2003.

Mignolo, Walter. *The Darker Side of Western Modernity: Global Futures, Decolonial Options.* Durham, NC: Duke University Press, 2011.

Miller, J. Hillis. *Communities in Fiction.* New York: Fordham University Press, 2014.

Miller, John F. *Propertius at Baiae: Apollo, Augustus and the Poets.* Cambridge: Cambridge University Press, 2009.

Moraña, Mabel. *Ángel Rama y los estudios latinoamericanos.* Pittsburgh: Instituto Internacional de Literatura Iberoamericana, 2006.

Ndiaye, Noémie. *Scripts of Blackness: Early Modern Performance Culture and the Making of Race.* Philadelphia: University of Pennsylvania Press, 2022.

Nelson, Benjamin. "Ovidian Fame: Garcilaso de la Vega and Jorge de Montemayor as Orphic Voices in Early Modern Spain and the *Contamino* of the Orpheus and Eurydice Myth." In *Ovid in the Age of Cervantes,* edited by Frederick de Armas, 203–28. Toronto: Toronto University Press, 2010.

Neruda, Pablo. *Canto general: Edición de Enrico Mario Santi.* Madrid: Cátedra, 2005.

Neruda, Pablo. *Canto General.* Translated by Jack Schmitt. Berkeley: University of California Press, 1991.

Newman, Karen, and Jane Tylus, eds. *Early Modern Cultures of Translation.* Philadelphia: University of Pennsylvania Press, 2015.

Newstok, Scott. *Quoting Death in Early Modern England: The Poetics of Epitaphs Beyond the Tomb*. New York: Palgrave Macmillan, 2009.

Nightingale, Andrea Wilson. "Plato's *Gorgias* and Euripides' *Antiope*: A Study in Generic Transformation." *Classical Antiquity* 11, no. 1 (April 1992): 121–41.

Osuna Rodríguez, Inmaculada. "Literary Academies and Poetic Tournaments." In *The Routledge Companion to Spanish Women Writers*, edited by Nieves Baranda and Anne J. Cruz, 153–67. London: Routledge, 2018.

Oswald, Alice. *Memorial: An Excavation of "The Iliad."* London: Faber and Faber, 2011.

Ovid. *Metamorphoses*. Translated by David Raeburn. New York: Penguin Classics, 2004.

Ovid. *Metamorphoses: The New, Annotated Edition*. Translated by Rolfe Humphries. Edited by Joseph D. Reed. Bloomington: Indiana University Press, 2018.

Ovid. *Metamorphoses by Ovid*. Translated by Stephanie McCarter. New York: Penguin, 2022.

"P. OVIDI NASONIS METAMORPHOSEON LIBER QVINTVS DECIMVS." The Latin Library. https://www.thelatinlibrary.com/ovid/ovid.met15.shtml.

Padrón, Ricardo. *The Spacious Word: Cartography, Literature, and Empire in Early Modern Spain*. Chicago: University of Chicago Press, 2004.

Páez de Valenzuela, Juan. *Relación breve de las fiestas que en la ciudad de Cordova se celebraron à la beatificación de la gloriosa patriarcha Santa Theresa de Jesus, fundadora de la reformación de Descalços y Descalças Carmelitas, con la justa literaria, que en ella uvo*. Córdoba: La Viuda de Andrés Barrera, 1615.

Pageaux, Daniel-Henri. *La lyre d'Amphion: De Thèbes a La Havane pour une poétique sans frontières*. Paris: Presses de la Sorbonne Nouvelle, 2001.

Park, James. "Ethnogenesis or Neoindigenous Intelligentsia: Contemporary Mapuche-Huilliche Poetry (Ethnogénesis o Neo Intelligentsia Indígena: Poesía Mapuche Huiliche Contemporánea)." *Latin American Research Review* 42, no. 3 (2007): 15–42.

Paster, Gail Kern. *The Idea of the City in the Age of Shakespeare*. Athens: University of Georgia Press, 2012.

Paster, Gail Kern. "Ben Jonson and the Uses of Architecture." *Renaissance Quarterly* 27, no. 3 (1974): 306–20.

Pelletier Du Mans, Jacques. *L'Art Poétique. Départi An Deus Livres*, 1555. Geneva: Slatkine Reprints, 1971.

Pérez y Gómez, Antonio, ed. *El ayre de la almena: Textos literarios rarísimos*. 40 vols. Valencia: Cieza, 1956–75.

Peureux, Guillaume, and Alain Vaillant, eds. *La poésie de circonstance (XVIᵉ–XXIᵉ siècle): Formes, practiques, usages*. Paris: Presses universitaires de Paris Nanterre, 2022.

Plato. *Gorgias*. Translated by Walter Hamilton. London: Penguin, 1960.

Prescott, Anne Lake. "Chivalric Restoration: From Bateman's *Travayled Pylgrime* to the Redcrosse Knight." *Studies in Philology* 86, no. 2 (1989): 166–97.

Puttenham, George. *The Art of English Poesy: A Critical Edition*. Edited by Frank Whigham and Wayne A. Rebhorn. Ithaca, NY: Cornell University Press, 2007.

Quevedo, Francisco de. "A Roma Sepultada en sus Ruinas." Biblioteca Virtual Miguel de Cervantes. cervantesvirtual.com/obra-visor/antologia-poetica--39/html /ffa6b3fe-82b1-11df-acc7-002185ce6064_2.html.

208 Bibliography

Quitslund, Beth. "'Without Pity Heare Their Dying Groanes': Metrical Psalms and the Poetry of Sacred Violence." *Religion and Literature* 49, no. 3 (2017): 152–62.

Rabelais, François. *"Bonnes gens, Buveurs très illustres, et vous goutteaux très précieux."* In *Oeuvres complètes.* Texte original et translation en français moderne, par Guy Demerson. Paris: Seuil, 1989.

Rama, Ángel. *La ciudad letrada.* Mexico: Ediciones del Norte, 1984.

Ramachandran, Ayesha. *The Worldmakers: Global Imaginings in Early Modern Europe.* Chicago: University of Chicago Press, 2015.

Ramanzani, Jahan. *Poetry and Its Others: News, Prayer, Song, and the Dialogue of Genres.* Chicago: University of Chicago Press, 2014.

Rancière, Jacques. *Aesthetics and Its Discontents.* Translated by Steven Corcoran. Cambridge: Polity Press, 2009.

Reed, Brian. "Idea Eater: The Conceptual Lyric as Emergent Literary Form." *Mosaic: An Interdisciplinary Critical Journal* 49, no. 2 (2016): 1–18.

Reitz-Joosse, Bettina. *Building in Words: The Process of Construction in Latin Literature.* Oxford: Oxford University Press, 2021.

Roche, Thomas P. *Petrarch and the English Sonnet Sequences.* New York: AMS Press, 1989.

Rowe, Erin Kathleen. *Saint and Nation: Santiago, Teresa of Avila, and Plural Identities in Early Modern Spain.* University Park: Penn State University Press, 2011.

Rowe, William. "Raúl Zurita: Language, Madness and the Social Wound." *Travesía* 2, no. 2 (1993): 183–218.

Schmidt, Michael. *The First Poets: Lives of the Ancient Greek Poets.* New York: Random House, 2010.

Shakespeare, William. Sonnet 18. The Poetry Foundation. https://www .poetryfoundation.org/poems/45087/sonnet-18-shall-i-compare-thee-to-a -summers-day.

Sidney, Philip. *The Defence of Poesy.* The Poetry Foundation. poetryfoundation.org /articles/69375/the-defence-of-poesy#.

Spenser, Edmund. *Complaints.* Luminarium: Anthology of English Literature. http:// www.luminarium.org/renascence-editions/complaints.html.

Stewart, Susan. *Poetry and the Fate of the Senses.* Chicago: Chicago University Press, 2002.

Stoler, Ann Laura. "Imperial Debris: Reflections on Ruins and Ruination." *Cultural Anthropology* 23, no. 2 (2008): 191–219.

Stoler, Ann Laura, Carole McGranahan, and Peter C. Perdue. *Imperial Formations.* Santa Fe, NM: School for Advanced Research Press, 2007.

Sutch, Susie Speakman, and Anne Lake Prescott. "Translation as Transformation: Olivier de la Marche's *Le Chevalier délibéré* and Its Hapsburg and Elizabethan Permutations." *Comparative Literature Studies* 25, no. 4 (1988): 281–317.

Sweeney, Anne R. *Snow in Arcadia: Redrawing the English Lyric Landscape, 1586–1595.* Manchester: Manchester University Press, 2006.

Taormina, Michael. *Amphion Orator: How the Royal Odes of François de Malherbe Reimagine the French Nation.* Tübingen: Narr Franke Attempto, 2021.

Thomás, Miguel. *Certamen Poético, en honor de la venerable madre Sor Catharina Thomasa Mallorquina, Monja canóniga reglar de San Agustin, Mantenido en la isla y ciudad de Mallorca, en la Sala de la Congregación de los Cavalleros, en el Colegio de Monte Sion de la Compañía de Jesús*. Barcelona: Gabriel Nogués, 1636.

Thompson, John. *The Founding of English Metre*. New York: Columbia University Press, 1961.

Torre, Osvaldo de la. "On Loss and Not Losing It: Neruda, Mistral, and Zurita in the Post-Dictatorship." *New Centennial Review* 14, no. 1 (2014): 129–52.

Torres, Isabel. *Love Poetry in the Spanish Golden Age: Eros, Eris and Empire*. Woodbridge, UK: Tamesis, 2013.

Urrea, Jerónimo de. *Discurso de la vida humana y aventuras del caballero determinado traduzido de frances por Don Jerónimo de Urrea*. Antwerp: Martin Nutius, 1555.

Valencia, Felipe. *The Melancholy Void: Lyric and Masculinity in the Age of Góngora*. Lincoln: University of Nebraska Press, 2021.

Vázquez, Miguel Ángel. "Poesía morisca (o cómo el español se convirtió en lengua literaria del islam)." *Hispanic Review* 75, no. 3 (2007): 219–42.

Vega, Garcilaso de la. "Oda ad florem Gnidi." In *Poesía Castellana*, edited by Julián Jiménez Heffernan and E. Ignacio García Aguilar, 270–73. Madrid: Akal, 2017.

Vega, Lope de. *Rimas sacras*. Edited by Ramón García González. Alicante: Biblioteca Virtual Miguel de Cervantes, 2003, https://www.cervantesvirtual.com/obra-visor /rimas-sacras--0/html/ffe59452-82b1-11df-acc7-002185ce6064_2.html#I_0_.

Vega, Maria José, and Cesc Esteve, eds. *Idea de la lírica en el renacimiento (entre Italia y España)*. Barcelona: Mirabel Editorial, 2004.

Vegas, Federico. "This World Heritage Site Is in Ruins, and That's Not by Accident." *New York Times*, July 7, 2021. https://www.nytimes.com/2021/07/07/opinion /venezuela-landmark-university.html.

Velasco, Jesús D. Rodríguez. "La *Bibliotheca* y los márgenes: Ensayo teórico sobre la glosa en el ámbito cortesano del siglo XV en Castilla. I: Códice, dialéctica y autoridad." *eHumanista: Journal of Iberian Studies* 1 (2001): 119–34.

Velasco, Jesús R. *Dead Voice: Law, Philosophy, and Fiction in the Iberian Middle Ages*. University Park: Pennsylvania State University Press, 2020.

Velasco, Jesús. *Microliteraturas*. Madrid: Cátedra, 2022.

Vendler, Helen. *The Art of Shakespeare's Sonnets*. Cambridge, MA: Harvard University Press, 1999.

Venuti, Lawrence. "The Poet's Version; or, An Ethics of Translation." *Translation Studies* 4, no. 2 (2011): 230–47.

Vickers, Nancy J. "Diana Described: Scattered Woman, Scattered Rhyme." *Critical Inquiry* 8, no. 2 (1981): 265–79.

Vinestock, Elizabeth. *Poétique et pratique dans les "Poemes" de Jean-Antoine de Baïf*. Paris: Honoré Champion, 2006.

Walcott, Derek. *Omeros*. New York: Farrar, Straus & Giroux, 1992.

Warden, John. *Orpheus: The Metamorphoses of a Myth*. Toronto: University of Toronto Press, 1982.

Williams, Raymond. *Keywords: A Vocabulary of Culture and Society*. 2nd ed. Oxford: Oxford University Press, 2015.

Winnicott, D. W. *Playing and Reality*. London: Tavistock, 1971.

Wordsworth, William. "The World Is Too Much with Us." Poetry Foundation. https:// www.poetryfoundation.org/poems/45564/the-world-is-too-much-with-us.

210 Bibliography

Wright, Elizabeth R. *The Epic of Juan Latino: Dilemmas of Race and Religion in Renaissance Spain*. Toronto: University of Toronto Press, 2016.

Yates, Frances. *French Academies of the Sixteenth Century*. London: Warburg Institute, 1947.

Yeats, William Butler. "Lapis Lazuli." Poetry Foundation. https://www.poetry foundation.org/poems/43297/lapis-lazuli.

Yiu, Mimi. "Sounding the Space between Men: Choric and Choral Cities in Ben Jonson's *Epicoene*; or, *The Silent Woman*." *PMLA* 122, no. 1 (2007): 72–88.

Zapata, Luis. *El arte poetica de Horatio / traducida de latin en español por don Luis Çapata*. Lisbon: Casa de Alexandre de Syqueira, 1592.

Zecher, Carla. "Ronsard's Guitar: A Sixteenth-Century Heir to the Horatian Lyre." *International Journal of the Classical Tradition* 4 (1998): 532–54.

Zurita, Raúl. *Anteparadise: A Bilingual Edition*. Translated by Jack Schmitt. Berkeley: University of California Press, 1986.

Zurita, Raúl. *Sky Below: Selected Works*. Translated from the Spanish and with an introduction by Anna Deeny Morales. Evanston, IL: Northwestern University Press, 2016.

Zurita, Raúl. *Song for His Disappeared Love*. Translated by Daniel Borzutzky. Notre Dame, IN: Action Books, 2010.

Zurita, Raúl, and Benoît Santini. "En Zurita, van a aparecer las ruinas, pedazos de poemas antiguos." *Revista Chilena de Literatura* 80 (2011): 253–62.

Index

"A Boscán desde la Goleta" (To Boscán, from the Goleta) (Garcilaso), 192–93n15

Act of Supremacy, 54

Acuña, Hernando de, 48, 172n9, 175n45, 187n31; "A un buen caballero y mal poeta: La lira de Garcilaso contrahecha" (To a good gentleman and bad poet: Garcilaso's lyre undone), 41–46, 54; *Cavallero determinado*, 47, 56–59; *coplas* of *arte menor*, 51; *quintillas*, use of, 49, 58

Africa, 121, 149, 157, 181–82n21, 182n40, 192–93n15

African and Africana studies, 179n96

African diaspora, 62

al-Bakri, Abu al-Hasan: *Kitab al-Anwar*, 60

Alciato: *Emblemata liber*, 7

Alexander VI (pope), 190n2

Algeria, 118

Allende, Salvador, 140–41

Almagro, Diego de, 123

Alonso, Dámaso, 104, 169n27

Alonso de Cervantes, 29–33; glosses, 34

Amarílis: "Epístola a Belardo," 123–24, 133

Amphion, 18–19, 21–23, 32, 34, 36, 64, 68, 76, 79, 81–82, 87, 90–91, 94, 96, 100, 102, 115, 118, 120, 123, 129, 135, 137, 142–43, 146, 159, 168–69n20, 172n55, 174n34, 183n45, 184–85n59, 197n1; Amphionic, 5, 8, 59; Amphionic logic, 187n31; Amphionic lyric, 15, 133–34; Amphionic poetry, 172–73n13; Amphionic renewal, 170n30; Amphionic rereading, 62; *Antiope*, basis for, 15; basis for defining action, 3; as "bright, unbearable fact," 11; building up cities, 7, 85–86; charm, association with, 28, 167n3; cheerful collaboration, 27; Christian conquest, and myth of, 124; as city builder, 8; civic power, 97; collaborative effort, 2–3; collective activity, 117; contexts, 10; disappearance of, 78; engraving of, 11; enthusiasm, representing of, 188–89n37; as inspiration, 63, 150; literary criticism, connection between, 178n85; lyre of, xiii–xiv, 2–3, 28, 70, 104; lyric culture, informing of, 104–5, 108–9; lyric tradition, 25, 59, 63; Mercury, association with, 127; messianic Christianity, 124; muses, 128, 144; music, 15, 123, 127–28; music of ruination, 127; myth of, xiii, 16, 37, 70, 105, 117, 124, 127, 132, 137; name, indicating dualities, 8; orators, association with, 172n12; poetic tradition of, 8; poetry contests, 111, 115; as polity, 2; sculpture of, 163–64; Spanish-American imaginary, shaping of, 119; as specific kind of poiesis, 2, 5;

Index

Amphion (*continued*)
stones, 28; suicide of, xiv; Thebes, association with, 127

Amphion's lyre, xiii–xiv, 2, 7, 34–35, 56, 65–66, 85–86, 119, 158, 160, 164, 172n12, 184–85n59; capacity to accomplish magnificent feats, 3; collective action, joining in, 8; images of, 4; materiality and ephemerality of social cohesion, 28–29; music of ruination, 128, 159; walls of Cocytus, 143; walls for Thebes, 15, 183n45

Anaxarete, myth of, 40

Angel, Luis Pérez: Academia Antárctica circle, 2

Anglican Church, 55; common meter, adoption of, 58

Anteparaíso (Zurita), 128–29, 143

Antiope (Euripides), xiii, 15, 183n45

Apollo, xiv, 21–22, 29, 43, 78, 94, 117; lyre of, 28

Aragon, Spain, 103

Aristotle: *Poetics*, 3; theory of the structure, 122

"A Roma sepultada en sus ruinas" (Quevedo), 78

Ars Poetica (Horace), 3, 19–20, 22, 25, 96, 100, 174n34

arte mayor, 51

arte menor, 51

Art of English Poesy, The (Puttenham), 5–6, 8

Ashbery, John: "Daffy Duck in Hollywood," 183n43

Augustine: *The City of God*, 168n10

Augustus, 20, 71, 171n51

"A un buen caballero y mal poeta: La lira de Garcilaso contrahecha" (To a good gentleman and bad poet: Garcilaso's lyre undone) (Acuña), 41–44, 46, 54; double entendres in, 45

Austin, John: *How to Do Things with Words*, 97

Aztec empire, 120–21; conquest of, as God's will, 129–32

Balbuena de, Bernardo, 139, 194n43; Christian conquest and myths of Am-

phion, 124; *La grandeza Mexicana* (The grandeur of Mexico), 124–26, 134–38; *Siglo de oro en las selvas de Erífile*, 137

Bateman, Stephen, 56–58, 178n82, 178n84

Beechy, Tiffany, 28

belonging, 3, 41, 61–62, 115, 132, 137

Black studies, 179n96

Boileau, Nicolas: *L'Art poetique*, 26, 63

Book of Common Prayer, 55

Book of the Courtier, The, 38

Boscán, Juan, 38, 51; "Letter to the Duchess of Soma," 52

Bourdieu, Pierre, habitus, 5

Britain, 77, 83, 85. *See also* England; Scotland

British studies, 179n96

"Buscas en Roma a Roma ¡oh peregrino!" (You seek Rome in Rome, oh pilgrim!), 65

Cacho Casal, Rodrigo, 135–37, 194n43

Cadmus, 124–25, 137

Calvete de Estrella, Juan Cristóbal, 50

Cañizares-Esquerra, Jorge, 191n7

"Canto a su amor desaparecido" (Song for his disappeared love) (Zurita), 128–29, 140, 151–52, 158; communal singing, 153; dedication to, 148, 159; *galpones*, set in, 149, 154; *Inferno*, allusion to, 147–48, 150, 155; *paisa*, experience of, 147, 153

Canto general (Neruda), 157, 196n82

Canzoniere (Petrarch), 65, 180n4

"Capital Accounts" (Joyce), 83

carmina, 27

Carson, Anne, 185n61

Cartas de relación (Letters of relation) (Cortés) 122, 192–93n15; as Amphionic, 129; destiny, as God's will, 129–30; subtext of, as remaking of Yucatán Peninula, 131

Cascardi, Anthony J., 96, 190n63

Castillejo, Cristóbal de, 52

Catalá de Valeriola, Don Bernardo, 115–17

Catholic Church, 54

Catholicism, 57

Index   213

Cavalcante, Guido, 148, 159
Cavallero determinado (Acuña), 47, 56–59
Cave, Terence, 95
Central University of Venezuela, Amphion sculpture, 163
Certayne Psalmes Chosen out of the Psalter of David, and Drawen into English Metre (Sternhold and Hopkins), 55
Cervantes, Alonso de, 29–34, 173n14, 174n22, 174n30
Cervantes, Miguel de, 100, 105–6, 108, 173n14, 186n12; *Don Quixote, Part II*, 23, 46, 96–104, 117–18, 186n15, 186n18, 188n36, 190n63; *Los trabajos de Persiles y Sigismunda*, 96; *Viaje del Parnaso* (Journey to Parnassus), 23, 93–97, 117, 170n39, 186n12
Charles the Bold, 46–47
Charles V, 46–49, 52, 54, 56, 120, 122, 124, 191n4; as modern Caesar, 192–93n15; outlawing of Islam in Aragon, 60
charm, 27–29, 172n9
Chihuailaf Nahuelpán, Elicura, 159–60
Chile, 140, 142–43, 146, 148, 157; "disappearances," 141
Choi, Don Mee, 185n60
Christianity, 72; messianic, 124
chusma, 94, 106
cities, xiii, 2–5, 21–22, 69, 88, 119–21, 123, 129, 131, 139–40, 160, 190–91n3, 192–93n15; archaic, 17, 27–28, 90; "bad" 169n25; "baroque city," 192n13; building up of, 7, 15–16, 81–82, 89–90; colonial, 155; conquistadores, 190–91n3; destroying of, 65; founding of, as pious act, 168n10; fratricide, 168n10; hollowness in, 127–28; imperial, 17, 82–83; theory of the structure, 122
City of God, The (Augustine), 168n10
civil society, 27
Clarinda, 3, 137; *Discurso en loor de la poesía* (Discourse in praise of poetry), 2, 133–34
codicia, 140, 154
Colipán, Bernardo: "Pulotre 1916," 160–61
collective, 11, 18, 34, 64, 96, 108, 110, 126, 150; action, 8; activity, 117; ef-

fort, 86; endeavors, 16; energies, 27; global, 148–49; human, 148; living, 16; lyric-making, 114; lyrics, 152; motion, 7; as *paisa*, 142–43; participation, 111; prayer, 58; rhythms, 5; sense of identity, 53; social collective, 8; social life, 28; spirit, 103, 107; voice, 120
colonialism, 46, 192–93n15; apologists for, 139
coloniality, 13, 23, 83, 170n35, 189n47
colonization, 127; ruination, as target, 140
Columbus, Christopher, 34
common meter, 55–56
Complaints (Spenser), 75–78, 184nn56–57
conceptual poetry, 83
concierto, 127
conquistadores, 119–20, 125, 132, 190–91n3
Convent of Discalced Carmelites, 109–11
copia, 107, 117–18, 135, 186n15, 190n64
copia dicendi, 95, 97
Coplas por la muerte de su padre (Manrique), 30, 32–34, 51–52, 173n17; glosses of, 174n22, 174n30
Cordero, Juan Martín, 53, 178n82
Córdoba, Spain, 109
Cortés, Hernán, 45, 121, 123–25, 132, 137, 191n4, 191nn6–7, 192n13, 192–93n15; *Cartas de relación* (Letters of relation), 122, 129–31, 192–93n15; conquistadores, 120; violence of, as divine inspiration, 130–31
Counter-Reformation, 61, 137
criollos, 127–28, 137, 139; Amphionic lyric, role of, 133

"Daffy Duck in Hollywood" (Ashbery), 183n43
Damsell, Sir William, 56
Dante, 16, 18, 150, 158, 195–96n67; Amphion, invoking of, 143–44; *canto* form, 134; *Divina Commedia*, 24, 140; *The Inferno*, 17, 119, 127–29, 140, 143, 144, 147, 148, 155, 193n27; music of ruination, 128; poetry of, as incorporated

214 **Index**

Dante (*continued*)
into foundation of Spanish-American imperial formation, 128; terza rima, 19, 128, 134

Darker Side of Western Modernity, The (Mignolo), 12–13

de Certeau, Michel, 192n12

decolonial studies, 59

Deeny Morales, Anna, 195n65, 195–96n67

Defence of Poesy (Sidney), 27

Défense et illustration de la Langue Française (Defense and celebration of the French language) (Du Bellay), 66–67, 168n16

de la Torre, Osvaldo, 196n83

Delattre, Aurélie, 188–89n37

"Desert of Atacama, The" (Zurita), 146–47

Diana, xiv

Díaz del Castillo, Bernal: *Historia verdadera de la conquista de Nueva España* (True history of the conquest of New Spain), 121

Dimock, Wai Chee, 90

Dirce, xiii

Discurso de la luz (Rabadán), 60

Discurso en loor de la poesía (Discourse in praise of poetry) (Clarinda), 2, 133–34

dispossession, 85, 131–32

Divina Commedia (Dante), 24, 140

Don Quixote, Part II (Cervantes), 23, 46, 96, 190n63; aspiring *letrados* in, 99; Doña Cristina, 117–18; Don Diego de Miranda, 97–98, 100–102, 117–18, 186n15, 186n18; Don Lorenzo, 98–104, 188n36; Don Quixote, character of, 97–104, 186n15, 186n18, 188n36; Dulcinea, thoughts of, 100; Knight of the Green Coat, false nature of, 97, 100–102, 117; Orphic and Amphionic lyrics, theme of, 101–2; poetry contests, 103; Sancho Panza, 97, 117–18; Sansón Carrasco, 97, 99; Spanish empire, portrait of, 103

Dworkin, Craig, 83

Du Bellay, Jean, 66

Du Bellay, Joachim, 15, 64–65, 79, 82–84, 137, 183n50, 184n54, 184n57; *Antiquitez de Rome* (The ruins of Rome), 23, 66–75, 77, 78, 80–81, 87–90, 138, 181n22, 184n56, 184–85n59; *Défense et illustration de la langue française* (The defense and enrichment of the French language), 66–67, 168n16

Durling, Robert, 19

"Easter, 1916" (Yeats), 160–61

efficacia, 4–5, 22

Egido, Aurora, 103–4, 169n27

Egypt, 81

Eliot, T. S., 160

Elizabeth I, 6–7, 54, 77

"El mar" (Zurita), 145–46

El Mercurio (newspaper), 147

Emblemata liber (Alciato), 7

England, 3, 5, 19–20, 35–36, 38, 54–55, 57, 73, 78, 83, 182n40, 187n31; Christianity, incorporating of in imperial view, 124. *See also* Britain

English Civil Wars, 36

English identity, 55; English language and iambic pentameter, 54

English Pilgrims, 191n7

Enlightenment, 78

"Epistola a Belardo" (Amarílis), 123–24, 133

Erasmus, 186n15

Esteve, Cesc, 3

Euripides, xiii, 70, 82; *Antiope*, 15

Europe, 3, 5, 17, 34, 59, 83, 109, 117, 139, 170n35, 182n40, 190n2

European Union (EU), 182–83n42

Eurydice, 21–22

extractivism, 46, 82

Faerie Queene, The (Spenser), 76

Ferdinand I (Spain), 52, 59

"Fig Tree and the Laurel, The: Petrarch's Poetics" (Freccero), 180n4

FitzGerald, Garret, 182–83n42

foedera (diplomatic pact), 7; as social collective, 8

Foucault, Michel: conducted societies, 192n12; *Security, Territory, Population*, 192nn12–13

Fra-Molinero, Baltasar, 45, 179n96
France, 3, 19–20, 23, 35, 48–49, 56, 64–66, 70, 73, 77–78, 180–81n14, 182n40, 187n31; Christianity, incorporating of in imperial vision, 124
Franco, Jean, 196n82
François I (France), 67, 124, 180–81n14
Freccero, John: "The Fig Tree and the Laurel: Petrarch's Poetics," 180n4
Fuchs, Barbara, 3, 178n88

Garcilaso de la Vega, 33, 51–52, 63–64, 101, 175n38, 192n15; "Ode ad florem Gnidi," 38–42, 44, 46, 175n44
Gascoigne, George, 55–56
gender, 46; gender norms, 41; gender politics, 39
Georgics (Virgil), 39
Glantz, Margo, 120
global North, 182n40
glossing, 16, 30–33, 173n20, 174n22, 174n24, 174n30
Golden Age lyric, 59, 61, 137
Gómez de Sandoval y Rojas, Don Francisco, 116
Góngora, Luis de, 62, 187n31
Gorgias (Plato), 15, 183n45
Greece, 2, 20, 81
Greene, Roland, 34–35, 180n4
Greene, Thomas M., 184–85n59; *The Light in Troy*, 90
Grossman, Allen, 5, 51, 169n26
Guillén de Castro, 187n31

habitus, 5, 28, 53
habla de negros (Africanized Castilian), 59; Black African life and Black personhood, 62
Hall, Kim F., 179n96
Hampton, Timothy, 107
Hapsburg Spain, 54, 77; La Marche's France, links to, 48
Hapsburgs, 34, 47–48, 56, 58
Hayot, Eric, 33
Heidegger, Martin, 33
Helgerson, Richard, 66
Hemans, Felicia, 78
hendecasyllable, 51–52, 56, 137

Henri II (France), 67
Henry VIII (England), 124; break with Catholic Church, 54
Hermes, xiv, 15, 70, 82, 183n45. *See also* Mercury
heroic couplets, 35–38
Herrera, Fernando de, 186n12
Historia verdadera de la conquista de Nueva España (True history of the conquest of New Spain) (Díaz del Castillo), 121
Holland, 182n40
Homer, 172n55; translations of, 185n61; *Iliad*, 170n30, 185n61; *Odyssey*, 16, 185n61
Hopkins, John, 56, 177n77; *Certayne Psalmes Chosen out of the Psalter of David, and Drawen into English Metre* (with Sternhold), 55
Horace, xiii, 4, 8, 13–14, 16, 21, 23–24, 28, 35, 38–39, 56, 63–64, 68, 82, 171n51; *Ars Poetica*, 3, 19–20, 22, 25–26, 96, 100, 174n34; charm, 29; *musa lyrae sollers* (songs of the lyric muse), 3–4, 104, 106, 128
How to Do Things with Words (Austin), 97
Huenún Villa, Jaime, 197n90, 197n94

Iliad (Homer), 170n30, 185n61
imitatio, 1, 10–11
Immediate Future, The (Joyce), 83
imperial formation, 11, 129, 180n8, 189n47, 194n52; empire, as term, 12; Hapsburg, 192–93n15; Spanish, 132, 138, 140; Spanish-American, 128
imperialism, 46, 82, 85, 192–93n15
imperium, 17, 64–65, 67, 124, 137–38; challenges to, 89; cultures of, 3; domestic, 181–82n31; English, 78; eternal, 73; Hapsburg, 96; Horace, poetics of, 19–20; language of, 85; and lyre, 73; lyric and polity, as interrelated, 4; Roman, 20, 66, 71, 79, 85; Spenser, as poet of, 75, 77; temporality of, 140
Incan empire, 3
Indigenous Americans, 139, 157, 196n82
indio, 139
Inés de la Cruz, Sor Juana, 62

216 Index

Inferno, The (Dante), 17, 119, 127–29, 140, 144, 147–48, 155, 193n27; "rime aspre e chiocce," 143
interés, 140, 154
interiority, 8, 10
Ireland, 23, 83, 85, 182n40; as Celtic Tiger, 182–83n42, 183n48
Isabel I (Spain), 34, 59
Islam, 186n15; outlawing of, 60
Italy, 56, 121; Italian academies, Spanish, French, and English writers modeling after, 103
Izenberg, Oren, 10, 107–8, 189n47, 190n64; Language poetry, 189n42

Jackson, Virginia, 25, 167n4
James R. Osgood and Company, 78
Johnson, Carina, 45, 122
Johnson, Carroll B., 175n38
Jones, Nicholas R., 59, 61–62, 179n96
Jonson, Ben, 15, 174n34; anaphora, 37; "ancient pile," 36; enjambment, 37; heroic couplets, 38; "To Penshurst," 35–38, 41, 123
Joyce, Trevor, 183nn49–50; "Capital Accounts," 83; iambic pentameter, replacing with octosyllables, 80, 83; *The Immediate Future*, 83; imperialism and neoliberalism, 85; lyre, 65–66; postmodernism of, 183n43; rewriting Spenser and Du Bellay, 80, 87–88, 90; *Rome's Wreck*, 13, 65–66, 79–91, 183n43

Kiely, Robert, 83, 182–83n42, 183n48
Kitab al-Anwar (al-Bakri), 60
Konuk-Blasing, Mutlu, 169n25

Laberinto de la fortuna (The labyrinth of fortune) (Mena), 51–52
La grandeza Mexicana (The grandeur of Mexico) (Balbuena), 124–26, 134–36; as celebration of Mexican city, 137; containment and organization, 137; hendecasyllables and tercets in, 137; signs, idea of, 138; Spanish imperial formation, 138; Thebes, as model, 138

La Marche, Olivier de, 59; *Le Chevalier délibéré*, 46–51, 54, 56–58
Language poetry, 108, 143, 189n42
"Lapis Lazuli" (Yeats), 12
L'Art poétique (Boileau), 26, 63
"Las cordilleras del Duce" (Zurita), 144–47
"Las espejeantes playas" (The sparkling beaches) (Zurita), 141–42
Las obras de Juan Boscán y algunas de Garcilaso de la Vega, repartidas en cuatro libros (The works of Juan Boscán and some by Garcilaso de la Vega, divided into four books), 55
Latona, xiv
"La United Fruit Co." (Neruda), 195n53
Laurens, Henri, 163–64
La vida nueva (Zurita) 128–29, 143
Le Chevalier délibéré (La Marche), 46, 59; Acuña's Castilian verse, translation of, 47–51, 54, 56; Bateman translation, 57–58; Christian allegory in, 47; English aristocracy, popular among, 57; propaganda, incorporating of, 47; rules of allegory, violating of, 49–50; terza rima, 51; *translatio imperii*, 50; Urrea's translation of, 51, 54, 56
Lee, Christina, 178n88
Leningrad, 189n42
Lepautre, Antoine, 11
Les Antiquitez de Rome (The ruins of Rome) (Du Bellay), 23, 64, 66, 67, 69, 80, 81, 87, 90, 181n22, 184n56, 184–85n59; aesthetics of desiccation, 74–75; Britain, power of, 77; Christian cosmos, 72–73; conceit of, 68; disenchantment, as theme, 73–74; ephemeral nature of all things, 75; fall of Rome, 70–71, 74–75; feminine conceit, 77; lyres of Amphion and Orpheus, invoking of, 70; "Nouveau venu, qui cherches Rome en Rome," 65; people in, 88; poetry-polis-self, 78; Quevedo translation, 73–75; Roman ruins, 138; romantic themes of, 78; Rome, rebuilding itself, 89; Spenser translation, 75–77; transmediation of, 66

letrados, 53, 99, 117
Levinas, Emmanuel: the face, 195n65
Lienlaf, Leonel, 159–60
Light in Troy, The (Greene), 90
Linus, 172n55
Lionetto, Adeline, 188–89n37
lira, 38
Lloyd, David, 183n49
Longfellow, Henry Wadsworth, 182n39; *Poems and Places*, 65, 78–79, 182n40
Lope de Vega, 186n12, 187n31
López Alemany, Ignacio, 53
Los trabajos de Persiles y Sigismunda (Cervantes), 96
Lugones, Maria, 175n44
lyre, 27–29, 32–33, 38, 49, 63, 66, 68, 81, 86, 144, 172n55; archaic, 39; eternal imperium, 73; invention of, by Hermes/ Mercury, 13; as metaphor for political, social, and cultural power, 90; Neoplatonic powers of, 64; power of, 8; social relations, 91; status and fame, as mechanism for, 117; tropes of, 35
lyric, 11–12, 23–24, 27, 29, 43, 59, 75–76, 94, 96, 101, 111, 116, 133–34, 140, 159–60; alphabet song, 3; civic life, 2–26; collective 114, 132, 152; contest lyrics, 105, 107–9, 114, 169n27, 188n36; and cultural memory, 60; English lyric, 54–55, 177n77; flourishing of, 3; happy birthday song, 3; "idea of," 3; lyric art, 35; lyric culture, 34, 104, 108–9, 113–14; lyric forms, 46; lyric poetics, 35–36; lyric poetry, 3, 8, 25–26, 82, 100; lyric poiesis, 4–5, 63; lyric reading, 10; lyric tradition, 15, 23, 25, 63, 133; *musa lyrae sollers*, 108–9, 113–14; national anthems, 3; New Lyric studies, 177n77; Petrarchan lyric, 64; as *poemi piccoli*, 3; *pöesies*, 3; politics, 53; *rimas*, 3; small poetry, 3; stipulative functions of, 25, 167n4; world-making power of, 56
Lycus, xiii–xiv

Mallorca, 114–16
Mallorquina, Sor Catharina Thomasa, 111–13, 115; holiness of, 114

Manrique, Jorge, 30–32, 173n17
Manrique, Santiago Rodrigo, 173n17; *Coplas por la muerte de su padre*, 30, 32–34, 51–52, 173n17, 174n22, 174n30
Mapuche poets and writers, 13, 24, 159, 161, 197nn90–91
Margaret of Austria, 48
Marino, Nancy F., 34, 174n22
Martínez Valdivia, Lucía, 55
Mary of Burgundy, 46–47
Mazzotti, José Antonio, 132
McCarter, Stephanie, 185n61
McGranahan, Carole, 11–12
Melehy, Hassan, 183n22
Memorial (Oswald), 185n61
Mena, Juan de: *Laberinto de la fortuna* (The labyrinth of fortune), 51–52
mercantilism, 46
Mercury, 13–15, 22, 28, 70, 94–96, 117, 127, 170nn38–39, 183n45; change, association with, 29. *See also* Hermes
Merrim, Stephanie, 121–22, 129, 192n13; the scriptural economy, 192n12
Metamorphoses (Ovid), 16–17, 39–41, 44, 69, 175n36, 185n61
Mexía de Fernangil, Diego, 133–34
Mexico, 124–25, 134–35, 137; Black population in, 62; Indigenous inhabitants, 139; vibrancy of, 138
Middle English poetry, charms and riddles in, 26
Mignolo, Walter: *The Darker Side of Western Modernity*, 12–13
Mistral, Gabriela, 196n83
modernity, xiii, 11–12, 24, 35, 108, 163–64, 170n35, 175n44, 189n47
Mohammed, 59
Montezuma, 129–31
Mora Curriao, Maribel, 160
Moriscos, 59, 61, 178n88; expulsion of, 23, 60, 117–18, 186n15; othering of, 178n88, 197n90; poets, 13, 179n89; as targeted population, 186n18
Morocco, 117–18
Mothers of the Plaza de Mayo, 148
Musaeus, 172n55

218 **Index**

musa lyrae sollers (songs of the lyric muse), 3-4, 23, 25, 27, 34-35, 38, 46, 61, 63, 76, 104, 106, 119, 128, 143, 145; common meter, 56; cultural memory, preserving of, 60; Islamic Spanish lyrics, 60; literary and social poiesis, value of, 108; lyric culture of, 59, 108-9, 113-14; oracles, 22
muses, 43, 50, 76, 128, 133-34, 140, 144; Spanish poetic topos of, 179n89
myth, xiii

Nancy, Jean Luc, 33, 174n27
Naples, Italy, 41-43, 63-64
neoliberalism, 85; neoliberal economics, 83, 157
Neoplatonism, 122
Neruda, Pablo, 158; *Canto general*, 157, 196n82; "La United Fruit Co.," 195n53
Niobe, xiv, 16
North Africa, 178n88
Nutius, Martin, 47

"Ode ad florem Gnidi" (Garcilaso), 38-40, 42, 44, 46, 175n44; lyric devices in, 41
Odyssey (Homer), 16, 185n61
Omeros (Walcott), 185n61
Orlando Furioso (Urrea), 46
Orpheus, 2-4, 21, 23, 39, 41, 44, 65, 68, 76, 78, 81, 96, 100, 168n10, 168-69n20, 172n55, 174n34, 184-85n59; as inspiration, 150; lyre of, 35, 63-64, 70, 77, 104; lyric culture, informing of, 108-9; myth of, 111, 168n11; Orphic law, 5; Orphic music, 111; Orphic poetry, 8, 22; Orphic power, 28; poetry contests, 111; speech act, 97; stones, 113-14
Oswald, Alice, 11, 170n30; *Memorial*, 185n61
othering, 45, 178n88, 197n90
Ovid, xiii, 20, 28, 35, 37, 100; *Metamorphoses*, 16-17, 39-41, 44, 69, 175n36, 185n61; *Primera parte del Parnaso Antártica de obras amatorias* (First part of the Antarctic Parnassus of the art of love), 133-34

Padrón, Ricardo, 94
Pageaux, Daniel-Henri, 178n85
paisa, 147, 149-50, 153, 157-58; solidarity, 148
Park, James, 197n90
Paster, Gail Kern, 168n10
Pausanias, 16
Pelletier du Mans, Jacques, 26
Perdue, Peter C., 11-12
Peru, 123
Petrarch, 33, 64; *Canzoniere*, 65, 180n4
Petrarchism, 1, 10-11; Petrarchan lyric, 64
Philip II, 47, 54, 56, 60, 175n47
Philip III, 47, 60-61
Pinochet, Augusto, 13, 140-41, 159
Piso, Lucius Calpurnius, 20
Pizzaro, Francisco, 123-24
Plato, 70, 82, 96, 122; *Gorgias*, 15, 183n45; *The Republic*, 169n25
Pléiade, 64
Poems and Places (Longfellow), 65, 78-79, 182n40
poésie de circonstance: social power and enthusiasm, 188-89n37
Poetics (Aristotle), 3
poetry, 6, 117; cultural memory, 15-16; identity, conflict in, 54; internal logic, 108; lyricization of, 34; poetic community, solidarity between poets and readers, 107; poetry makers, community of, 115; poets, as political leaders, 157; purpose of, 169n26; social justice, 157; verse form, cultural and political significance of, 57
poetry contests (*certámenes*), 103-4, 106, 137, 187n31; Amphion, association with, 111; collective spirit, 107; community and society, tension between, 115-16; contest lyrics, 108-9; lyrics, 107-8; lyrics, aesthetics of, 105; lyrics, dismissal of, 169n27; Orpheus, association with, 111; social poiesis of, 111; stones, conceit of, 113-14
poetry festivals, 109, 137, 187n31; community and society, tension between, 115
Poetry of the Earth: Mapuche Trilingual Anthology, 160-61, 197n90

poetry tournaments (*justas*), 103
poiesis, 2, 34, 48; Amphionic, 5, 8, 59; literary, 108; lyric, 4–5, 8, 14, 59, 63, 96, 147; social, 108, 111
polis, 122, 139, 142–43, 184–85n59
polity 2, 4, 8, 10–11, 24, 105, 115, 141, 143
Ponsonby, William, 75–78
Portugal, 29, 34, 182n40, 190n2, 192–93n15
Portuguese empire, 190n2
post-dictatorship culture, 141
Prescott, Anne Lake, 47, 49, 55, 57
Primera parte del Parnaso Antártica de obras amatorias (First part of the Antarctic Parnassus of the art of love) (Ovid), 133–34
Propertius, 20
Protestantism, 54; as True Religion, 56–57
"Pulotre 1916" (Colipán), 160–61
Purgatorio (Zurita), 128–29, 145
Puttenham, George, 7, 10, 28, 63, 168–69n20; *The Art of English Poesy*, 5–6, 8; English experience, as different from Greek and Latin, 6, 7; worldedness of, 6
puys, 103
Pythagoras, 16–17, 69

Quevedo, Francisco de, 62, 65, 73–75, 78
quintillas, 58
Quitsland, Beth, 55

Rabadán, Mohamed: *Discurso de la luz*, 60
Raeburn, David, 17
Rama, Ángel, 122, 190–91n3, 192n13
Ramachandran, Ayesha, 34
Rancière, Jacques, 132; world-making, 175n44
redondillas, 93, 113
Reitz-Joosse, Bettina, 167n3
Renaissance, xiii, 19, 23–24, 35, 37, 41, 59, 64–65, 80, 124; architecture, theories of, 125; "courtierization," 101; court poetry, 53; cultures of imperialism, 3; English, 83; humanist ideas, 13–14, 20, 76, 83, 90, 122–23, 133, 137–38, 168n10,

186n18; imperial expansion, 13; lyric, 83; poetic contests, 103; poetry, 8, 25; polis, interest in, 122; sonnet, 86; space, planning of, 122; sprezzatura, 107
Republic, The (Plato), 169n25
Requerimiento (Requisition), 119, 157, 190n2
rhetoric, 80
Rhodes, 81
Rodríguez, Inmaculada Osuna, 103, 187n31
romances (ballads), 2, 51, 93–94, 104, 106
Roman Republic, 71
Romantics, 10–11
Rome, 3, 22–23, 26, 66, 69, 71, 77, 79, 88, 89, 138, 168n10, 181n22; fall of, 70
Rome's Wreck (Joyce), 13, 65–66, 80–81, 86, 88, 90–91, 183n43; "Blockwork," 82, 87; "great ghosts" of Rome, 79, 83–85, 87, 89
Rudd, Niall, 171n51
ruination, 13; colonization, 140; music of, 127–29, 159
Ruines of Rome, The (Spenser), 65, 78–81
"Ruines of Time, The" (Spenser), 76–77

Sappho, 172n55
scriptural economy, 192n12
Security, Territory, Population (Foucault), 192nn12–13
self-fashioning, 1, 10–11
Seneca, 16
Sidney, Mary, 76
Sidney, Philip, 36, 38; *Defence of Poesy*, 27
Sidney, Robert, 35–36
Siglo de oro en las selvas de Erifile (Balbuena), 137
Silliman, Ron: *Tjanting*, 189n42
slavery, 192–93n15; apologists for, 139
social formation, 11
sociality, 11
social life, 10
social poiesis, 111
Socrates, 15
solitude, 10–11
Songs and Sonnettes (a.k.a. *Tottel's Miscellany*) (Tottel), 55

220 **Index**

sonsoneto, 53

South America, "Antartica," as term for, 167n2

Southern Cone, 159

Spain, 3, 13, 19–20, 29–30, 34–35, 48–49, 51, 54–58, 73, 100, 102, 109, 115, 118, 121, 123, 128, 131, 137, 175n47, 178n88, 182n40, 187n31, 190n2, 192–93n15; Black population in, 62; Christianity, incorporating of in imperial vision, 124; culture of letters, 96; imperial formation, 132, 138, 140; Jewish population, 59–60; Moriscos, expulsion of, 23, 60; as new Rome, idea of, 192–93n15

Spanish America, 134; colonial enterprise, 139; original sin, foundations in, 126–27; polis of, 139

Spanish empire, 96, 103, 114, 190n2

Spanish Hapsburgs, 47–48, 94, 128, 138, 182n40

speech act, 97, 119

Spenser, Edmund, 82–84, 86–90, 183n50; twenty-first-century view of, 79; *Complaints*, 75–78, 184nn56–57; *The Faerie Queene*, 76; *The Ruines of Rome*, 65, 78–81; "The Ruines of Time," 76–77; "View of the Present State of Ireland," 65

Statius, 16

Steelsius, Johannes, 47

Sternhold, Thomas, 56, 177n77; *Certayne Psalmes Chosen out of the Psalter of David, and Drawen into English Metre* (with Hopkins), 55

Stewart, Susan, 8, 168n18, 169n26

Stoler, Ann Laura, 11–12, 65, 87, 140, 180n8; ruination, 13

subjectivity, 33, 91, 108

subject-self, 1

Surrey, Earl of (Henry Howard), 55

Sutch, Susie Speakman, 47, 49, 55, 57

Sweeney, Anne R., 54–55

synalepha, 176n60

Taybilí, Ibrahim, 179n89

Technochtitlán (Mexico), 121–22, 130–31

Teresa of Ávila, Saint, 103–4, 109, 111, 116

terza rima, 19, 51, 128

Thebes, xiii–xiv, 2, 15–18, 22, 28, 127, 131–32, 137–38, 154, 183n45; Mars's dragon, 124–25; myths of, 19

Thomás, Don Miguel, 111, 114–16

Thompson, John, 55

Tjanting (Silliman), 189n42

Tlaxcala, 121, 129

"To Penshurst" (Jonson), 35, 41, 123; as example of Renaissance Amphionic poetics, 37–38; as nostalgic, 36

totalitarianism, 142, 146

Tottel, Richard: *Songs and Sonnettes (Tottel's Miscellany)*, 55, 177n77

Trauailed Pilgrime, The (Bateman), 57–59

Treaty of Tordesillas, 119, 190n2

Tudor, Mary, 54

Tudors, 58

Tunis (Tunisia), 192–93n15

United States, 140, 182n40

Urrea, Jerónimo de, 42–45, 50, 56–58, 172n9, 175n47; *Orlando Furioso*, 46; Spanish caballero, habitus of, 53–54

Valdepeñas, Rodrigo de, 174n22, 174n30

Valencia, Spain, 105

Valesio, Giovanni Luigi, 13

vates, 5

Vázquez, Miguel Ángel, 59–60, 62, 179n89

Vega, María José, 3

Velázquez, Diego, 120

Veracruz, Mexico, 120, 191n6

Viaje del Parnaso (Journey to Parnassas) (Cervantes), 23, 93, 94–95, 170n39, 186n12; false poets, 117; galleon scenes in, 96–97, 117, 170n39

"View of the Present State of Ireland" (Spenser), 65

villancicos: as Amphionic poetry, 61–62; Christmas carols, 61; *coplas* and *estribillo* in, 61

Villanueva, Carlos Raúl, 163–64, 197n1

Villanueva, Francisco Márquez, 186n15

Virgil, 28, 35, 184–85n59; *Georgics*, 39

Vitruvius, 136–37

Walcott, Derek: *Omeros*, 185n61
Wars of Religion, 73
"Wasteland, The" (Eliot), 160
Williams, Raymond, 107; formation, as social form, 11
Wilson, Emily, 185n61
Winnicott, D. W., 1–2
Wyatt, Sir Thomas, 33

Yeats, W. B., 15–16; "Easter, 1916," 160–61; "Lapis Lazuli," 12
Yiu, Mimi, 174n34
Yucatán, 123, 192–93n15; inhabitants, as orderly political units, 120–22; Neoplatonic principles, 125; as ordered city, 122; as spoils, 122

Zapata, Luis, 26
Zethus, xiii–xiv, 15; builder of cities, 82, 90, 115, 183n45; labor of building, 16

Zeus, xiii
Zurita, Raúl, 13, 24, 143, 146, 195n58, 195n65, 195–96n67; adhesion, trope of, 195n55; Amphionic music and poetics of, 128–29, 142, 146, 150, 158; "Canto a su amor desaparecido" (Song for his disappeared love), 128–29, 140, 147–55, 157–59; Chilean polis, engaged with, 142–43; Christian themes, 147; *codicia* and *interés*, shaped by, 140, 154; Dante, as poetic model, 140, 143–44, 147–48, 150, 155, 158; "The Desert of Atacama," 146–47; "Las cordilleras del Duce," 144–47; "Las espejeantes playas" (The sparkling beaches), 141–42; *La vida nueva*, 128–29, 143; Orpheus, as inspiration, 150; *paisa*, 142–43, 148, 150, 153, 158; personal associations, with Dante, 143; *Purgatorio*, 128–29, 145